S. Hawson .   9-95

GW00360616

DATE BOUGHT

6|91

Introducing Policework

Introducing Policework

Mike Brogden
Liverpool Polytechnic

Tony Jefferson
University of Sheffield

Sandra Walklate
Liverpool Polytechnic

London
UNWIN HYMAN
Boston   Sydney   Wellington

© Mike Brogden, Tony Jefferson and Sandra Walklate, 1988
This book is copyright under the Berne Convention. No reproduction
without permission. All rights reserved.

Published by the Academic Division of
Unwin Hyman Ltd
15/17 Broadwick Street, London W1V 1FP

Allen & Unwin Inc.,
8 Winchester Place, Winchester, Mass. 01890, USA

Allen & Unwin (Australia) Ltd,
8 Napier Street, North Sydney, NSW 2060, Australia

Allen & Unwin (New Zealand) Ltd in association with
the Port Nicholson Press Ltd,
60 Cambridge Terrace, Wellington, New Zealand

First published in 1988

British Library Cataloguing in Publication Data

Brogden, Michael
    Introducing policework.
1. Great Britain. Policework
I. Title   II. Jefferson, Tony   III. Walklate, Sandra
363.2'3'0941
ISBN 0-04-363012-X
ISBN 0-04-363008-1 pbk

Library of Congress Cataloging in Publication Data

Brogden, Michael
    Introducing Policework.
Bibliography: p.
Includes index.
1. Police.   I. Jefferson, Tony.   II. Walklate, Sandra.   III. Title
HV7921.B695 1988   363.2   88–90
ISBN 0-04-363012-X (alk. paper)
ISBN 0-04-363008-1 (pbk.: alk. paper)

Typeset in 10 on 11 point Bembo by Fotographics (Bedford) Ltd
and printed in Great Britain by Billing and Sons, London and Worcester

Contents

Preface and Acknowledgements

The literature on policework now traverses a number of disciplines – psychology, sociology, politics and history – and a variety of theoretical traditions. A student entering the field might be forgiven for being daunted by the sheer (and ever-expanding) volume of the work. Yet search for a route map to help guide the intrepid traveller, a map that offered a concise overview of the various contributions *and* showed how these might be linked in a systematic and coherent way, would prove fruitless. That absence provided our starting point – a decision to try to 'plug that gap' by drawing on and pooling our various specialist knowledges on the subject.

The irony of such an enterprise is that the more necessary such a text becomes, because of the bewildering variety of writings on policework, the more difficult it becomes to write. Being foolhardy types, we decided to step in where 'angels (probably wisely) fear to tread' and 'have a go' before the task became not just difficult but impossible. This means, of course, that we will almost certainly offend 'some of the people, some of the time' (though hopefully not 'all of the people, all of the time').

In any event, we bear collective responsibility for what follows, and have incurred the usual debts to various people. In the first place, we would like to thank all those whose works we have used (and abused) and generally 'bent' around our argument. We have usually learnt something, even from (perhaps 'especially from', in some cases) those with whom we disagree. In addition, we are indebted to all those friends and colleagues who variously contributed to (and suffered) our efforts. Mike would particularly like to thank Bob, Jo, Don, Marge and his co-authors for their friendship and support through 1986–7. Sandra would like to thank Margaret Langford for the speedy and efficient typing of draft chapters. And Tony wishes particularly to thank the following: all those friends and colleagues 'down under' who provided accommodation, hospitality and 'good times' during his sabbatical spent lugging the book around Hong Kong and Australia, especially Dave Brown, Maureen Cain, Kit Carson, Russell Hogg and Eugene McLaughlin; Claire Smythe, for reading and commenting (without standing upon ceremony) on draft chapters, and producing the index; and Claire Davidson and Gladys Quaye, for typing the final text so proficiently.

Introducing Policework

1 Introduction

In so far as policing implies functions related to the social control of others, we have all, at one time or another, acted as policemen or women. Older children police younger brothers and sisters; parents police their children; school prefects police other pupils; and so on. In addition to this 'amateur' policing undertaken occasionally by all of us, some groups of workers have a policing or control role built into their jobs. Examples of such workers include:

(1) youth workers, teachers, and social workers who have statutory responsibilities which include a control function, broadly conceived. They might also be said to have a control function in relation to the dissemination of ideas – an ideological control function;

(2) private security police, like Securicor, hired to guard property in transit;

(3) state employed police with a *specific* mandate to guard particular institutions like defence establishments (MOD police) and others such as nuclear energy plants;

(4) those agents (stewards, 'bouncers') employed by night clubs and similar establishments to control the behaviour of users.

Policing then, as a form of social control, is widespread, either as a small part of a particular occupation's much *broader* remit (as in the case of social worker, youth worker, etc.), or as an exclusive part of an occupation with a much *narrower* remit (as in the cases of private security, police guardwork, bouncer, etc.).

If we were concerned generally with policing or social control all these groups of workers, and others, would be part of our subject matter. But we are not. Our concern is much narrower, namely, 'the police' – 'bobbies', 'coppers', 'pigs', or simply the 'boys (and girls) in blue'. The police is an occupation defined by its *specific mandate* (given in the oath which all must take), its *specific powers* and its *specific form of accountability*. The mandate entails upholding 'law and order'. The powers to fulfil this include a range of extra powers over and above those of citizens. And the form of accountability is accountability *to the law*, not to politicians or more generally to the 'democratic' polity. All of these are *unique* – specific to police officers of the state. It is this specific form of policing only – the police, their everyday practices and policies, including issues about accountability – that concerns us in what follows.

Responsibility for upholding the law implies two things:

(a) enforcement of the criminal law;
(b) maintaining order when criminal violations occur during social unrest, political protest and industrial action.

Since the powers granted to police to effect both of these are often *discretionary*, that is, are powers which require officers to employ their judgement as to whether a criminal or disorderly act has taken place, this also makes police responsible, in many instances, for *defining criminality*. Both the above activities of criminal law enforcement and order maintenance imply a need for information or *intelligence gathering*. Finally, since maintaining order in the face of unrest, protest and industrial action (i.e. conflict) consists of restoring a consensus, policework is also about *securing and maintaining consent* (or ideological control, in order to facilitate the reproduction of order). In short, 'blue-uniform' policing or state policework implies a range of functions, namely, enforcing (and sometimes defining) the criminal law, maintaining order, intelligence gathering, and securing consent, all directed towards a singular end: upholding the general legal framework of the state – by persuasion if possible, violently if necessary.

The forms of state policework have varied in time and place. Sometimes the police force has not been part of the state. This may occur in situations where legitimacy has been withdrawn from the legal state; for example, the use of Catholic ex-servicemen by the community to conduct general policework duties in Catholic West Belfast (Boehringer, 1971). Sometimes the state will claim the mantle socialist or popular with consequent differences in the form of policework. Differences such as these will affect the relative emphases given to the four functions. Those which emphasize intelligence gathering and maintaining order can be called versions of '*high*' policing; those emphasizing enforcing/defining the law and securing consent, versions of '*low*' policing. The first account of a preventive police in Europe suggests its midwives were the ministers of Louis XIV (Brodeur, 1983). This was a form of high policing – police concern with the affairs of state which stretches from the times of Fouché in the eighteenth century to the present Sûreté (Criminal Investigation Department). The primary police commitment is the defence of the realm, which makes the enforcement of the current Prevention of Terrorism Act one lineal descendant.

An early example of 'low policing' is a historical experiment which rarely receives as much as a footnote (Emsley, 1983). In the French Revolutionary context of 1848, a transient police agency guarded the streets of Paris under Minister Cassidière. That body of 'montagnards' elected its own officers, and recruited and promoted members on the basis of their political commitment to the new revolutionary state. Police priorities were directed against those who committed crimes against property or persons, not against public disorder. Critically their function was to conciliate on the street, not repress on behalf of the state. Brady has described a contemporary version of such a policing system in Cuba (Brady, 1982).

We, of course, are concerned with state policework in the modern British state and its historical development. Though like all systems of state policework it has 'high' and 'low' aspects, it has always emphasized its 'low' aspects. As we shall see in more detail in Chapter 4, the introduction of modern policework in England was only possible on condition that its 'high' aspects – associated with France – were played down and its 'low' aspects emphasized.

'The police must be stable, efficient, and organized along military lines.' Thus Robert Peel, the Home Secretary in 1829, established the concept of a military-based structure of law enforcement administration (quoted in Stinchcombe, 1979, p. 50). 'Given the fear and distrust with which earlier proposals for a full-time, paid police had met . . . it was a logical strategy to equate the police with a more familiar structure – could not order and discipline which were the hallmarks of the military provide restraints against potential power abuses of the police?' (ibid.).

A defining feature of that New Police was its lack of aggressive weaponry. An unarmed institution encompassing a small number of personnel (3,300 police officers to London's 1.3 million population at the time) made the style of policing more important than any calculation of strength. Authoritative bearing and persuasive powers were consequently more important to the British police than a display of naked coercion. The first Commissioners, Rowan and Mayne, believed that the London police had to control the streets not through numerical supremacy but through unquestioned respect for their legitimacy and only secondly through a perception that they represented an institution of formidable reserve capacities. This authority was owed not to persons but to a single uniform temperament, to a code of conduct, and to the peaceful style of work of the constable.

The Metropolitan Police was to be confined to preventive patrol, and restricted officers to two relatively apolitical forms of intervention – situations in which a citizen could request their attention, and problems on the street that officers could see required attention. Wearing a highly visible uniform on street patrol was assumed to act as a preventive deterrent. Proactive policing by continual patrol and in the symbolic uniform was meant to seem preventive but not threatening.

Further, there was the ambiguous question of control. In London, the New Police were to be state-influenced but not state-directed. Formally separate from the Home Office, they remained open to guidance from that ministry but not subject to its commands. In the provinces, with the emergence of bodies similar to the Metropolitan Police over the succeeding half century, a similar relationship developed between the police and their local watch committees (themselves supposedly representative of the wider community) who appointed them but whose powers to control them remained unclear.

The Commissioners had argued that there should be no separate officer class – that higher ranks should be promoted on the basis of peer advancement, not through external recruitment – for example, from a military class or from a special academy. The police were to be of the people and drawn directly from them. In particular, the origin of their powers lay in common law – principally every citizen's rights of arrest and prosecution. One consequence of this assumption of citizen powers – and of the failure of the original parliamentary legislation to specify police duties – meant that a whole variety of tasks could fall to the lot of the police as well as those duties which had a very direct relationship with the law.

From this initial model, the police forces of England and Wales developed to their present structure of 43 individual forces with a complement of some 128,000 officers and 35,000 civilian support staff. But in that century and a half, specialization of function and specification of tasks had proceeded apace. The early patrolmen were general dogsbodies in a largely undifferentiated force. Expansion, and the division of labour over the succeeding years, produced a much more complex structure with the typical force in the 1980s encompassing many horizontal as well as vertical divisions, with much of the general craft skill of the constable being lost to a variety of specialist units.

More particularly, some of these specialist units, such as the CID and the Special Branch, are more concerned with 'high' than 'low' aspects of policing. Today, it may be a moot point whether we still have a 'low' police or whether we are on the road to a 'high' police. The question is sometimes put another way, 'Is Britain becoming a police state?' We shall be in a better position to answer a question like that at the end, not the beginning, of our passage through this book.

Currently, an enormous literature on state policework exists. Part of our purpose is to summarize what is known. But we also intend to steer our own course through the material. So each chapter will constitute both a summary, setting out different positions, where applicable, and an argument which offers our own 'resolution'. The intention is that each chapter can be read on its own, yet will also form part of a developing argument which places each body of literature within an overall framework. In that way we hope to satisfy both the 'dipper' and the 'all-through' reader. Finally, assuming we do our job tolerably well, you should be in a better position to make sense of stories about police in your daily newspaper; and conversely, you should be able to use such stories to 'test' the arguments presented in this book. To assist you in this process, the following run-through of chapters will include references to relevant stories about the police gleaned from browsing through at random two weeks of the *Guardian* newspaper. In the book's conclusion, we will return to the issues posed by these articles to enable you to check whether the intervening chapters have indeed helped clarify your thinking.

We start in Chapter 2 with the psychological approaches to policework. These share a focus on the individual police officer, his or her attitudes and skills, and how these might be improved, especially through training, in the interests of 'better policing'. The inner city riots and 'better value for money' – key features of the Thatcherite years – have provided a boost to this kind of work and considerable revamping of formal training programmes. But the individualistic focus of this work, with its attention largely to formal rather than informal learning processes, considerably restricts its explanatory scope.

None the less, the theme of training constantly recurs in media stories. In a follow-up to the biggest police story of our chosen fortnight, the gaoling of five police officers for their 'vicious and unprovoked attack on five schoolboys in north London' some four years earlier, in August 1983 (*Guardian*, 17 July 1987, p. 2) – the infamous 'Holloway Road' incident – the question posed was how to avoid police mobile support units (from which the five gaoled PCs were drawn) roaming 'around the streets together in the van looking for trouble' (Brian Hillard, quoted in *Guardian*, 18 July 1987, p. 17). The police answer emphasized rigorous selection and training: 'a concentrated two-week programme focusing on self-discipline, teamwork, physical fitness, and professionalism' (Scotland Yard, ibid.). Will such an 'answer' prove adequate to prevent more 'Holloway Roads'?

Chapter 3, with its focus on microsociological approaches to policework, takes us beyond the individual officer and the formal learning programme into the profane social world of policework and its informal modes of socialization: to the idea of policework as the outcome of situationally specific interactions, informed largely by the values of the 'cop culture', values which get picked up informally by watching older more experienced hands at work. But, while both the situating of policework within a social context and alertness to informal dimensions of training have provided important insights to understanding police behaviour, the approach remains limited none the less by the narrowness of its social gaze. Methodologically and theoretically microsociology has difficulty dealing with events beyond its chosen field of vision, namely, the immediate social situation and the interactional dynamics of the groups involved. Thus it has difficulty dealing with the broader social functions of policework and the ensuing predictability in the social patterns of police activity.

To focus one of the key themes of this chapter, the notion of an informal 'cop culture', consider another aspect of the Holloway Road incident – the four-year time-lag between the crime and its punishment. Indeed, the attack almost went unpunished until media attention, a public outcry and an offer of immunity from prosecution to witnesses who had not personally taken part in the assault, persuaded three officers to break with the erstwhile impregnable code of loyalty to their fellow officers and start telling the truth. What is it about policing that promotes and sustains such loyalty, a loyalty that can, as this incident showed, override their clear (sworn) duty to uphold the law?

We move next, in Chapters 4 and 5, to historical approaches. These necessarily tackle Chapter 3's missing question, namely the social functions of policework, though the answers given depend on the theoretical presuppositions employed. We identify three broad approaches – the evolutionary, which stresses the development of policework to deal with 'obvious' social problems like crime and disorder, the class-based, which stresses policework's role in class control, and the accidental, which emphasizes local, contingent factors in explaining changes – and then tell the story of policework from pre-Norman times to the end of the nineteenth century (Chapter 4) and thereafter, in Chapter 5, the tale of twentieth-century policework. The story to the end of the nineteenth century is one of the replacement of a communal, unpaid, reactive police function by police forces staffed by full-time paid police officers with proactive as well as reactive police functions. The twentieth century witnesses further changes, especially the growth of centralization, specialization and professionalization. Yet, despite these changes and despite the different explanations given by the three theoretical approaches, the focus of policework remains, we argue, remarkably stable: namely, working-class lives, livelihoods and leisure pursuits. Such a focus has narrowed over time as structural changes created divisions between the 'respectable' and 'rough' working class, as the 'rough' became more youthful, and as some forms of crime became 'professionalized', but it endures nevertheless, and thus confirms the importance of a historical approach in shedding light on the social functions of policework.

Can a historical understanding help in thinking about current problems in the Metropolitan Police? In a story about the new Commissioner, Mr Peter Imbert, he stressed his commitment to 'partnership policing' – evidenced in such schemes as neighbourhood watch, crime prevention, victim support and local consultative groups – but admitted they were working well only in the 'leafy suburbs' and not where they were most needed, namely the inner city (*Guardian*, 27 July 1987, p. 2). Will such schemes ever work in the inner city? And if not, why not?

Chapter 6 looks at the social functions of policework today. This provides a sort of contemporary 'test' of the historical evidence; but it also broadens its focus to include other important social divisions apart from class, namely, age, race and gender. It thus also acts to complement the earlier microsociology chapter by providing a macrosociology of policework. In relation to each of the social divisions looked at in detail, the evidence points towards age, race and gender, as well as class, being the occasion for different *and* discriminatory policing. We end by offering an explanation of how a series of biases cumulatively produce such discrimination against the relatively powerless. These biases involve elements of the law, organizational deployment, police practices and the stereotypes used by the occupational culture.

A number of stories of police brutality during our fortnight are relevant to this chapter. Obviously the Holloway Road incident, which involved five youths, some of whom were black; then there was an article on Greenham peacewomen preparing to stay, even if Cruise is removed. In the course of this it was revealed that 'most of the 20 or so campers at the yellow gate yesterday . . . said the police or military had been brutal to them' (*Guardian*, 24 July 1987, p. 1). Further, in the aftermath of the Stalker affair, there was an article announcing a government investigation into the Royal Ulster

Constabulary's 'elite undercover squad. . . at the centre of allegations
of a shoot to kill policy' (*Guardian*, 16 July 1987, p. 1). Three more
stories, linked with the issue of oppressive policing, involved the
policing of the black community. The first was a report by a black US
judge criticizing police handling of the investigations into the murder
of their colleague, PC Blakelock, hacked to death in 1985 on the
Broadwater Farm Estate during a riot. Police behaviour was, she said,
'affected by their anger at the murder of a colleague' (*Guardian*, 20 July
1987, p. 2). The next day, the *Guardian* reported two of Britain's new
black MPs criticizing police activities in Notting Hill, namely the
'crackdown' on drug pushing known as Operation Trident. The
'swamping' use of stop and search powers echoed Swamp 81 (the
forerunner of the Brixton riots in 1981), as did the police response in
pointing to the number of drug-related arrests and the high level of
community support for their activities. The following day, Wolverhampton police reported defusing an incendiary device left outside a
police station, the second time that year the Wolverhampton police
had been so targeted. The presumed motive: revenge for the over-
forceful arrest of a young black man in February, which proved fatal
(*Guardian*, 22 July 1987, p. 4).

Youth, peacewomen, 'terrorists', black people: is it just coincidence that these stories of police oppression and brutality centre on
these particular social groups? Or do these groups share certain
characteristics that might help explain their similar treatment? And if
they do, what is it they have in common?

Understanding the relationship between the elements identified in
Chapter 6 as crucial in producing policing biased against the relatively
powerless, namely elements of the law, organizational deployment,
police practices and the stereotypes used by the occupational culture –
how they interact to produce the present discriminatory policing of
the powerless – is the key to understanding the difficulties of controlling policework, which is the nub of the debate about police
accountability. This is the subject of Chapter 7. The divisions in the
debate – between those wanting only the present legal controls and
those wanting some form of control by a democratic body, and
between those opting for 'rule-tightening' and those stressing the
need to co-opt the 'cop culture' – are critically explored. But the nub of
the matter, we argue, is the relationship between rules and the cop
culture. And we argue that the cop culture is 'allowed' to take the form
it does *because* of the permissive legal structure – hence the need to *start*
with these legal rules. However, such a change still does not address
the question of the content of policing, a question, we argue, which
necessarily engages the notion of public justice.

Accountability was implicated in many of the newspaper stories, including, obviously, those dealing with brutal and oppressive policing. In addition, there were three other relevant stories: one the report by Her Majesty's Chief Inspector of Constabulary high-lighting (yet again) the need for 'highly skilled supervision' of riot squads to 'avoid confrontation tactics' (*Guardian*, 16 July 1987, p. 5). Since the report also referred to plastic bullets and CS gas, a postscript mentioned the continuing row between Northumbria Police Authority and the Home Secretary (later resolved in favour of the Home Secretary, *Guardian*, Law Report, 20 November 1987, p. 5) over whether the latter had the power to bypass them and supply chief constables with plastic bullets and CS gas without local authority agreement. Several days later, a story appeared about local authority leaders demanding a meeting with ministers over the index-linked police pay award that they, the local authority, were going to find difficulty in funding. Then there was a story about the proposed review of the guidelines concerning the investigation of senior police officers, after the débâcle of the Stalker affair (*Guardian*, 23 July 1987, p. 32). Who should decide – local authorities or the Home Secretary – whether chief constables should have CS gas and plastic bullets at their disposal? Who should direct their use? And, once again, is highly skilled supervision, more rigorous selection and training going to be sufficient to prevent more 'Holloway Roads'?

Chapter 8 takes up the relatively neglected issue of public justice in looking at how far the post-Scarman 'monitoring' developments – PACE, consultative committees, neighbourhood watch, lay visiting, crime surveys, monitoring groups – are likely to produce effective policing. For us this means policing that would be regarded as just by those routinely on the receiving end – the relatively powerless groups highlighted in Chapters 4, 5 and 6.

Two final stories take us back, appropriately enough, to our starting point: the distinction between 'policing' and 'the police'. The long-running story of alleged child sexual abuse in Cleveland produced a report of a police surgeon refusing to let the controversial paediatricians responsible for the upsurge of allegedly abused children taken into care examine a three-year-old girl whose father had been arrested for suspected indecency (*Guardian*, 18 July 1987, p. 4). The second story concerned the appointment of a director for the new Serious Fraud Office, 'the new [non-police] agency which will investigate cases such as those at Guinness, Lloyds of London and Johnson Matthey' (*Guardian*, 20 July 1987, p. 4). Why are these criminal areas – the abuse of children, massive frauds – not obviously the job of the police? Though clearly serious, why is police involvement subordinate – in the first case to the paediatricians and social workers, in the latter to a civilian-led group (of accountants, lawyers and attached police) accountable directly to the Attorney-General – rather than pre-eminent?

Finally, in the Conclusion, we invite you to 'test' our arguments against the media police stories introduced here.

2 Psychology: Attitudes, Skills and Management

Introduction

Psychology is concerned with the structure and functioning of individual mental processes and their relationship to behaviour. Like all disciplines of academic study, it embraces a range of different concepts and theories, but in psychology these are bound together by their commitment to offering explanations by reference to *individual* characteristics of human beings. Here we are interested in assessing the extent to which such an individualistic level of explanation is relevant to understanding policework. Psychologists interested in policework have focused on three questions; the kinds of *attitudes* possessed by police officers; the kinds of *skills* required of police officers; and the *management* problems involved in harnessing such attitudes and skills in the production of 'good police practice' – arguably the overriding interest of psychologists in this area.

Generally, the questions and initiatives suggested by psychology, particularly with regard to training, have been more readily embraced by police organizations than those suggested by sociology, partly because it is dominated by a traditional notion of science and partly because of its reputation for practical relevance. Since 1979 and the advent of the first Thatcher government, and more particularly since 1981 (the year of widespread inner city riots) there has been increased interest in what psychology might offer the police service. This can be understood as a result of a number of factors.

In the first place, 'budgeting for the household' has been one of the key themes of the Thatcher years which has had its impact on every aspect of public expenditure. The drives for efficiency and value for money have been felt in the police service, as in other sectors involving public finance. Home Office Circular 114, 1983, 'Manpower, Effectiveness and Efficiency in the Police Force', established some of the guidelines within which police forces were expected to operate and organize their resources given that:

The constraints on public expenditure at both central and local government levels make it impossible to continue with the sort of expansion which has occurred in recent years. (Home Office Circular 114/1983)

This meant attending to priorities and objectives in the interests of more effective (the ability to achieve goals) and efficient (value for money) use of resources.

The Home Secretary therefore attaches importance to the determination of objectives and priorities in the police service, and to the allocation of resources and the deployment of police and civilian manpower in a way that will most effectively and efficiently secure those objectives and priorities. (ibid.)

This has led the Merseyside force, for example, to introduce a strategy of 'planned policing', while others like the Metropolitan Police and Northamptonshire have adopted a 'management by objectives' strategy, in the interests of the more economical use of limited resources. And, as we shall see, such strategies also involve certain management assumptions concerning motivation and job satisfaction for the police officer – psychological issues relevant to our final question, and to which we shall return. (On the question of financial constraints on policework, and on the 'inherent' conflict between 'effectiveness' and 'efficiency', see Jones and Silverman, 1984.)

In the second place, specific events and in particular the inner city disturbances of 1981 and the subsequent Scarman Report, have enhanced the role of psychology. The Scarman Report suggested a range of proposals and recommendations with respect to police recruitment, training, supervision, discipline, and policing methods. Of specific interest here is the attention given to recruitment and training, especially as these relate to police racism.

Efforts must be made to avoid racially prejudiced people entering the police service. I recommend that the work currently being undertaken in the Metropolitan Police designed to identify scientific ways in which evidence of racial prejudice can be identified should be vigorously pursued with the support of the Home Office and that the results should in due course be incorporated into the procedures for selecting recruits to all police forces. (Scarman, 1982, para. 8.29)

The lack of recruitment from ethnic minorities (to which we return in Chapter 5) is also commented on by Lord Scarman and ways of improving on this were suggested as of urgent concern. In a similar vein, Scarman recommended that training should prepare the recruit for policing a multiracial society: which meant a longer training more sensitive to ethnic differences (para. 8.30). Human Awareness Training discussed below on (page 20) is mentioned especially in this context (para. 5.21).

The implicit concern within these proposals to establish a police service comprising individuals with 'acceptable' attitudes and good policing skills has provided some considerable impetus to psychological studies relevant to policework and, in particular, a contribution to the questions posed at the outset, namely those concerned with understanding the *attitudes* of police officers, policing *skills*, and *management* (or *organizational behaviour*).

Police Attitudes

Most studies on this issue affirm the existence of particular police attitudes, the most recent examples being the Scarman Report, the work of Coleman and Gorman (1982), and the reports of the Policy Studies Institute on the Metropolitan Police (1983). In discussing the nature of police officers' attitudes, psychologists have asked three kinds of questions: first, do police officers possess certain kinds of attitudes because they possess a particular kind of personality; that is are they predisposed to particular attitudinal responses? Alternatively, if police officers are not predisposed towards particular attitudes, psychologists have been concerned to develop an understanding of how they acquire their attitudes. This has led them, thirdly, to focus especially on the impact of the formal training process on attitude formation.

Is there a 'Police Personality'?

The most common connection made between the idea of a police personality and the idea of predisposition is through the concept of *authoritarianism*, which is discussed in the classic text *The Authoritarian Personality* (Adorno *et al.*, 1950). Although Adorno and his colleagues were specifically concerned with anti-semitism, their model of the authoritarian personality type has been much more widely applied.

Balch (1972) offers a clear account of the characteristics of authoritarianism:

(1)   Conventionalism: rigid adherence to conventional middle-class values.
(2)   Submissive uncritical attitudes to idealized moral authorities.
(3)   Aggression: tendency to be on the lookout for and to condemn, reject and punish people who violate conventional values.
(4)   Anti-intraception: opposition to the subjective, the imaginative, the tender-minded.
(5)   Superstition and stereotypy: the belief in mystical determinants of the individual's fate; the disposition to think in rigid categories.
(6)   Power and toughness: exaggerated assertion of strength and toughness.
(7)   Destructiveness and cynicism; generalized hostility.
(8)   Projectivity: the disposition to believe that wild and dangerous things go on in the world.
(9)   Sex; exaggerated concern with sexual 'goings-on'.

Balch concludes that, with the exception of superstition, the police officer is a classic example of the authoritarian personality, a finding which overlaps with Reiner's review of the sociological literature on the 'cop culture'. Building on Skolnick's (1966) 'working personality' and summarizing what is known, Reiner (1985a, pp. 87–103) lists the core characteristics of 'cop culture' as, 'mission–action–cynicism–pessimism', 'suspicion', 'isolation/solidarity', 'conservatism', 'machismo', 'racial prejudice' and 'pragmatism'.

The question remains, however. Are these characteristics psychologically predispositional or learned? There are technical problems in a comparative review of this literature, since studies use different scales of measurement, fail to use control groups, and fail to match adequately their samples. Nevertheless, we can usefully examine the evidence through the two main methods of comparison used, comparison of police officers with the population at large, and comparison of successful and unsuccessful officers (Burbeck and Furnham, 1985). As we shall see the predispositional evidence as a whole is less than convincing.

One of the most recent studies comparing police recruits with a sample of the general population was reported by Coleman and Gorman (1982). They compared matched groups from recruit constables (48), probationer constables (36) with an average of twenty months' service, and the general population (30), on a number of scales, particularly focusing on conservatism, dogmatism and authoritarianism. They concluded that 'the police force attracts conservative and authoritarian personalities' (Coleman and Gorman, 1982, p. 1; and see also page 17 below), a finding in line with Potter (1977) and Cook (1977). Burbeck and Furnham (1984) also found that 319 applicants to the Metropolitan Police 'displayed higher levels of extrovert instability on Eysenck's Personality Inventory (EPI) than the norm'. This study included all those who applied, before selection took place, and might be evidence for the 'predispositional' explanation, though the authors had reason to believe that there was 'extensive "faking good" on the part of the applicants'.

'Predispositional' findings such as these suggest three possibilities: certain kinds of individuals choose their occupation to fit their personality, police officers are recruited from an authoritarian section of the population, or in the process of recruitment other personality 'types' are sifted out. The first possibility requires that the nature of the occupation be narrowly defined and understood, something for which there is little evidence. Indeed, the evidence points towards the ordinariness of police officers: 'if there is a police type, he is eminently unexceptional' (Bradley, Walker and Wilkie, 1986, p. 164). The second possibility is that police recruits originate from an authoritarian section of society. Once again, the findings point towards the typicality of police officers. Both Cain (1973) and Reiner (1978), for example, indicate that the majority of their samples were officers from social class III backgrounds, in particular from the manual working class. In socio-economic terms, this hardly sets them apart from the population as a whole (cf. Bradley, Walker and Wilkie, 1986, p. 163), though the current high pay levels and mass unemployment may be making the occupation more attractive to sections of the middle classes.

Given this predominance of manual working-class recruits, the question is therefore asked whether this sector of the working class possesses authoritarian attitudes. Again, the evidence is inconclusive. For example, Coleman and Gorman (1982) found their recruits more authoritarian, yet Bayley and Mendelsohn (1969) in the USA did not. A more developed notion of this thesis suggests that police officers suffer, in common with others from the lower middle class and the working class, from 'status anxiety'. In becoming a police officer, individuals enter a non-manual occupational. Those from the manual working class therefore experience upward social mobility and become 'marginal' because they then 'belong' to neither class (cf. Bradley, Walker and Wilkie, 1986; and Reiner, 1978). The marginality of such a position, it is suggested, leads police officers to embrace traditional middle–class values more readily than the middle class, which creates a similarity of viewpoint between them and what Balch (1972) refers to as the 'silent majority'.

Members of the 'silent majority' are certainly not fascists, any more than policemen are, but they seem to have many authoritarian characteristics: conventionalism, authoritarian aggression, stereotypy, cynicism, and projectivity. From this point of view, policemen appear to be good representatives of white middle or working class America. (Balch, 1972, p. 117)

However, there is an interesting dimension to this question not dealt with by Balch but mentioned by Reiner (1978). He reports that while police officers make up about 0.6 per cent of the working population, in his sample 14 per cent came from police backgrounds. The sample breaks down further, with those from police backgrounds most heavily concentrated in the CID (46 per cent) or in senior posts (22 per cent of inspectors). Thus it could be that there is also an inter-generational transmission of attitudes and values which has not yet been explored. But even if police are not more authoritarian than the general population, 'the "normal" degree of authoritarianism is disturbing in an occupation which wields considerable powers over minorities' (Reiner, 1985a, p. 101).

Finally, the third explanation for the authoritarian characteristics found in police officers suggests that 'types' without such characteristics are weeded out. The question of the impact of the selection process has become increasingly important in England and Wales particularly in the last 10 years. Until recently forces in England and Wales were understaffed, and anyone who could meet the minimum physical and educational requirements stood a good chance of joining the police force. However, currently, forces are generally meeting their authorized numbers (a result of the generosity of the Edmund Davies pay award of 1978 and the alacrity with which the incoming Tory government of 1979 implemented it) and, given the rise in unemployment, have more applicants than vacancies. Thus the question of selection has become very pertinent.

The research relevant to this question has attempted to compare successful and unsuccessful police officers. One problem, as Burbeck and Furnham (1985) report, is the different criteria of failure used by researchers: failed trainees, resignations, unsatisfactory ratings, unselected candidates. Given this range of problems, the evidence to date appears unclear with respect to selection processes. Be that as it may, there is an alternative way of understanding the notion of a 'police personality'. Such an alternative lies in understanding it as a learned response to doing a particular kind of job in a particular kind of organizational setting, rather than as a predisposition. In this kind of explanation, the 'police personality' is a consequence of the job in question rather than a predisposition.

Balch (1972) re-examines the characteristics of authoritarianism from this point of view. Suspiciousness, for example, is often cited as a characteristic of police officers, possessed as a consequence of the danger of the job, but also as a consequence of specific training. Conventionalism is another police characteristic, resulting from their involvement in a disciplined paramilitary organization; as McNamara (1967) suggests, when in doubt follow the rules. Similar comments might be made with respect to the remaining characteristics of authoritarianism. Indeed, some of the predispositional psychological data point to the importance of the learning process. At this juncture it becomes useful to complete the earlier quote from Coleman and Gorman:

> The findings suggest that the police force attracts conservative and authoritarian personalities, that basic training has a temporarily liberalising effect, and *that continued police service results in increasingly illiberal/intolerant attitudes towards coloured immigration.* (1982, p. 1, italics added)

To review: it has been established that police officers do appear to possess particular attitudes, but that these attitudes do not mark them out in any way as being particularly different from the population from which they are recruited. The evidence here leads to the conclusion that the notion of police officers being predisposed to particular attitudes because they are of a particular personality type is, to say the least, problematic. Indeed, this evidence can be much more strongly drawn on to support the view that some sort of learning process takes place for police officers which enhances and heightens those attitudes they already possess as a consequence of being fairly typical members of the lower middle/working class. In other words, the longer an individual is a police officer, the more likely it is that s/he will express conservative and authoritarian attitudes (see Coleman and Gorman, 1982, p. 1, and Cochrane and Butler, 1980). The view that some sort of learning process takes place the longer one is a police officer has led the attention of psychologists to be focused on the role that the formal training process has on the formation of police attitudes.

Police Attitudes and Training

In considering this question we need first to remember that learning
processes can take place formally, through training programmes
specifically concerned with the transmission of skills – an issue we
discuss later in this chapter – but also informally, through on-the-job
learning from other colleagues. This issue embracing the idea of an
occupational culture is dealt with in Chapter 3. We must also be aware
that both formal and informal learning processes take place within a
wider social context than either training or the occupational culture,
and that both will be affected. That issue, the impact of wider society
on police behaviour, constitutes the subject of Chapter 6. With these
provisos in mind, let us turn first to what we know about police
attitudes and the role of training in their formation.

Probably the most unacceptable police attitude is racial prejudice.
For this reason, we adopt it as our chosen example. The incidence of
prejudiced attitudes and the use of racist language among police
officers has been recorded by Cain (1973), Reiner (1978), Southgate
(1982), Coleman and Gorman (1982), Holdaway (1983) and Policy
Studies Institute (1983). However, such a finding constitutes only a
starting point for inquiry. There is, for example, an important distinction to be made between *prejudice* – a concept referring to the expressed
attitudes of respondents, and *discrimination* – a concept referring to
behaviour.

Thus police officers may be racially prejudiced without necessarily
acting on those prejudices to produce racially discriminatory
behaviour, as the Policy Studies Institute (1983) reports suggest.
Additionally, it is important to distinguish *individual* prejudice or acts
of discrimination from the *institutional* kind which stems not from the
intentions of members but from the effects of the institution's
practices. This means that racial discrimination can occur in policework as a result of individuals acting out their prejudices and/or as a
result of institutional practices which have the effect of discriminating
against a particular racial group, sometimes even despite the best
intentions of police officers as individuals (an issue dealt with more
fully in Chapter 6). The distinction between these two forms of
prejudice and discrimination are nicely brought out in the following
quotation, as is the importance to be attached to institutional prejudice:

> The crucial source of police prejudice is societal racism which places
> ethnic minorities disproportionately in those strata and situations
> from which the police derive their 'property'. This structural
> feature of police–ethnic minority relations bolsters any prior
> prejudice police officers have. (Reiner, 1985a, pp. 102–3)

It has to be said that there is much confusion about this distinction, as the debate generated by the Scarman Report demonstrated. Lord Scarman himself seems unable to grasp the concept of institutional discrimination because he equates racism only with intentional behaviour (Scarman, 1982, p. 105).

What role can training play in eliminating racial prejudice and other undesirable attitudes? There is no doubt that many see it as important since it routinely figures as an element in any strategy of police reform in the aftermath of particular policing disasters. In the British post-Scarman context, for example, a critical re-evaluation of police training occurred. Thus, many would agree with Bahn's view of the training environment as the 'psychological crucible in which occupational identities are forged' (Bahn, 1984, p. 392), even though they might not use his terminology. This need not deny the importance of other significant elements in the forging of police identity – the distinctions made between the police and the public, in the manner of dress, expected behaviour, specific powers and so on, nor what Bahn (1973, p. 1069) sees as the 'counter training of the informal networks established during this period'.

The recent shift in emphasis in police training is nicely caught in this early quotation as to what was wrong with the old.

> It can be said of police training schools that the recruit is taught everything except the essential requirements of his calling, which is how to secure and maintain the approval and respect of the public who he encounters daily in the course of his duties. (Reith, 1952, quoted in Bull, 1984, p. 123)

The essential movement entailed is away from a narrow interpretation of the police task, for which technical knowledge of the law is the primary prerequisite and military discipline the manner of its acquisition, towards a much broader interpretation of the role as one requiring greater social and self-awareness and improved interpersonal skills. This movement is also evident in American police training – what Lundman (1980) calls the change from the 'military' to the 'non-stress' academy.

In Britain, the general movement usually now entails a specific emphasis on the need to make community and race relations an integral part of training. It also, perhaps, implicitly recognizes the potential disjunction between the police perception of the public's judgement of their performance (which they see in terms of law enforcement) and the public's evaluation of that performance (which values interpersonal skills) (Jones and Levi, 1983).

The components of the new training include factual learning, i.e. learning what is 'known' especially about community relations, self-awareness and interpersonal skills. Included in the former category would be Banton's (1973) four principles of police training in community relations: the need for an understanding of citizenship and of the way in which scapegoating, prejudice and discrimination crucially moulds the experiences of ethnic minorities. More generally, the Metropolitan Police's Human Awareness Training (HAT) and Racial Awareness Training (RAT) – comprising interpersonal skills, self-awareness and community relations – falls within the new, as does Southgate's recommendations for race relations training: factual learning, plus training designed to produce appropriate *attitudes* and effective *behaviour*.

Evaluation of the new training programme of HAT is ongoing. Bull and Horncastle (1986a) report a 17 per cent drop in complaints per officer who have undergone HAT training. Criticisms of relevance emphasize the disjunctions between classroom and simulated exercises and 'real policing'. (An evaluation of the impact of HAT on the street is proposed.) Implicitly such criticisms raise the issue of the role of the informal culture. Criticisms of this order encompass officer dissastisfaction with relevance, and the feeling of some that outside experts fail fully to appreciate policework and procedures (Southgate, 1984).

Criticisms of adequacy range from attacks on the core assumptions upon which such courses are built, questioning the inadequate definitions, such as that of racism, employed (cf. Banton, 1985) – to a failure to follow up fully the implications of an emphasis on interactive skills, namely their situationally dependent nature, and hence the need to 'encourage the use of reflection in order to understand how action is continually modified by context, and the meanings ascribed by other participants in the situation' (Jones and Joss, 1985, p. 222).

This final criticism neatly highlights the central problem with the purely psychological approach to attitudes and associated training programmes, that face-to-face encounters are seen as devoid of learned rules. Thus the question of whether or not police officers are prejudiced as individuals is less relevant than understanding the contextual processes whereby prejudicial outcomes are produced. The importance of this relationship between immediate context and prejudicial outcome is well brought out in the psychological literature dealing with particular police skills, to which we now turn, though we shall have to await the discussions in Chapter 4, 5 and 6 before seeing how the broader historical and social context prestructures policework encounters.

Policing Skills

The previous section mentioned the innovations that are taking place in the general skill training of police officers. However, training has a longer history of equipping a police officer with a variety of more traditional skills, to do with the law and the collecting of evidence, associated with the police officer's job. These we can usefully divide into skills connected with observation, those connected with interrogation, and situational skills – those connected with the handling of interactions with the public. Attention will be paid to the psychological evidence relevant to these skills and to the limitations of a purely psychological understanding of them.

(a) *Observational Skills*

Observational skills demand a recognition that the senses, memory, perceptual processes, and expectancy play an important part in contributing to what we 'see' and remember. Bull *et al*. (1983) mention the 'tendency of the police to recall or perceive intentions not actually present' (p. 19). That is referred to as a 'confabulation factor'; the tendency to fill in the gaps of what is seen by imputing intentions which are not present. Much experimental research has shown that while police officers appear capable of remembering more details of dress and appearance than members of the general public (see Bull *et al*., 1983), this process of confabulation leads them also to report things more frequently which are not present, and particularly to report these in a suspicious manner. The complex psychological processes involved in observation outlined above have implications for the validity to be attributed to identification processes, eye witness testimonies (see Irving, 1983), and so on. More generally, when it is recognized that police officers do not operate in a series of random or *ad hoc* situations, but in recurrent and predictable ones, it should not be difficult to see how those tendencies of confabulation and over-suspiciousness bear down heavily and in a prejudicial manner on particular groups, and how the resulting stereotypes are regularly reinforced in the process. The question of which stereotypes are regularly reinforced we return to in Chapter 6.

(b) *Interrogation Skills*

The most precisely stated formal police pronouncement on psychological phenomena I heard in the seventies came from the police evidence to the Maxwell Confait enquiry. Three boys, one of

them retarded, had been sent to prison for a murder they were subsequently shown not to have committed . . . I believe to this day
that the senior detective in the case did not knowingly falsify the
evidence or unduly oppress his prisoners. Yet all the psychological
phenomena which could so easily have accounted for the confessions were systematically denied by all the police witnesses. They
steadfastly refused to acknowledge even the possibility of dynamic
phenomena which are a part of all such dialogues. (Irving, 1983,
p. 2)

Irving goes on to suggest that in addition to not recognizing the
psychological phenomena involved, this case also illustrates the
police bias in favour of forensic evidence (in this case faulty) over other
evidence. However, this example aptly illustrates the focusing of
police attention on interrogation (which the police prefer to call inter-
viewing) as an activity in itself without reflecting upon the
importance of the context within which interrogation routinely takes
place. The report of Softley (1985) on interrogation indicates that in
their samples nearly half the suspects interviewed made a confession,
and over two-thirds gave information which would help secure a
conviction in court. Clearly, then, interrogation constitutes a very
significant part of policework, the purpose of which is to persuade the
accused to confess or accede to incriminating evidence. The skills
vary:

> At its most impressive, the art of interrogation involves mere
> gestures, slight inflections to the voice, the smallest hints of an
> underlying threat or inducement, usually of a psychological kind.
> At its crudest, tactics involve downright trickery and bargaining
> over overtly stated material threats and inducements. (Irving,
> 1985, p. 13)

And although, on occasion, this process may give rise to an awareness
that the accused is not the appropriate person to be interrogating if
other evidence is also inconclusive, the likelihood, from the evidence
available, that this is considered an alternative equal to the possibility
of a confession appears to be small.

What underlies this psychological relationship of questioner and
questionee and the clear desire of police to obtain confessions, is the
context of the interrogation process, namely the structural investment police have in successful prosecutions and the structural power
they have in the situation. Thus, while some police officers may
acquire better interrogation skills than others, and some defendants

might be confession prone, the parameters to their relationship are *structured* prior to the particular encounter. The Police and Criminal Evidence Act (PACE) 1984 has recognized these problems to a certain extent, as Irving argues.

> If the tactics or circumstances of the interview look dodgy to the court, it's up to the prosecution to prove that they did not oppress the suspect or render his admission unreliable. (Irving, 1985, p. 14)

However, the absence of an absolute exclusionary rule gives discretion to the courts to decide what is and is not fair in interrogation, with the onus on the police to present detailed and accurate records of what proceeded. Such records must also be available to the suspect and must be verbatim. The requirement for contemporaneous note-taking has, ironically, led to a loss of interrogation skills (McKenzie and Irving, 1987). PACE also provides the foundation for tape recording of interviews and establishes an independent prosecution service. While these initiatives cannot prevent unrecorded contacts occurring (both Kinsey, 1981, and Merricks, 1983, report an increase in interviews outside the police station after the introduction of tape recorders), and while a suspect's total experience of custody still retains some significant discretionary elements, the burden of accounting for their actions has clearly increased for police officers. Whether this will reduce the investment in, and hence reliance upon, confessions, the crucial existing contextual feature, remains to be seen. Our own verdict on this form of accountability we discuss in Chapter 7.

(c) *Situational Skills*

Situational skills fall within the orbit of that kind of training already discussed, namely HAT and RAT. However, here the intention is to discuss both the relevance and limitations of a purely psychological approach to the handling of aggressive or violent situations as particular exemplifications of more general problems.

Two common types of situation in which a police officer's response is crucial in determining outcomes are the pub brawl and the dispute between neighbours. Recommendations of a 'cool, firm professional response which heightens awareness of the punishing consequences of further action' (Bull *et al.*, 1983, p. 102) are designed to draw attention to the officer's response as the key to 'cooling out' the situation rather than escalating it. The outcome of such situations, however, is not only dependent on the officer's reading of the situation, but also the way the situation 'reads' (i.e. affects) the officer, as the police use of firearms illustrates.

The shooting of Stephen Waldorf in January 1983, and of Mrs Cherry Groce in September 1985, are but two incidents which in their separate ways had escalating consequences. Bull and Horncastle (1986b) argue that improved firearms training conceived in a purely technical way will not tackle incidents of this sort. What is required, they suggest, is an understanding of the officer's psychological state at such moments. An understanding, in particular, of the way in which fear and anxiety result in a reduced ability to recognize alternative courses of action and to communicate, which can lead to tunnel vision and panic. They state:

> If an armed criminal is expected to be in a house which a police officer knowingly enters, that officer may well 'see' any moving human as the gunman. The officer's expectancy (or 'set') will be so high that the brain will decide that anything even loosely approximating a gunman is the gunman, and any movement is an attempt to shoot the officer. Until this approach is adopted, there will be more people shot than is necessary. (Bull and Horncastle, 1986b, p. 13)

Some argue that women generally have the necessary 'gentling' effect:

> In dealing with hot-tempered, wrathful complainants, the women seem to have a 'gentling affect' seldom manifested to male officers . . . The very womanness of the former placated the actors, and prevented them from acting as angrily as intended. Women, it seems, have a pacifying quality that men lack, and that is a distinct asset in policework. (Sherman, 1975, p. 75)

While there is a danger in this statement of reinforcing stereotypes about women and gentleness, as if 'gentleness' were a quality inherent to women, there can be no doubt that viewed as a technique that can be acquired, the art of pacification is a very relevant situational skill. (We return to the question of women and policework in Chapter 6.)

In assessing the contribution and limitations of psychology to understanding the eruption or inhibition of violence, it is necessary to distinguish between two kinds of context: the immediate and the wider. A training approach alert to the kinds of contextual approach advocated by Bull *et al.* (1983) – the immediate context – could indeed improve the ability of officers to handle themselves in particular situations, such as those just discussed. But, to understand why it is that police routinely find themselves in particular situations facing particular sorts of people in particular predefined ways requires an understanding of the wider context of policework – the institutionalized practices of a police force. Knowledge of this context may not always prevent the officer pulling the trigger inadvertently, for once the officer finds himself or herself in a particular situation, the immediate context will prove more pressing. But it will help the rest of us understand why those officers were reacting in those ways against those sorts of people – vital knowledge for all interested in comprehending *patterns* of policework, a knowledge well beyond the ability of psychology to deliver.

Behaviour in Organizations: Management Initiatives

What is not to be denied is that situations like those described above are the sharp end of stress-inducing circumstances as experienced by the police officer. The incidence of stress and stress management in the police force has provoked considerable research by psychologists. Some argue that changes in management style would alleviate such stress.

Home Office Circular 114/83, which we have already mentioned (above on page 12), indicated an official endorsement of the management style of 'policing by objectives' as a means of improving police effectiveness (ability to meet goals) and resource management (value for money). The implications and impact of any particular management style, though, has wider effects than just redirecting resources. Any style of management is geared towards maximizing, if possible, the production rate of the employees and will therefore work upon their motivaton to produce. Arguably, as the availability of information processing techniques has greatly increased, and as the job of the police officer has become increasingly diversified and complex, the nature and style of police management of finite resources have become more crucial. And at no time more so than in a period of general economic restraint in which all public organizations are required to demonstrate their 'value for money'. In addition, research has increasingly indicated that the nature of the police organization and how the police define their job is having deleterious unintended consequences on the officers and the general public. Plumridge states:

> To the constable 'on the ground' it all too often seems that his role requires great maturity and sensitivity and the wisdom of

Solomon, whereas the organisation of which he is a part, in an insensitive punishment-centred manner, demands submissiveness, deference and immaturity. (Plumridge, 1985, p. 176)

He suggests one resulting effect is stress. In addition, the work of Jones and Levi (1983) already cited indicates a difference between the police and the public in terms of job evaluation, with the public rating the 'service role' of the police officer much more highly than the police officers themselves. A further source of job satisfaction or dissatisfaction for police officers comes from their relationships with colleagues, and their view of career prospects. Kinsey's survey of police officers on Merseyside reports that 'high morale amongst police officers is more a function of relationships within internal sub-cultures and working groups than of relations with the public or senior officers' (Kinsey, 1985a, p. 111). In consequence,

> while politicians and senior officers sing the virtues of the foot patrol officer, a number of recent participant studies have concluded that for many younger officers the job is both of low status and, more often than not, cold, wet and miserable. For the more ambitious – an increasing problem possibly, when, as now, educational qualifications on entry are rising – such work is seen as little more than a necessary first step to promotion and the more specialised and glamorous aspects of police work . . . If this is so, any policy geared to increasing the numbers of foot patrol officers within the force may be met with opposition from those whose support and motivation it is most important to encourage. (ibid., p. 97)

The relationship between organizational commitment to foot patrol work, and the reality whereby it is in practice treated as the most dispensable (cf. Jones, 1980) undoubtedly fuels patrol officers' dissatisfaction since it adds a level of organizational hypocrisy. The 'top-down' managerial style typifying the traditional police organization alledgedly leads to (in extreme cases), 'outlets likely to be found in alcoholism, disturbed families and aggressive sports; could it also be that the outlet is found in aggressive acts "on the streets" in situations of low visibility' (Plumridge, 1985, p. 181).

Against this background, Bull *et al.* (1983) again provide a useful review of the relevance of psychological research to the problems faced by managers in general, but police managers in particular. They offer ideas on the manager's role, how to achieve effective communication, leadership, motivation, and how to evaluate performance. With respect to motivation they suggest,

> that goal setting is a technique for planning and improving subordinates performance. For the greatest benefit to be gained, goals need to be specific, difficult to attain, but attainable, and accepted. Goal setting can confer motivational influence on knowledge of results, and feedback can improve the effectiveness of goal setting . . . Set goals. (Bull *et al.*, 1983, p. 185)

A style of management has recently been initiated in this country which has, as intrinsic to it, the setting of goals; examples of it include planned policing on Merseyside, and policing by objectives in the Metropolitan Police and Northamptonshire.

Policing by objectives (PBO), of which planned policing is a variation, is an American import, with the text by Edgar and Lubans (1979) constituting the PBO bible. It is a management style intended to improve efficiency and effectiveness by rational planning. At each stage in the planning process goals become more and more specific until they are put into action on the ground. These actions are empirically evaluated and assessed, and then fed back into the management hierarchy for the cycle to begin again. It is, therefore, a dynamic system, intended to render an organization more responsive to its members and as a result ensure greater commitment from those below to the goals of the organization. In this way, it is hoped that the resistance of the rank and file to being managed may be overcome. It is also intended – through greater effectiveness and efficiency – to render the organizaton more accountable. On Merseyside, for example, the force goals for 1985 were: to achieve a closer relationship between the local community and the police; to increase the number of positive contacts between the police and young people; to develop the professional skills of police officers; to identify offences which cause the public concern. At a subdivisional level, these goals are variously interpreted so that in Birkenhead, for example, focus was placed on more visible beat policing, a quicker response to calls for assistance, and drug abuse. Whereas in the district of Rainhill attention was paid to burglary, vandalism, the number of psychiatric patients escaping from the psychiatric hospital, and the development of Home Watch schemes. In this way, specific local priorities are set, evaluated, and assessed in the light of the wider force goals.

However, the limits of such a purely psychological approach is revealed in a study conducted by Reuss-Ianni (1983). She documents the rise and fall of a 'management by objectives' (MBO) plan which

illustrated, for her, the discrepancy between management cop culture
and street cop culture, and which the MBO initiative failed to overcome.

> While we assumed that headquarters was well intentioned and
> expected the MBO program to improve efficiency and add
> accountability at the precinct level . . . At the precinct level super-
> visors as well as street cops ridiculed as well as resented the fact that
> they were being asked to come up with numbers which were
> meaningless to them in terms of actual precinct work. (Reuss-Ianni,
> 1983, p. 113)

Whether this explanation of failure is correct is something we
return to in Chapter 7. For the moment, its importance lies in its
demonstration of the limitations of concentrating on goals of
improving efficiency, increasing motivation and job satisfaction, and
reducing stress, purely through the concept of management style.
This we shall call the 'ideal' concept of how organizations work. What
is required to move beyond this level of analysis and to understand
why management initiatives fail is (1) an understanding of how
organizations really function; and (2) an understanding of the
relationship between the police mandate (the 'extra-organizational'
level), the organization and routine police behaviour. The former we
can, again, call the immediate context, the latter the wider one.
Relating behaviour to its contexts in this way, both immediate and
wider, may reveal why certain behaviours are so apparently
impervious to management direction; it certainly reveals the need to
move beyond psychology.

Overview and Conclusion

This review of the evidence from the psychological approach to
policework has for the most part proved inconclusive. The notion of a
police personality in the predispositional sense is not proved, but a
consideration of it has revealed some of the characteristics police
officers share with the general public, namely their ordinariness and
working-class background. The evidence that police officers possess
certain attitudes and that these attitudes are learned is more persuasive
than the evidence for predispositional attitudes. This psychological
approach has led to an emphasis on the formal training process, to a re-
examination of training procedures, and has drawn attention to the
impact training procedures can have on attitude formation. This has,
however, overlooked two important features contributing to the

formation of a police identity: the informal learning environment; and the wider structural environment in which the police officer and the police organization works. Because of these oversights, the management initiatives designed to improve efficiency and effectiveness may not achieve their goals – though they may lead to improvement in the police officer's psychological environment.

While human beings and their mental processes and dispositions may reflect certain characteristics, what enables us to communicate and understand each other is not so much our individual predispositions, attitudes, and motivations, but what we hold in common with each other. This ability to engage in concerted action based on shared understandings of the situations in which we find ourselves broadens our understanding of the basis from which our attitudes and behaviour are constructed. Thus, in the context of policework, it is more meaningful to talk of performance rather than personality traits, of the social construction of attitudes rather than natural predispositions, of what is considered to be acceptable police practice rather than policing skills, and of the need to understand the ways in which such practices are perpetuated within particular management structures. This does not mean to say that each police officer cannot stamp his or her individual personality on the job, or that, for example, some of these ways of doing the job cannot be improved upon by re-examining the training procedures and by examining the general relevance of the psychological approach to understanding particular situations (see Ainsworth and Pease, 1987). What it does stress, however, is that looking to psychology for an understanding of policework constitutes only a small part of the picture in which police officers construct their work, framed by wider social and historical processes.

Suggestions for Further Reading

Ainsworth, P., and Pease, K. (1987), *Police Work* (London: Methuen).
Bradley, D., Walker, N., and Wilkie, R. (1986), *Managing the Police* (Brighton: Harvester).
Bull, R., Bustin, B., Evans, P., and Gahagan, D. (1983), *Psychology for Police Officers* (Chichester: Wiley).

3 Microsociology: Policework as Concerted Action

Introduction

At the end of Chapter 2 we highlighted the problems associated with explanations of what police officers do, couched simply in terms of their individual psychology, and began to touch upon more social understandings of why police officers appear to share such observed characteristics. Such social understandings embrace a variety of sociological approaches, from the more traditional onwards. These approaches, loosely referred to here as microsociology, represent the most common and developed attempts to produce a social understanding of policework. Predominantly, these focus attention on the processes whereby human beings construct and monitor the understandings they have of the social world. They draw attention to the notion that understandings held in common with other human beings are the means by which the social world is understood and perpetuated. This kind of analysis of policework has led to the 'discovery' of 'cop culture'; that is, an uncovering of the rules, norms and values which construct and guide the attitudes and behaviours of police officers. Personality then becomes role performance, attitudes become socially constructed responses to situations rather than individual predispositions, and the ultimate behaviour produced becomes an activity better understood by reference to the social processes which encourage the production and reproduction of such behaviour. This chapter, therefore, is concerned to uncover what this approach can tell us about the social world of the police officer and the rules which guide it. We shall also be concerned with its limits as a guide to understanding policework.

The Theoretical Base of Microsociological Studies

Microsociology is rather a loose term potentially covering a range of different concepts from different theoretical frameworks; symbolic

interactionism, dramaturgy, and phenomenology being the frameworks currently employed most frequently, though role theory was
influential on earlier studies as we shall see. Here, symbolic interactionism will be employed as the overarching framework, with the
others introduced as and where appropriate.

The ideas of symbolic interactionism, popularly associated with
the work of George Herbert Mead, can be located in a longer tradition
of American philosophical thought, namely pragmatism. Pragmatism links the writings of Mead with Thomas, Dewey and Cooley,
all of whom were concerned to construct an image of human
behaviour as neither determined by internal forces (predispositions)
or external forces (environmental/ecological determinism), nor a
matter of free choice. Action is considered to be a product of the interaction between these various constraining forces *and* the interpretive
abilities of the individual.

For Mead, human beings are capable of a range of actions from the
simple reactive response (moving away from something which
burns) to the more complex symbolic responses such as the use of
language. It is this capacity for the use of symbols which, in Mead's
view, frees the human being from the stimulus response chain of the
behaviourist. The human being sees an *interpreted* world, that is a
world which is given meaning and significance by the symbols
attaching to it. Thus symbolic interactionism is concerned to understand how human beings acquire an understanding of these symbols
and how in interaction with others they negotiate and monitor their
shared understandings of the social world. For Mead, this concern
emphasized the importance of understanding the process of socialization, the emergence and continuation of the self, and the process of
interaction.

These ideas became popular particularly in the 1960s with the
emergence of different schools of thought building on different
aspects of Mead's work. The work of Becker and Blumer, among
others, in the 1950s and 1960s claimed to adopt the authentic Meadian
approach of symbolic interactionism. They embraced participant
observation (involvement in the world of the researched, as participating observer) as the primary technique whereby it would be
possible to achieve a sympathetic understanding of the actions of
others. This has led to a range of studies on the police, designed to
uncover their norms and values, using this technique. Within this
tradition, Becker was primarily responsible for introducing the
notion of labelling theory (understanding how the same behaviour
acquired different labels), which has also been influential in looking at
policework.

Becoming a Police Officer

Howard Becker, in classic interactionist mode, documents the
process whereby an individual becomes a marijuana user. This
involved not only acquiring an understanding of the norms and values
associated with marijuana smoking, but also involved acquiring the
'know-how' of smoking: how to do it; where and when this was
appropriate. Becker attempts to provide a 'blueprint for action' for
anyone entering this world. In the same way interactionists attempt to
outline a blueprint for action in the process of becoming a police
officer. This process includes not only being aware of the formal
training process (discussed in Chapter 2), but also being aware of how

> The motive for patrol officers' actions comes from particular
> interests defined within their occupational culture. This includes an
> array of 'recipe' rules which guide him on how to get the job done in
> ways that will appear acceptable to the organization. (Ericson,
> 1982, p. 14)

The formal training programme takes place in controlled circumstances not unlike those circumstances described by Goffman (1968)
in the total institution of a mental hospital. This equips the
probationer with the formal requirements of a professional identity
and with an understanding of the legal and organizational rules within
which s/he will work. In addition, embryonic images of what being
a police officer is about, being 'one of the boys', 'serving the
community', also have their beginnings in the training centre. These
images of police work are confirmed or discounted in the peer group
relationships they construct there (see Van Maanen, 1973, and
Hopper, 1977, on the training of policemen in the United States, and
Ehrlich-Martin, 1980, on policewomen). These embryonic images
are made more 'real' in the next stage of training where, under the
guidance of a relatively experienced officer, the probationer takes to
the street. As Punch says,

> while intensive anticipatory socialisation had taken place in
> training, there was nothing quite like the real thing and that the role
> of law-enforcer, with its overtones of gravity and propriety, has to
> be learned in encounters on the streets. (Punch, 1979, p. 91)

Chatterton's study of policework on the streets of Manchester
demonstrates how young trainees are transformed into 'practical
coppers' (Chatterton, 1979). The 'common sense' (or 'recipe rules') of

the police subculture is absorbed as the police officer becomes street-wise.

> In this job it's not always possible to work to the book. Common sense plays a large part in police work and that's the angle that the practical copper sees the rules from. That's one of the ways you can tell the good bobby from what we call the plastic policeman – the bookman who doesn't know what the job is all about. (Quoted in Chatterton, 1979, p. 83)

In the canteen, in the slack hours of the early morning, as well as under pressure on the street, the junior officer learns about the job, the accepted ways of dealing with practical situations. Punch, again, gives some idea of the importance of this introduction to the rules on the ground:

> an important role was played . . . by the verbally transmitted folk-lore of the station and the 'war stories' of the older hands . . . With such folklore and nostalgic myth the policeman's culture was transmitted from one generation to another . . . this lore confirms images of good police work and implicitly prepares the constable for unforeseen circumstances. For the training does not adequately prepare for the initial immersion in patrol work with its anxieties and new responsibilities in real, rather than simulated situations (Punch, 1979, pp. 87–8)

Learning how policework is done then involves the probationer in acquiring not only a formal knowledge of the law and so on, but crucially an understanding of the informal norms and values of the police subculture.

A 'Working Personality'

This subculture has certain key features equipping the officer with a 'working personality' (Skolnick, 1966; note the difference in implication of 'personality' here, with its emphasis on construction through the activity of 'working', in comparison with the previous chapter). Reiner (1985a, ch. 3), adequately documents the research consensus on these features. He summarizes the key characteristics of this personality (mentioned above on page 14) as being 'mission–action–cynicism–pessimism', 'suspicion', 'isolation/solidarity', 'conservatism', 'machismo', 'prejudice' and 'pragmatism'.

These features of the 'working personality' mean that a police officer is likely to think s/he is doing an important job, preserving law and order from anarchy and that this involves excitement and a degree of commitment not experienced in other occupations. At the same time, the motives of offenders with whom s/he routinely comes into contact are likely to be cynically dismissed. S/he is required to be suspicious as a result of both formal and informal training. It is seen to be an essential part of the job which in part isolates him or her from other sections of the community. This isolation also happens as a consequence of the demands of loyalty (sticking together in the event of criticism from outsiders) and commitment (the need to be impartial and hence beyond reproach) to the job. Failure in achieving the right degree of social aloofness can result in disciplinary action; as happened in the case of John Stalker, deputy chief constable of Greater Manchester, in the summer of 1986, allegedly for associating with known criminals – albeit unwittingly.

This need to maintain the right social distance may also act to distance police sympathies from ordinary people and then serve to reinforce that conservatism other evidence reveals – for example, the American evidence which suggests that police officers support the right politically, and Reiner's evidence that police officers hold conservative moral views (Reiner, 1978, ch. 2). More generally, interactionist studies reveal that this conservatism takes the form of a traditional male dominated culture with alcohol and heterosexual activities being central to it, and one which condones the expression of prejudicial attitudes, towards blacks and women for example (a point to which we return in Chapter 6). The final feature of pragmatism leads an officer to want to get from A to B without thinking too much about the future or how working practices might be changed. These characteristics equip the officer with a day-to-day attitudinal and behavioural framework for his or her activities. Through this 'working personality' an officer learns how to resolve the dilemma of occupational autonomy s/he faces on the streets.

Occupational Subculture and Occupational Autonomy

The context which undoubtedly provides the foundation for the emergence of an apparently autonomous subculture (though the microsociologists do not generally recognize this, nor its implications) is the legal one – characterized by the doctrine of constabulary independence on the one hand, which makes police accountable not to a statutory authority but to the law itself (a point we return to in much greater detail in Chapter 7), and discretion in law enforcement on the other. As Doreen McBarnet has tellingly put it, referring to discretionary law enforcement:

> in vague cases like Breach of the Peace, the offence exists *because* the police say they observed someone loitering, drunk, 'bawling, shouting, cursing and swearing', to quote the daily menu for the district courts. (1978, pp. 205–6, italics in original)

Within this highly permissive legal context, the occupational subculture equips them with the knowledge of how to deal with their substantial (legally granted) discretion on a day-to-day basis. And management initiatives to control the rank and file officer continually have to contend with this legally sanctioned discretion and the 'space' it offers the occupational subculture.

The organizational context is what begins to account for particular features of the culture, such as the need for secrecy. Cain, in expressing the dilemma faced by a police officer in doing his/her job, neatly summarized the essence of this organizational context.

> If a 'war on crime' is demanded, and bureaucratic evidence of success in the form of arrest or clear up rates, then infringement of the rules in order to achieve these objectives become an occupational necessity. Not only is illegality (police primary deviation) engendered, but also secondary deviancy in terms of secretiveness, and the formation of the close-knit, self-protective colleague organization which makes secrecy possible. Such an organization renders the police as impervious to exhortation from the top of their own hierarchy as to the requirements of courts, lawyers, and concerned members of the public. (Cain, 1979, p. 146)

The occupational culture of policework provides the means by which police officers, faced with the dilemma of managing the two demands for legality and efficiency, which in organizational terms means clear up rates (or crimes solved), are able to conceal their 'solution' from external scrutiny.

Other features of policework which interactionists suggest serve to strengthen the culture and its apparent autonomy include the social isolation demanded of the job and the low visibility of much of its activities. Social isolation, cultivated in part to contend with the need for 'impartiality', is enhanced by shiftwork and, at one time, geographical isolation in police housing, though this is much less common now. Suspiciousness, too, contributes by helping to develop a common view of the elements posing a threat to 'law and order', and hence to themselves. This results in the following type of viewpoint:

> We're a tightknit community. We've got to stand by each other because we're getting it from all angles. We get it from outside, the general public, we get it from solicitors, from QCs, we get it from our own bosses. (Quoted in Reiner, 1985a, p. 97)

Low visibility of much of rank and file policework is also held to be crucial in sustaining occupational autonomy. This renders much of what police officers do invisible to senior officers and unrecorded.

> Everything is potentially police business if either a citizen or a policeman makes it so. Many of these encounters go unrecorded; others may be recorded in the constable's pocket book. Few will ever find their way to a central information system. (Cain, 1979, p. 147)

Bittner's work illustrates how such invisibility permits the officers the freedom to interpret their role. In Bittner's (1967) North American study of Skid Row, the place where the 'down and outs' hung out, the officers leant more towards keeping the peace (without involving the legal process) rather than towards law enforcement. Traditional empirical studies confirm the point. Willis's (1983) study of stop and search in London and Luton not only revealed that black youths were more likely to be stopped than white youths (a point we examine in more detail on pages 129–30), but also that two-thirds of the stops occurred independently of the knowledge of senior officers.

Within the context of a powerful cop culture, technological developments, such as the advent of panda cars, may be co-opted and management initiatives subverted. Holdaway (1983, pp. 134–8), for example, has noted the intermeshing of equipment with the values and norms of the culture. The drama of the car chase illustrates the premium placed upon excitement within the subculture and the way in which squad cars have been incorporated into this.

Cain (1973), whose theoretical framework was not strictly speaking within the interactionist tradition (despite using participant observation methods among others), but the more traditional one of role theory, introduces the notion of 'easing' behaviour (how to make life easier on the beat, from the timing of arrests to the knowledge of cafes and pubs where appreciable service (free meals and drinks) will be offered), as a key to recognizing how the norms of the subculture equip the police officer with the knowledge of what is and is not acceptable practice on the beat.

Chatterton notes the importance of learning 'good stories' to be able to offer reasonable and acceptable accounts of one's activities, as a means by which the officer maintains a measure of autonomy on the street. Socialization into the occupational subculture through, for example, learning about excitement, 'good stories' and 'easing' tactics, obviously demands allegiance and loyalty to one's colleagues. This loyalty poses problems for management, critically the problem of control.

> the problem of policing from an administrative perspective is always to what degree it is possible to control the lower participants. (Manning, 1979, p. 65)

Scarman (1981) also notes the problem. The police organization may require a return to the 'local bobby' image, but unless this takes account of the assumptions of the subculture, it will not have an easy passage. The 'good story', in this context, becomes more than just rendering an acceptable account of action. It can become the means of resisting the control of the police command. In similar vein, programmes such as 'policing by objectives' (see above pages 27–8) can be scuppered if they fail to recognize the norms and values of those on the street. Though it should be added that, given the overarching framework of constabulary independence, as currently interpreted, attempts at managerial control operate in a very difficult climate (a point which has implications for accountability as we shall see in Chapter 7). But the occupational culture does not just pose problems of control for management; the knowledge it equips the officer with, the loyalty and secrecy it demands, operate as mechanisms of control in a number of ways.

Policework as Control Work

The interactionist contribution to the analysis of policework as a form of control stems from Becker's (1963) initial input into 'labelling theory'. Briefly, Becker wished to understand how some individuals or groups in society were recognized and labelled as rule breakers while others, who may have behaved in a similar way, were not. Becker argued that labelling was dependent upon the way in which the behaviour was perceived by others. Deviance was a quality in the eye of the beholder, not the act itself. Thus, whether taking property is regarded as theft or a justifiable 'perk', or a violent act is regarded as a criminal assault or a 'deserved' punishment or 'retribution', is dependent on which labels are applied – the condemnatory or the legitimizing sort. From this point of view, deviant behaviour needs to be understood by reference to the differential power of social groups or organizations to label an act normal or abnormal, legitimate or illegitimate. To interactionist writers few social groups have as much power as the police to designate behaviour in this way. As we have seen, the discretionary power of the police officer permits inter-pretation of their role. The permissive nature of the law allows the officer to define much petty criminality on the street, and, in the next two chapters, we look at how such definitional power has been used historically. What will be considered here is how the occupational culture exerts control over the officers themselves; further, how it equips the officers with knowledge which results in patterns of control in street encounters; and, finally, how the police organization can control and direct the nature of these encounters. The cumulative effect of looking at these dimensions of control will hopefully reveal both the knowledge to be gleaned by this level of sociological analysis, and its limitations.

Occupational Culture as Control: the Example of Police Violence

The work of Westley (1970) on the use of violence and the importance of secrecy, and of Manning (1980) who has argued that physical force is sanctioned by the 'realities' of policework even when it is ruled out by law and departmental regulation, draw attention to how violent situations are negotiated by police officers. Observe this example (taken from Baldwin and Kinsey's study of policework in the Lothian force) of how the station sergeant maintains a balance between the formal control by the Police Regulations and the practice on the ground:

> We had this caper last week – the kids breaking into the shop. OK, we did the usual . . . if you don't tell us the truth you're going to get bounced all over the station. But there was never any intention of lifting a finger to any of them. A few quiet words of threat to give them the idea we knew who we had. But there was no intention to beat the shite out of them if they didn't tell us. If you do that they'll swear blind to anything – just 'cos they're getting their head kicked in. There's no point . . . we'll get them another time anyway . . .

But then you've got the other situation where they start to cut up rough. And whenever they start cutting up in this station – in any station – they've lost. If they take a swing at a cop it's fatal . . . The only deterrent is to hit him back fucking harder than he hit you and to let him know that it's not just one – there's two and a half thousand of us that'll keep on hitting him. (Baldwin and Kinsey, 1982, p. 50)

Several writers have documented this balancing act, especially in the manner of gaining evidence and obtaining confessions in British police stations (Holdaway, 1983; McConville and Baldwin, 1981). The occupational subcultural values of secrecy and of colleague loyalty are central to controlling the flow of potentially explosive information, and hence each other, as the efforts by the Metropolitan Police to discover who used violence against youths in Tottenham in 1983 (mentioned in Chapter 1 above) more than adequately illustrates (*Policing London*, no. 22, July–August, 1986, p. 11). In addition one of the paradoxes of policework is that the resort to violence may be acceptable to the external audience, the public. Manning suggests,

While an officer risks sanctions – seldom severe – for using violence inappropriately, there is also the possibility of a hero's rewards. There is very little possibility for accolades for the avoidance of violence. (Manning, 1980, p. 144)

The endorsement of occasional violence by the public supports the use of it as a potential strategy by the occupational culture. The use of violence then serves as a critical example of the power of the occupational culture to control its members through secrecy.

Occupational Culture and Control in Street Encounters

The occupational culture equips the police officer, as has been seen, with a 'working personality', one which, according to Reiner, operates with particular views of the social structure (see Reiner, 1985, pp. 94–6), despite the abstract notion that the 'impartiality' of the police places them 'above politics'. Such views of the social structure, the 'respectable' and the 'roughs' (Cain, 1973), those who threaten the police role (Holdaway, 1983), and so on, sensitize the police officer to particular features of face-to-face encounters which encourage him or her to define situations in particular ways. According to Black (1971) in a study conducted in North America

The probability of arrest increases when a suspect is disrespectful towards the police . . . Even disrespectful complainants receive a penalty of sorts from the police, as their complaints are less likely to receive official recognition. (Black, 1971, p. 1108)

In similar vein, Piliavin and Briar (1964) have documented the importance of demeanour (bearing) in juveniles in North America, with the wrong demeanour increasing the likelihood of arrest. These responses are overlain by a broader way of thinking about the appropriate relation between people, time and space.

[They] were the wrong people, the wrong age, in the wrong place at the wrong time. (Cohen, 1979, p. 131)

This way of thinking is shared by the organization, as police training manuals reveal (cf. Powis, 1977). From the occupational sub-culture the officer learns who to expect to be doing what, where and when. Such learning equips the officer with sets of expectations of what will be demanded of him or her in different places at different times and what members of the general public might be doing in these places at these times. It is this situationally located learning which produces (as we shall see in Chapter 6) the discriminatory pattern of police attention focused upon young working-class males, and, in the inner cities, on black youth, as the stop and search figures, for example, reveal (Willis, 1983; Policy Studies Institute, 1983; Southgate and Ekblom, 1986).

But to understand fully why control in face-to-face interactions operates with the particular stereotypes it does, we must turn to the wider organizational direction of policework in order to understand how resources and manpower become concentrated in particular areas.

The Organization as a Means of Control

Cicourel (1968) examined the relationship between police organization and the level of reported crime. He argued that it is police officers at various levels of decision-making who structure the crime problem by deciding which reported crimes to record and thus make 'official'. Wilkins (1964) developed this point with his notion of deviancy amplification; where the amount of social deviance can be magnified as a consequence of the control exerted. Young's work (1971) provides a pertinent example of this. He considered the cumulative effect of police action against marijuana users in Notting Hill. The activity, once stigmatized by the police and the judiciary, became more secret and therefore, perversely, more pleasurable. The more pressure (in terms of police raids, street trawling for potential users, and court appearances) that was applied, the more the problem amplified: more drug use came to light, the habit became more attractive, or users became more alienated from conventional law-abiding society. In these ways, Young argues, deviant activity can be amplified as a result of control initiatives.

As part of a critical development of writers such as Young, Ditton (1980) suggests that to talk of crime waves is misleading. It is better to refer to 'control waves'. By this Ditton suggests that the police as an agency of social control directly create new ways of dealing with suspects or offenders which in themselves amplify the 'crime problem'. For example, in the case of minor road traffic and juvenile offences, chief officers have considerable latitude in deciding whether to prosecute the offender or to issue a caution. Steer (1970) found that the prosecution rates for adult offences were in part a function of the local chief constable's preferences. Ditchfield (1975) suggested that the new practice of making cautions official rather than unofficial (as happened prior to the Children and Young Persons Act, 1969) had the effect of giving more young people a criminal record (what Stan Cohen, 1979, pp. 346–50, refers to as 'widening the net'; see also Pratt, 1986) – a point we return to in Chapter 6. Once that record was acquired, once juveniles had been formally labelled, they were likely to move further into the criminal justice system. Eric St Johnstone (a former Chief Inspector of Constabulary in England and Wales) argued that the initiative of encouraging specialist drug squads generated a 'control' wave of drug offences. (The relationship between specialization and amplification is dealt with more fully in Chapter 5.)

Specific organizational initiatives and decisions lead to differential emphasis being placed on different criminal activity according to the organization's concern with it. It may also lead to different constabularies having different priorities and therefore different practices for the same kind of criminal activity according to its status locally as a problem (see, for example, Farrington and Dowds, 1985, on crime recording in Nottinghamshire). There is, however, a broader framework of priorities in the allocation of resources and manpower which reflect a similarity rather than a difference of practice; that is, the way in which inner city areas, council estates, shopping centres, 'red light' districts receive very similar kinds of attention in resource allocation across different forces. This reflects broad assumptions of where crime which 'demands' the attention of these resources occurs. The explanation of this broader framework is beyond the concern of this chapter. Little can be learned about this broader framework from microsociological studies. It is within this broader framework, however, that the specific actions of individual officers on the street become explicable. It enables an understanding of *why* an officer is at that place, at that time, perhaps concerned with a particular activity (see Chapter 4 and 5).

The occupational culture equips the police officer with knowledge of what is appropriate or inappropriate behaviour in specific circumstances. The officer does not simply read off the appropriate response from this subculture, but constantly monitors and reflects on the situation, balancing consciously and unconsciously the various demands made of him/her at any specific instance. The extent to which he/she does this competently will now be explored.

Competence and Expertise

In Chapter 2 attention was paid to the notion of 'policing skills'; those techniques deemed necessary for an officer to acquire to do her/his job successfully. We have now seen how the acquisition of such skills occurs, not in the vacuum of the classroom but from the processes of interaction with colleagues within the framework of the police organization. For the interactionist, the competent officer is not one who necessarily can exhibit the 'policing skills' (though this may be part of his/her verbal and behavioural pattern) but is one who can give the impression of competence in a way which is acceptable to colleagues, the wider community, and the courts. The concept of role has been central in analysing this process, though it has been employed in two different ways. The first approach employs traditional role theory, a theoretical framework which predates symbolic interactionism. This attempts to relate the dominant features of the role to the performance of that role, to the expectations of what is required of the person playing the role, and to interaction with others. The second approach stems from the work of Goffman, and represents a particular development within symbolical interactionism. He uses the metaphor of the theatre as a way of depicting social interaction, the idea that social acts are 'performances' constructed with particular 'audiences' in mind. Each of these approaches has been applied in understanding the way in which police officers negotiate specific situations.

In the 1960s two major English studies of policework took the path of role theory, Banton (1964) and Cain (1973). Cain was especially concerned to map out the relationship between a police officer's own definition of the job and the way in which that definition depended upon the expectations and reactions of other parties: family, colleagues, and the local community. Cain suggested that the police role varied according to the type of community which was being policed. She illustrated this by contrasting urban policework with rural policework. In the latter case, she says:

> The crimes may have been defined as 'petty' by city men, but they were defined as important by the rural man who had to deal with them. The people of the community defined them as important, and had power to define them for their policeman. (Cain, 1973, p. 71)

In the rural area, the police officer lived locally, associated regularly in leisure hours with non-police officers and was an integral part of local social life. What constituted policework, therefore, was derived from what the local public thought it should be. Conversely, in the city, with its relatively heterogeneous population and apparently anonymous social life, role definitions were derived from the occupational culture of policework rather than the community. This approach leads to thinking of a competent officer as one whose role performance is constructed by reference to the expectations of others.

For Goffman (1959), however, interaction is much more a process of impression management in which social actors use the drama-turgical skills of 'dramatic realisation' and 'expressive control' to convince others of their competence and worthiness. Manning's work (1977) is the clearest application of Goffman's concept of role to policework.

> in their everyday work the police . . . must dramatize the *appearance* of control. That is, they must segment their audiences so that certain presentations are available only to some segments of the society; they must control the information available on their actions in order to be effective . . . they must display a unity of purpose and of action regardless of the varying statuses and roles of police personnel and of their own political, moral, and personal attitudes; they must decrease the amount of information available to their public that indicates the dirty, the boring, the ineffectual, the illegal or potentially immoral; and they must through the management of appearances create the sense of commitment to and enforcement of rules and tenets on which there is only an 'as if' public agreement. (Manning, 1977, pp. 17–18, italics in original)

Thus from the process of becoming a police officer onwards, techniques of impression management are developed. Competence is demonstrated by fitting the appropriate appearance to the appropriate occasion. Moving in on a street busker, giving directions to a member of the public, intervening in a domestic dispute, taking part in a drugs raid, all require a display of competence and expertise, not just dependent on the expectations of others (as in Cain's work), but also dependent upon how the officers themselves interpret, signify, and construct appearances in all these instances. This approach suggests policework should be understood as a process of negotiation in which the officer weighs up the alternative strategies, on a stage bounded by the demands of the organization and occupation on one side, and the public and the courts on the other. Fielding (1984) has looked at how the officer acquires the confidence to negotiate his/her world, by focusing on how the process of becoming a police officer means learning how to recognize and respond to situations. The recruit's ability to handle situations changes as his/her knowledge and experience grows. This knowledge is not necessarily ever complete. A police officer continues to negotiate, interpret and differentiate situation from situation in acquiring greater knowledge and experience. He/she may choose to specialize in certain types of encounters; drugs, cheque frauds, etc. But all will acquire the competence to negotiate for themselves what makes the job manageable for them.

Microsociology: Summary and Assessment

The sociological perspective focused on here has offered an understanding of policework qualitatively different from that discussed in Chapter 2, yet it has been concerned with the same issues; the attitudes and behaviour of police officers. The perspective drawn on here has highlighted the way in which those attitudes and behaviours are the product of the concerted action of police officers, reflecting the understandings of the world they have and hold in common with each other. The observed patterns of similar attitudes and behaviour of police officers are not to be understood by reference to the psychology of individuals. This means that, while individual officers may or may not have particular personalities, motivations, etc., the explanation for their similarly expressed attitudes and observed behaviour lies within understanding the powerful controlling effect of the norms and values of the occupational subculture. It can be seen that these norms and values equip the officer with the kind of knowledge necessary to enable him or her to negotiate their day-to-day activities. The norms and values of the subculture constitute a framework for the officer on the street which helps him/her resolve the dilemma of how to deal with this autonomy.

It is important to note, however, that none of this *necessarily* entails that the officer simply 'reads off' the appropriate response from what is seen to be acceptable to the subculture, nor is that subculture *necessarily* unchanging. Returning to the original image of the human being underpinning the interactionist tradition discussed at the beginning of this chapter, the norms and values of the subculture are negotiated by police officers in each situation in which they find themselves. Thus space is created for a degree of individuality in the form of different policing styles (cf. Reiner, 1985a, pp. 103–6. For a structural account of the origins of police styles, see Wilson, 1968). Interactionist accounts such as those mentioned operate well as descriptions of day-to-day policing. They offer valuable insights into how police officers do their job, and add a welcome level of *profane reality* to counteract the idealistic notion of how organizations function implicit in 'policing by objectives' schemes. The question of 'why', however, is less satisfactorily dealt with. This becomes clearer when a more critical stance is adopted towards the material in this chapter.

First there are methodological problems. While the advantage of interactionists' primary research method – participant observation – lies with the researcher gaining a realistic experience of the social world s/he is interested in, everything depends on how comprehensively that social world can be revealed by participation and observation alone. Two sorts of error become possible: that resulting from participants successfully concealing aspects of their world from the researcher; and that resulting from the inability to take into account unobserved processes, beyond the immediate 'world' under observation, that nevertheless affect the social world being studied.

The first type of error is well illustrated by Punch's *Policing the Inner City* (1979). Punch spent six months attached to the same group of officers, and, despite his apparent acceptance by, and involvement with, these officers, and the detailed material produced, the partial nature of his account later became clear. He himself reported the following, after leaving the field of investigation:

> One evening, I went to Itan's flat for a celebration and several policemen began talking excitedly about corruption. I learnt more in that evening, thanks to the liberating effects of alcohol, than in all my fieldwork. It was not so much a series of shocking personal revelations . . . but more a subterranean police culture which had

largely escaped me, suddenly emerged . . . Hansard Tom
explained, 'How much do you think that you found out when you
were with us?. . . Well, we only let you see what we wanted you to
see. You only saw about fifty per cent. We showed you only half the
story.' (Punch, 1979, p. 13)

That which Punch did learn forms part of a more recent work,
Conduct Unbecoming (1985), and it could be argued that, eventually, he
did manage to uncover the whole picture. Be that as it may, the fact
remains that the success of participant observation is partly dependent
on the willingness of respondents to reveal all. Since secrecy is a key
component of the occupational culture, and since police clearly have a
lot of dark secrets they would prefer not to reveal, comprehensive
revelations seem unlikely. And, by definition, the extent of police
secrets will remain unknown.

The second sort of error, that stemming from the inability of
participant observation to take into account processes that have not
been directly observed, can be partly overcome by using a combination of methods. Thus observational techniques can be combined
with other sources of data collection, particularly in-depth interviews
and questionnaires. The Policy Studies Institute Report, *Police and
People in London, Vols 1–4* (1983), is a good example of the way in
which these techniques can be made complementary while retaining a
feel for the detailed reality of day-to-day policework. Such a strategy,
however, does not necessarily bring all the unobserved processes to
light, as Cain observes:

Explanations will be bounded by what the researcher has been able
to see or discuss . . . Effectively this precludes the possibility of
understanding the ways in which the institutions of society affect
one another. Usually it precludes understanding of the upper
echelons of the organization since senior people tend to work in
individual offices, rather than in units which can economically be
observed . . . the explanation is new [but] it is bounded by the
organization studied, and the senior personnel are not studied.
(Cain, 1979, p. 146)

The tendency of only the relatively powerless to be studied within
organizations is not a new phenomenon within sociology. In the
context of policework, however, it does affect how the data are to be
meaningfully analysed.

The theoretical problems of the approach result from the partiality of the observations and the over-reliance on accounts of those studied. The former problem is well captured in the following quotation:

> In short, whilst the daily happenings, on the streets and in the locker room, are examined in all their apparently kaleidoscopic variations, the law, the formal organization, its policies and senior officers are all assumptive categories: essentially unexamined. (Grimshaw and Jefferson, 1987, p. 8)

Most of the work discussed in this chapter has focused solely on the day-to-day activities of those at the base of the police hierarchy. In so doing a picture of 'normal policework' has been drawn in which 'easing' behaviour, the 'working personality', secrecy and loyalty are some of the key features. None of these features reveal how, if at all, the law, formal organizational policy or senior officers impinge on this world, and hence must render explanations of these features partial at best. Grimshaw and Jefferson (1987) point, for example, to divisional differences in policing, where the role of the superintendent plays a crucial part in establishing the acceptable parameters of police-work for that division, and in producing differences in the responses of the occupational culture. Understanding the possible kind of impact of these features, of the law and of the organization, is crucial before the political implications of the approach – with regard to accountability, for example – can be properly assessed. This we deal with in Chapter 7.

Underlying the theoretical problem of incorporating unobserved processes is the relationship between the occupational subculture and the social groups and divisions that collectively make up the wider structure of society. This relationship has been hinted at here in two main ways. First, in the observation that the police subculture operates with particular views encouraging racial and sexual stereo-typing on the part of individual officers. Although Holdaway (1983) suggests that the racial stereotyping does not lead to a form of policing black people that is any different to normal policing this still leaves unexamined the question of how such 'normal' practices relate to the wider structure of society. Is that the kind of policing society demands? If so, why? If not, why are such practices routine? Secondly, it has been suggested that, through the direction of man-power and resources, crime is on occasion as much a function of this process as it is a function of actual criminal activity. While inter-actionism has cast some light on how and why particular crimes emerge as particular problems at particular points in time, it fails to explain why the broader framework of resource allocation is similarly structured across different places at different times. The answer to both these questions must lie in understanding what cannot be directly observed: the historical emergence of the police as an organization, and the police's relationship to the wider structure of society (see Chapters 4, 5 and 6).

In conclusion, it can be seen that the psychological approach and the microsociological approach offer different explanations of policework. Both remain inadequate. While police officers may operate with individual characteristics which inform their policing style within the norms and values of the subculture, without locating this subculture socially, in a wider legal, historical and social process, still only a small part of the whole picture of policework has been painted.

Suggestions for Further Reading

Cain, M. (1973), *Society and the Policeman's Role* (London: Routledge & Kegan Paul).

Ericson, R. V. (1982), *Reproducing Order: A Study of Police Patrol Work* (University of Toronto Press).

Holdaway, S. (1983), *Inside the British Police* (Oxford: Blackwell).

Manning, P., and Van Maanen, J. (eds) (1978), *Policing: A View from the Street* (Santa Monica, Calif.: Goodyear).

4 Policework Histories

(i) From the Anglo-Saxons to the Consolidation of the 'New Police'

Introduction

In moving beyond the microsociological focus on what can be directly observed, we turn here and in the next chapter, to historical studies of the emergence of the police and then, in Chapter 6, to studies of the police's relationship to the key social divisions constitutive of the wider structure of society. The historical studies deal with the changes, through time, of the relationship between the institution of police and society. The main point of studying history is to provide a sort of test bed – a retrospective test of current ideas or hypotheses; and, similarly, to enable us to distinguish between significant changes ('what's *really* new') and more superficial ones ('what simply *appears* to be new'). In other words, studying the history of the relations between police and society can help us better understand these relations in the present – which is the focus of Chapter 6.

However, historical evidence does not explain itself but requires interpretation. And the same evidence can be interpreted differently, depending on one's theoretical presuppositions. Broadly, we can talk of three different theoretical attempts to make sense of the historical facts about policework; namely, the evolutionary, the class-based and the accidental.

The first of these emphasizes the *evolutionary* character of developments in policing, regarding these as progressive and, once the police 'idea' caught on, incremental. It stems from a general view of the world which tends to equate change with progress and sees both as stemming from the rational adoption of 'good' ideas. In its relatively uncritical, incremental approach to progress, and its idealism, it can be characterized broadly as conservative.

The *class-based* approach emphasizes the relation between

developments in policing and changes in the political economy or
class relations. From this perspective, police have an intimate role to
play in protecting the material interests of the dominant class against
those of subordinate ones and hence in sustaining and reproducing
class inequalities. It stems from a general vision which sees material
interests, not ideas, determining the rate and direction of change, as
economic developments throw up new classes to rise up and depose
old ones. Its critical approach to the idea of change and development
marks it out as radical.

The *accidental* view of history emphasizes the importance of local
contingencies and unforeseen accidents. The best ideas of mice and
men, including the rational pursuit of class interests, are laid to waste,
in this view, by historical 'mistakes' and 'accidents'. The result is that
no pattern, neither a history of progressive ideas nor of succeeding
class interests, is discernible in history. The best one can do is to trace
and explain the local and accidental in all its bizarre uniqueness. Its
parent vision is a pragmatic view of the world, and its merely sceptical
notion of change places it somewhere between the conservative and
radical approaches.

In approaching the literature, we will highlight the differences
between approaches and their relative strengths and weaknesses in
accounting for the 'facts'. Our own preferred reading, which will
become evident, is one that *prioritizes* changes in class relations and
their resulting impact on developments in policework, but without
making other factors, such as ideas and local contingencies, redundant.
Any reading that tries to squeeze the data exclusively through one
or other of the theoretical grids will be found wanting, unable to
accommodate the richness of the empirical data; by the same token,
any reading that fails to connect the police developments to changes in
class relations will, as we hope to show, end up mistaking the trees for
the wood. Partly, it is a question of distance. The closer one gets to any
particular development, the more striking seem local and contingent
factors. The further away one gets, the more one is struck by clearly
discernible trends, such as the growing influence of the central state,
overriding local contingencies. But near or far, failing to ask 'who
benefits?' or 'whose definition of crime or order prevails?', risks
producing the sort of naive idealism it is the job of a social scientific
approach to question.

Contrasting pre-Norman, Anglo-Saxon policing with the present
we can clearly discern a general shift from a locally based, unpaid,
non-specialist form of policing to one which is centrally influenced,
salaried and increasingly specialized. But, to rest content there would
be to risk suggesting the shifts have been unilinear and inevitable. And

viewed from this end of the telescope, this may seem to be the case. But tracing the changes through the centuries reveals an altogether more contingent picture; it also enables us to understand better *why* these shifts took place *when* they did. With that objective in mind, let us now turn to the histories.

Pre-Modern Policing

The histories of 'pre-modern' policing have tended to be recounted within a conservative evolutionary framework. More recently, critical class-based approaches have begun to make an appearance, but the relative absence of detailed local histories of police for this period has effectively precluded the 'accidental' approach altogether. Consequently, rather than attempt to sketch how each of these three approaches handled the same basic data and then offer our own synthesis—something we shall do for the later period—we shall simply sketch the agreed bones of the police story up to the early nineteenth century, mentioning such competing interpretations as have appeared in the literature, and offering our own synthesis as and when necessary *en passant*.

The first identifiable form of policework, one that dominated England until the end of the thirteenth century, was the *tything* system. Saxon law required every citizen over the age of twelve to form a group with nine of his neighbours called a tything. Each tything was committed to undertake related functions—to apprehend and deliver to court any one of its members who had committed a crime, to hold suspects in custody before trial, to present information on wrongdoers in the tythings, to ensure the payment of the king's taxes, and to maintain the forest and game laws. In turn, groups of tythings were formed into a hundred, whose headman (commonly the 'reeve') enforced judicial and administrative power under the king. The system is generally represented as being a voluntary (i.e. unpaid) law enforcement function – but it rested on severe fines imposed on all the members if the reeve failed to perform his functions.

Its surface attraction was its *localism*, a feature that is one of the major ideological continuities in conventional conservative portrayals of Anglo-American policework. The tything signified a decentralized police system, responsive to local community needs, and conducted on an unpaid basis. But this conventional version of the tything system fails to acknowledge the unequal and divided society in which this first police system was constructed. It fails to recognize that 'local' can connote local elites as well as local communities. Simply to contrast local with the centre obscures the different interests at the local level which, prior to the Norman invasion, meant Saxon lords and their allies on the one hand, and their local communities on the other.

After 1066, as the tything system was systematized into the *frank-pledge* in those parts of southern England directly under Norman control, the social division between the police agents and the policed became more evident. For as frankpledge sought to take control away from the locality and place it directly within the governance of the monarch, elite interests became directly associated with the centre. Under frankpledge, the tything fines went into the king's treasury. The tything was supervised not by the provincial nobility but by the king's appointee – a sheriff. Further, when in default, tything members were brought not to local manorial courts but to the central courts of the king's justices. The frankpledge came to represent the maintenance of an alien authority, a compulsory economic and political relationship. Even if the early tything system's 'voluntari-ness' was ultimately backed by coercion, the new system, dominated by alien 'non-local' interests, was more so.

The more mandatory the frankpledge became, with its rules those of king's specification rather than of local elite or community, the more it fell into disuse. As compulsion, it depended upon loyalty that could not be guaranteed, a contractual fealty in which the benefits to the local community and elites were few – for example, in the failure to resolve immediate social problems such as dealing with outlaws. By the time of Henry III, the assizes could be delayed for up to seven years, during which period the tythings had to pay for the custody of the suspects and to bear other financial costs. The frankpledge could only operate effectively as long as the policing system conferred benefits to the local community (with which it was not concerned), or directly served the interests of the ruling elite – and these it was incapable of carrying out effectively.

Out of the local dissatisfactions with both the frankpledge and tything-men systems, there emerged an alternative: parish constables. Although given formal recognition by the Statutes of Winchester (1285), that legislation only unified existing local developments. It imposed from the top what had already grown organically from below. One person from each parish would serve as unpaid constable for a year, primarily to arrest offenders and to deliver them to the local court. Citizen powers of arrest were reinforced by the specific obliga-tion on the constable to conduct arrest. With the aid of the night watch in the larger towns, the constable carried out a preventive system of patrol. Through the hue-and-cry, which required every citizen to help pursue an offender, the constable legally obliged other citizens to conduct reactive policing. And with concomitant minor judicial powers, the officer could sometimes brand, mutilate, whip and fine those who met communal disapproval. With a wide mandate to maintain community law and order, the position was voluntary, the primary allegiance to the locality.

The Justice of the Peace Act, 1361, re-established the supremacy of the central state, giving the new justices the conjoined powers of law enforcement, of judiciary, and of administration in the counties. Drawn from the petty nobility, the justices derived their power from the king, not from the community. Their primary allegiance was to the throne. Over time, the constables became general factotums for the justices, running lowly errands. Their relative status was enshrined in the Leet Court, where the magistrate judged, and the constable 'fetched and carried'. This specific relationship became generalized, as the judicial powers spread from that forum to ensure the rule of the nobility on behalf of the king over the local community. The constable, in so far as the office had possessed any local independence, was incorporated in the larger collective judicial system of the central state. The job had become that of a servant rather than that of a volunteer, a relative menial concerned with all the unwanted tasks of the parish rather than a narrower function of law enforcement. The volunteer was slowly transferred into a paid official, with obligations to taskmasters outside the locality, and with a growing responsibility to act as a control agent against the lower social strata.

The decline of the status and authority of the constable between the Middle Ages and the onset of the Industrial Revolution has been well-documented. In the orthodox conservative histories, the office has been best remembered through the image of Shakespeare's Dogberry, an incompetent, inefficient, feckless fellow (Critchley, 1978; Trevelyan, 1941; Rowse, 1950). In them, the constable's status loss related to the widening in his humdrum duties. As with other parish offices – the surveyor of highways and the overseer of the poor – substitutes were hired from the lowest strata of the community. Some of the citizens liable for the constable's post could buy a 'Tyburn Ticket' – a certificate issued to anyone who apprehended a felon and which could be sold to another person, thus allowing the latter to escape parish constable duty. The constable's function became one of forced labour, based on either threats or on minimal remuneration. From within this evolutionary framework, the parish constable was an idea whose time was fast running out.

The picture looks different when we recall the extent of society's social divisions, whose boundaries the constable increasingly patrolled. This is because the period marks the slow rise to supremacy of a capitalist economy. At this stage, the use of property as capital is only beginning to get under way, but in its wake is establishing new polarizations, as land previously held in common is enclosed for 'profitable' development as a capital investment, and many of those previously using the land for subsistence purposes find themselves landless. Until the eighteenth century the position of constable, according to more recent radical histories, was more attractive to the yeomanry and to similar strata than has been recognized in conventional accounts. The consequent polarization of a stable tenantry on one side, and the landless poor on the other side (with the enactment of political measures such as the Enclosure Acts), meant the local squire-archy and the landed nobility increasingly had an economic interest in separating and controlling the latter. According to Sharpe (1983), the constable in the divided late mediaeval village played increasingly a class-control function. From within this class-based framework, incompetence takes on a different meaning. According to Robinson (1978), constables were only portrayed as inefficient at policing the poor because they failed to control their own class in a way that satisfied the local gentry. Their loyalties, irrespective of their new position as a servant of the local squirearchy, remained to their class peers.

But critically, whether or not the constable was incompetent, whether or not the hiring of a paid substitute resulted in inferior work, there was a wider structural source of problems for the policing duty. The constable was caught between the ideal of social order promulgated by the central governmental elites and by the church, and the differing local (elite and community) notions of social order (Sharpe, 1983). What London and the justices regarded as a legal priority – such as the enforcement of the gaming laws – was not seen in quite the same way by those who had more communal notions of surviving off the land. Priorities in ideas of policing were increasingly marked by differences in social class and in geographical location – the provinces or London. By the end of the eighteenth century, the state had become increasingly intrusive in local affairs. The constable was the cutting edge of a massive shift away from local communal justice towards state public justice. 'Public order' was an ambiguous term, and the constable could only rarely satisfy the conflicting viewpoints:

> When comparing police forces over time, what we should have in mind is a spectrum with external 'state' control at one end, and 'internal' community control at the other. The exact location of

police controls on that spectrum will . . . differ from society to society . . . in early modern England . . . that location was moving towards the state's end of the spectrum. (Sharpe, 1983, p. 14)

A similar point could be made about the office of the justice of the peace. Like the constables, the magistrates increasingly found the task of mediating justice on behalf of central government, without economic or significant political reward, irksome and time-consuming. Delegation became relatively common, to the lower squirearchy and yeomanry and in the municipalities to the new stratum of shop-keepers and traders. For the latter, the incentive to surrender working hours was sometimes directly economic. The justices came to depend for their incomes partly on the fines – which in other times would have gone direct to the king's treasury – and partly on bribes. Direct economic benefits became increasingly important in the possession and sale of this higher office in the policing system. What was sauce for the magistrates inevitably became gruel for the constable.

The economic transformation of the office of justice had two other effects on the policing system. The new social stratum assuming the justice position had different definitions of criminality from the concerns of the previous incumbents. For example, shopkeepers as justices in the expanding cities increasingly defined policing in their own interests. The street traders and itinerant hawkers suffered accordingly. Secondly, where justice was directly linked to economic reward, punishment became more tuned to financial restitution than to physical penalties. Without understanding these economic changes, changes in the law enforcement system become difficult to decipher.

With the growth of mercantile capitalism, the objects of police-work were gradually reconstructed. Guarding the transit of goods on the highways, and their storage in dockside warehouses, became new policing priorities. Later in the eighteenth century, with the rise of industrial capitalism, yet further new policing tasks were defined – 'theft' from work became a priority (Phillips, 1977; Hay, 1983), and other specific tasks such as tracing counterfeiters (Styles, 1980) were assumed. The new paid specialist grew out of the changing productive relations of the country. The 'local' character of police-work concealed different ideas about social control. The assumed homogeneity of local society was increasingly revealed as a fiction by conflicts between those with property to defend and those without. And policework was a central component in the struggle.

Payment for policing was not, of course, new. Throughout the Middle Ages, merchants had commonly employed private reactive guards (agents required to respond only *after* a crime had been

committed) and the widespread utilization of gamekeepers across
continental Europe represented the most visible apparatus of paid
policing for the common people. But in Britain, towards the end of
the eighteenth century, there was an explosion of paid forms of
enforcement.

Legal change assisted these changes in policework. Old legislation
such as the Vagrancy Statutes and Stop-and-Search Powers were
adapted for use against footpads (Chambliss, 1971; Brogden and
Brogden, 1984). New legislation enabled policework to become
more concentrated on particular objects or persons since it tied reward
to particular results. The William and Mary Act, 1742, for example,
provided that anyone who captured and successfully prosecuted a
thief would receive a forty-shilling reward or could take possession of
the latter's property. A royal pardon was available for any offender
who betrayed to the law officers two others – in paying one felon, the
law captured two more. McMullan (1982) has described the medley of
practices in which recruits from the criminal underworld were sent
back to profit from reporting on other criminal activities.

The most visible institutional example of these changes was the
London Bow Street Office, from the middle of the eighteenth
century. The Fielding brothers, as the resident paid magistrates at the
commercial hub of the trading capital, innovated in several ways.
They appointed paid thief-takers, introduced a preventive horse
patrol of the surrounding district (Phillips, 1980), and circulated the
hue-and-cry crime sheet, as part of a co-ordinated information system
for tracking down fugitives. The Bow Street Patrol itself operated
mainly as a preventive force on the capital's thoroughfares, but also
conducted entrepreneurial thief-taking operations at a national level
(Radzinowicz, 1955).

Also, by the end of the eighteenth century, private paid policing
was institutionalized to protect mercantile goods in the riverside
warehouses of the seaports. (Stop-and-search powers, for example,
were first codified not for the city streets but to control potential
'lumpers and glutsmen' (Ascoli, 1979) from molesting merchant
ships on the Thames, Mersey and Avon.) The Thames River Police
emerged as a private company in 1798, to be followed soon by similar
bodies in Bristol and in Liverpool. As the first waged police, paid
largely on a preventive principle rather than by immediate result, they
represented a further step away from the voluntary principle.

But not all policing was following the specialist path. Throughout
the country, Associations for the Prosecution of Felons emerged to
protect the property of the new manufacturing classes (Hay, 1983),
and occasionally to service the requirements of lower-class victims of

petty theft and of assault (Brewer and Styles, 1980; King, 1984). Further, remnants of the old voluntary procedures remained: the hue-and-cry (as written into the Statutes of Winchester), which required every citizen to help pursue an offender; and the posse comitatus (literally the power of the county), which required all males between the ages of 15 and 70 years (on pain of fine) to help the justice and his servant, the constable, to assist in the preservation of public order, especially in the case of riots and of other disturbances. Paid policing, often with a mandate unrestricted by parish or by urban habitat, was linked with a hotchpotch of the old voluntary, non-specialist policing, encompassing constables, night watch, and magistrates.

Summary

By the beginning of the nineteenth century, policing in mainland Britain had assumed the following characteristics. The formal system was primarily reactive – with occasional preventive patrol elements. But that reactive system nevertheless depended in the cities on a kaleidoscope of informal pre-emptive and infiltrative techniques (Rock, 1985). It was largely victim-based. Consequently, it was cheap and little burden on city and central state finances. The thief-taker had come to dominate the policing system of the eighteenth century as the intermediary between offender and victim, committed not to the capture of felons but to the restitution of goods for a price. Private entrepreneurship had assumed an increasing role in police-work. Finally, elements of an organized system were emerging through the agency of private manufacturers and merchants in recruiting private bodies such as the Thames River Police (Spitzer and Scull, 1977).

Local policing was conducted by a variety of agencies with little co-ordination (Emsley, 1983). In London, for example, policing functions were conducted variously by justices (through the Bow Street patrols), by the night watch, by the prosecution associations, by the thief-takers, by the militia (the countrywide agency compulsorily elected from the respected classes), and by the army. In a few instances the voluntary principle remained intact. The policing function was conducted by a civilian armed only with citizen's rights of arrest and prosecution – though sometimes with truncheon or sabre.

In sum, in Britain, with the emergence of industrial capitalism, there were contrary trends reflecting the tension between central state and the tradition of local communal rights. Voluntary policing was disappearing under the increasing pressures to criminalize the poor, and the tighter coupling of law enforcement to the economic requirements of the class system of the new capitalist social relations. Economic commitment to trade and to production was not so much directing law enforcement away from the general priorities of public order as increasingly encompassing specialist defence of particular rights of merchant, shopkeeper and manufacturer. The pre-industrial age closed with the ascendancy of the privately employed specialist.

High Noon for the Parish Constable and the 'Thief-Taker' – the Rise of the 'Professional Police'

The most written-up period in the history of modern policework is that covering the late eighteenth and the early nineteenth centuries: the period that witnessed the birth of industrial capitalism and of Peel's 'new' police – the 'plague of the blue locusts' (Storch, 1975). Consequently, for our purposes, it provides the most comprehensive testing ground for the three historical approaches – conservative, radical and accidental. While the notion of the 'new' police implies novelty, historians differ whether the moment is best thought of in terms of its disjunctive features or in terms of its continuities, with an older consensus favouring the former and a newer one the latter. In looking at our object of concern – namely how well the three contrasting approaches account for the particular features characterizing the 'new' (locally based but centrally influenced salaried bureaucracy with a range of general, proactive tasks, i.e. activity designed to seek out or prevent crime), against the backdrop of our account of the 'premodern' period – elements of continuity, as well as new features, are clearly discernible.

In explaining what factors give rise to the new police, *conservative* histories emphasize one or more of three things:

(1) the importance of the 'mob', the fears by the respectable city dwellers of a new urban working class which might come to rule the streets;
(2) fear of crime, which dominated the official reports of the period;
(3) 'social disorganization', resulting from the complex processes of urbanization and migration.

Underlying these there tends to be an unwritten law of administrative progression, by which all the developing public agencies of early nineteenth-century Britain became standardized at varying stages in response to the pressures of industrialism, and collectively contribute to the 'pacification' of Britain (cf. Critchley, 1970). *Radical* commentaries relate the rise of professional policing to the crisis deriving from the transition from a predominantly agricultural and mercantile capitalist economy to an emergent industrial capitalist society. The police role as an agency of *class* control is always resisted – which means the pacification of society is always only partial. The *accidental* approach stresses how the particular local venue was critical in the development of policework. In a major collection of essays, Bailey has suggested that modern policework stemmed from specific provincial problems and circumstances:

> The evolution of professional policing was determined by the complexities and traditions of local towns and cities, the peculiarities of their security and crime problems and the unique features of their municipal structures. Professional policing developed through a series of . . . makeshift practices and policies. (Bailey, 1981, p. 18)

Conservative histories

(1)   Critchley (1978), in the major orthodox text, assumed that *riots* were the precipitating factor in the formation of the New Police. Lyman (1964) has pointed, for example, to the preceding Queen Caroline street disorder as playing a major part in the emergence of the Metropolitan Police. More recently, several American studies have emphasized the role of urban dissent and have followed the major contribution of Silver (1967) in elaborating on the riot theme (Walker, 1977; Maier, 1970). Intolerance of public disorder increased as street manifestations were transformed from symbolic protest against particular targets to general, material destruction. Urban property owners increasingly called for organized protection. As the slum dwellers spilt over the boundaries of the growing rookeries, that older politics of the street collided with the new bourgeois standards of the industrializing city.

(2)   *Rising crime levels* feature in many accounts produced at the time. Alarms about the apparent extent of the new crime phenomenon apparently featured prominently in the original parliamentary debate. Edmund Chadwick's (selective) production of witnesses for the Royal Commission of 1839 (which paved the way for many of the provincial forces) gave most weight to crime. Many of the more conservative historians (following their doyen, Charles Reith) have taken it for granted that the creation of the New Police was a direct

response to rises in reported crime, which in turn were considered to be a consequence of over-hasty urban growth. This view was also prominent in many of the early American accounts (Lane, 1967). Briefly, it was assumed that the traditional watch/constable system was ineffective in the face of the crime wave, generated by the new 'indisciplined' urban population.

(3)   A more developed version of this thesis appears in the work of those writers who draw principally upon Chicagoan theories of *social disorganization*. They link the rise of the New Police to the processes of immigration and of urbanization which according to the Chicago school theorists (cf. Park and Burgess, 1925), produced areas of social disorganization (areas without a stable set of cultural values) in their wake. Police departments were established in the main to control the migrant poor and the tramping phenomenon (that characterized both Great Britain (Jones, 1982) and the United States (Harring, 1983) at different times) on behalf of the urban elites. People control rather than crime or riot control, until the newcomers could be socialized by the institutions of education and factory toil, was the *raison d'être* of early organized policework (Johnson, 1979).

Underlying these accounts is an evolutionary notion of the growth of bureaucracy. The traditional view has been that the New Police arose as part of the general movement within early industrialism to regulate the disorderly edges of society through bureaucratic institutions (Radzinowicz, 1955). The same model of organization that apparently served well in times of external conflict, with its discipline and rule-bound hierarchical position, could similarly be utilized for 'ordering' the city. 'Citizens and city fathers alike [thought that a] regular force of patrolmen answering to a central office and on duty round the clock was a conveniently flexible instrument of administration' (Lane, 1980, p. 8). An instrument of city government, the new municipal police were available for miscellaneous tasks. Following Critchley, a school of early writers have dealt with the 'English' police as a form of administrative evolution. The consolidation of waged police in the capital was soon imitated in the provinces. The tentacles spread across the nation as city governments recognized the virtues of bureaucratic organization as an essential and ubiquitous instrument of authority.

The most recent and forcible representation of this thesis has been by Monkkonen (1981). Cities adopted paid policework agencies as part of the shift from class-based politics to liberal pluralistic urban administration. As traditional municipal elites gradually abandoned their monopoly of local power, the management of city affairs could no longer work on a personal, particularistic basis, and the new industrial ideas of rule-based, impersonal, universalistic standards became the appropriate tool. Ideas of waged policework and of policing organization were 'contagiously diffused' from larger cities to the smaller as part of a gradual innovation process. Once an urban unit reached a critical demographic size, it imitated the forms of police organization and control practised by the larger municipalities.

Usually these traditional Whig histories incorporate a 'pacification' thesis – giving police a central vote in the pacification of English society. The general claim is that despite initial opposition from the working and 'criminal' classes, waged policework, as an arm of a neutral state, slowly advanced across Britain to gradual public acceptance.

Recent American research within this tradition (Walker, 1977; Fogelson, 1977) has proffered a more sophisticated version of these histories. Initial inefficiencies, lack of appropriate services to all social classes, and occasional corruption and brutality, were all gradually ironed out. Four indices are used as measures of progress in police–public relations. Technological innovations made the organization more efficient in responding to public distress. Rising educational standards of police officers assisted in the development of more harmonious relations. An apparent relative increase in the crime clear-up rate throughout the century suggested a growing public acceptance and improved police response to public worries over crime. Wider police involvement in social service tasks in working–class communities assuaged police–class relations.

There are evident problems with such theses. The riot explanation has lost much of its appeal. As more recent writers have suggested (especially Monkkonen, 1981), there were few such precipitating conflicts and often (especially in the United States) a long interval between mob violence and the creation of the New Police. Furthermore, the evidence of rising crime prior to the 1830s is unsubstantiated at best. Even if it was simply a question of perception of rising crime, then that in itself was no reason for the urban leadership to respond with a uniformed police instead of using the army and other traditional measures (Monkkonen 1981). Lane (1980), for example, has repudiated his earlier commitment to the social disorganization model of explanation, stressing instead how urban conditions of life put a premium on co-operation, personal discipline and regular routine.

More generally, there is the problem of evolutionism: of assuming a natural sequence of events in which the public (or key decision-makers) automatically recognized that uniformed policework was the rational and only possible response to such social problems. In particular, in response to the more sophisticated version of those histories noted above, organizational and technological innovations – from the preventive beat system to the later call-box (Johnson, 1979) – can be seen as attempts to control the lower ranks as much as to develop a better police service. Higher educational standards arguably alienated police officers further from the class that received the brunt of coercive policework. Clear-up rates, as we now know, can be improved in various artificial ways and hence are little more than organizational measures with little relevance to police success in combating crime. And, finally, the extent of the service role is usually over-stated – a police officer could not intervene in local disputes in working-class neighbourhoods without the support of the coercive power of the state, and consequently was neither universally invited nor welcomed. More generally, prior to the development of the New Police, the conventional reaction to rising crime in particular had been through changes in the penal measures, not through modifications in the powers and status of the policing agency.

Further, there is the problem of mistaking symptoms for causes. Riots, crime, urbanization and migration are symptomatic processes. To rest content with explanations at this level is to offer, at best, partial explanations. More importantly, such myopic explanations can seriously distort the analysis. Critically, these processes need to be contextualised within the broader political and economic changes then taking place – a structure that radical class-based approaches take very much to heart.

Class-Based Histories

More critical writers, with debts variously to Marx and to Foucault, have located waged police development within the crisis of the onset of industrial capitalism. The new social relations of emergent capitalism required novel devices for regulating social behaviour, for keeping the lower classes in their place once the former mechanisms of control associated with feudalism had broken down in the urban centres. This disciplinary movement, evident in the similarity between policework and other systems of social control, from the prisons (Foucault, 1979; Ignatieff, 1978) to the mental asylums (Scull, 1979), reached its Victorian zenith with the formation of colonial police organization in the imperial territories of Africa, of Asia, and of the West Indies (Brogden, 1987). In other words, the emergent class struggle could only be settled and the new working class disciplined, by novel and dependable agencies of coercion and legitimation. A new waged police, combining both those elements, was a major weapon in that struggle (Harring, 1983).

Further, the financial burden could be shared without losing authority over policework. As traditional private property protection became costly to the urban middle class and to the new manufacturers, property owners, and merchants, policing was socialized and its costs transferred from the private to the public sector (Spitzer and Scull, 1977). In Harring's words, 'the creation and expansion of the police was part of a broader development of capitalist social institutions . . . [the] trend towards the socialisation of the expense of the reproduction of capital . . . and a number of heretofore private social functions, welfare, public health, and police protection' (Harring, 1983, p. 8). Influenced by American studies (Harring and McMullin, 1975; Harring, 1983), it has been suggested that the primary duty of the New Police was to confront the emergent working class whenever it threatened bourgeois order – in industrial dispute, political protest and social unrest – bourgeois property, or, more generally, bourgeois notions of respectability and public propriety. From within this framework, the New Police were almost directly subordinate to local industrial and elite interests. These accounts (cf. Scraton, 1985) suggest a continuing, confrontational relationship between the police and working-class people during the first century of modern policing. Considerations of class advantage were the driving force behind such policing, considerations rooted in the economic struggle underlying a developing capitalism and imperialism.

This latter reconstruction of the social relations of policework is however problematic in various ways. If – as the evidence suggests – police arrests consisted largely of the chaff of the street population (e.g. costermongers, street pedlars, drunks, prostitutes, and young people 'committing a nuisance'), then there is no simple radical or materialist explanation of that practice. Street pedlars, for example, may have damaged the profit margins of the new shopkeeping class, and doubtless some of the Christmas-Box payments (Brogden, 1983) were indirect inducements to the police to act as the agents of the latter in a minor class struggle. But no hawker posed the same threat to the stability of the industrial capitalist order as did the emergent working class of Victorian England, who were not policed in as direct or as continuing a manner as suggested. Ethnic, religious, and sectional factors (Jones, 1982) complicated the accounts of police–industrial worker confrontations. The energy of state-waged policework was spent essentially in harvesting the streets.

Moreover, especially in the United States, industrialists were often willing to turn to private police agencies, rather than to the state-waged police, in order to defeat the unions and to secure their property. In Britain the local Watch Committees, bodies of local councillors responsible for policing in the boroughs (towns) after 1835, were often reluctant – certainly in the early years – to use their police employees to serve what they regarded as the interests of a particular employer. This question, that of the *indirect* relation between capital and policework, signified by the transition in payment systems from direct payment by results to wages paid by the state regardless of results, and by the important notion of independent accountability to law, *not* to the direct employers, renders problematic any radical accounts that attempt to 'think' the relation between class and policework in ways that ignore these important mediations.

Accidental Histories

Critics of these two perspectives have fallen back on what amounts to an 'accidental' version of policing history. Irrespective of what was intended – a humane service to a wider public or, alternatively, the class control of an emerging working class – what actually happened was arbitrary, chaotic, and without systematic patterning. The class relations of the Victorian police from this perspective varied in time and place (Reiner, 1985a), as local exigencies determined the parameters of the relations between the New Police and the social classes. Thus modern policework was not a uniform national response to perceived social problems but stemmed from municipal initiatives, a localism that ensured idiosyncratic and parochial features of the New Police at the outset. Only later were those peculiarities ironed out. Field (1981) documents the apparently arbitrary and accidental development of the Portsmouth police. Weinburger (1981), in a detailed Birmingham study, has claimed that nineteenth-century policing must be placed within the pre-existing structure of local government, since it was local imperatives rather than national ones which produced the design and function of paid policework. Similar points are made in the early American studies (Lane, 1980; Richardson, 1970).

But what this final, accidental version of police history fails to allow for is that which remains the strength of the class-based approach despite all its shortcomings, namely, that the same social stratum was subject to discretionary law enforcement. The wealth of empirical material now appearing on the history of Anglo-American policework has highlighted this irreducible core, a core glossed over by both conservative and accidental versions of history. Moreover, the accidentalists' stress on difference also overlooks the growing organizational similarity between forces, a similarity that time only enhanced. While it is undeniable that policework did appear initially in different localities and in slightly varied forms, as a result of local economic, political and social conditions, the underlying dynamic was clearly more uniform, less *ad hoc*, impelled increasingly by national developments, rather than the local and peculiar.

Clearly, then, no one single account of the rise of the New Police, and the spread of that institution across mainland Britain throughout the middle of the nineteenth century, can be sufficient on its own. Moreover, all of the approaches have some merit: conservative accounts because they emphasize the consensual and bureaucratic features, even if neither is adequately contextualized nor sufficiently qualified. Particular local factors contributed to the timing of policing innovations. Indeed, in so far as the idea of compromise, namely, that the New Police were designed as a compromise between the interests of the emergent central state and the interests of the citadels of local power (the provincial mercantile and manufacturing class) underpins the accidental thesis, it adds an important dimension missing in class-based accounts. And class-based structural accounts, in linking developments in policing to developments in industrial capitalism and the changing class structure have obvious merit in addressing the broader functions of policework. An adequate account clearly has to be sensitive to all these dimensions, though without necessarily giving all equal weighting. Before attempting such an account, we should first summarize the position once new policing had become formally established countrywide by the late nineteenth century, and then bring the history briefly up to date. In attempting these tasks, since less has been written about these moments than the earlier ones we will resort to the strategy used in outlining the 'pre-modern' phase, namely: sketch the bones of the story, mention competing interpretations where applicable, and offer where necessary our synthesis.

Summary of the Position by the Late Nineteenth Century

Around 1890, just after the Local Government Act 1888 had established the broad administrative framework which survived essentially intact until the 1964 Police Act (the provisions of which are briefly dealt with below on pages 159–60), the following broad picture can be discerned, even if interpretive emphases differ somewhat. 'Control' of the police was locally based, resting partly in the hands of the judiciary and partly in the hands of elected councillors in the counties (through the medium of the hybrid Standing Joint Committee comprising one-half magistrates and one-half councillors) and wholly in the hands of the elected Watch Committee in the boroughs. How real such control was in practice seems to have varied between boroughs and counties with the greater formal powers of Watch Committees associated with greater control of policework generally. Influence from central government was small, with the basis for more direction being laid through several media:

(a)   a central government contribution (initially one-quarter in 1856, rising to one-half in 1874) to be granted only upon a successful inspection for efficiency;
(b)   statutory powers to enforce the consolidation of smaller forces under certain circumstances;
(c)   the requirement after 1856 for police authorities to submit crime statistics to the Home Secretary.

And chief constables, as constables, formally enjoyed an independent status – an independence that today is right at the heart of current controversies over police accountability (see Chapter 7) – with, once again, a difference in practice between the countryside, with its powerful autocratic chiefs, and the towns, whose chiefs appear to have been more beholden to their stronger Watch Committees.

Though there is a fair level of agreement about the difference between the situation in the countryside and that in the towns, what is more contentious is how this tripartite relationship for the management of policework – involving central and local government elements and the chief constable himself – worked in practice. For example, Critchley, an exemplar of the conservative tradition, suggests that central influence was negligible right up until the eve of the First World War (Critchley, 1978, p. 176), a view partly contested by Scraton (1981, p. 38), who cites in support the importance of the much earlier centrally influenced specialization in relation to both crime and political subversion. There are also different perceptions of the powers of police authorities and chief constables. One radical view regards the history of police authorities as one of a gradual loss of powers (a sort of de-democratization) and that of chief constables as the opposite (as a consequence in part of professionalization). An alternative radical position suggests that such a view overlooks the enduring centrality of the doctrine of constabulary independence and thus overstates the police authorities' starting position – they were never as powerful, formally, as suggested – while understating that of chief constables – their independent status always made them potentially powerful, even if in practice they tended to be less assertive in the nineteenth century (Jefferson and Grimshaw, 1984). What we suggest is that by the late nineteenth century, the picture is still one of a largely locally based system, but with a smidgen of central influence, generally dominated in the countryside by fairly powerful, independent chief constables and, in the towns by the Watch Committees, especially those of strong mind and faced with a compliant chief constable.

The objects of policework remained the same as previously: the maintenance of order, both in the field of political protest and of industrial conflicts, and 'the prevention and detection of crime', the all-embracing phrase covering essentially the policing of the whole way of life of the new class of street people with its illegal street economies, 'survival' crimes and 'offensive' recreations and pastimes. Order maintenance was still executed with the use of troops, if necessary, to supplement the civil power. In Geary's evocative phrase, the standard tactic in industrial conflicts consisted of 'stoning and shooting': pickets stone-throwing prompting shooting by troops aiding police. Crime-work – the 'routine attempts to control petty crime, street economies and pastimes' (Scraton, 1986, p. 36) – had undergone certain changes, partly consequent upon changes in policing method and partly the result of changes in the structure of the working class itself. The open resistance of working-class communities to the early crude crackdown on the recently criminalized and illegal aspects of working-class culture had gradually and unevenly given way to a pragmatic and grudging acceptance – as police learnt the delicate art of negotiated (or community) policing (i.e. how to turn a proverbial blind eye to certain infractions in the interests of the greater good of maintaining order or community acceptance) and the working class had become structurally segmented into its 'respectable' and 'rough' wings (Brogden, 1982). The resulting alliance between the respectables and the police based upon shared notions of 'public propriety' (Phil Cohen, 1979, p. 124) enabled crackdowns on the 'roughs' (the casually employed heirs to the now increasingly ostracized 'old' street life and cultures) to take place with the consent of the 'respectables' (the regularly employed, skilled and organized workers, increasingly committed to the new institutions of working-class political and social life: the church, and rational and uplifting recreational pursuits). In so far as the labour market consigned the young to the casual, unskilled, unorganized end of the spectrum (cf. Phil Cohen, 1979), policing the 'rough' began to take on a more youthful hue, a process exacerbated by the 'discovery' of adolescence as a 'dangerous time', both troubled and troubling. This 'discovery' had obvious implications for policing. 'Trouble' needed to be watched and controlled, in the interests of 'order'.

Differences between accounts centre on the extent and speed of change, and the underlying causes. Conservative accounts stress how quickly and extensively police won over the working class. Operating with minimum force, good-natured tact and absolute impartiality, the New Police quickly demonstrated not only how unjustified were early fears about a snooping, intrusive presence, but also how valuable police could be in protecting the lives and properties of the working classes. The result was acceptance by the working class as a whole, and the isolation of a criminal minority. The causes of such changes were the increasing recognition that the idea of police was a good and beneficient one whose time had come, and the concomitant recognition that opposition to policing was increasingly anachronistic and 'luddite' – a brake on 'progress'.

Radical accounts emphasize the time taken to overcome initial resistance and the partial and contingent nature of the ultimate acceptance: partial since acceptance was more confined to routine policing than the policing of political protest and industrial conflict where confrontation remained characteristic, and since it was confined to some sections of the working class rather than others; contingent since liable to be withdrawn if the terms of the 'negotiated truce' were changed or broken by the police, changes liable to be precipitated by changes in economic, political or social conditions. The starting point for such accounts are the structured or endemic conflict between police and public in our society. Because the society is marked by multiple inequalities, the maintenance of law and order in such a society is necessarily a conservative function not a progressive or beneficient one. The best that can be hoped for without far-reaching structural change is to keep the level of coercion within certain tolerance limits through constant vigilance, public protest and effective mechanisms of accountability.

'Accidental' accounts, as might be expected, stress variation – the different rates at which, and the different extents to which, police became accepted. The various local histories now emerging demonstrate the diversity in this respect. Exploring the causes of such variation may draw on conservative or radical assumptions, or may remain agnostic.

A broad summary of the objects of policing around the end of the nineteenth century would emphasize their continuing role in the policing of disorder, their more focused attention on an increasingly youthful 'rough' working class, and a growing public acceptance of policing. Such acceptance was more obvious in the area of crime than disorder, with some groups rather than others, and at some times rather than others. It was also subject to considerable regional variation.

5 Policework Histories

(ii) The Twentieth Century

Introduction

Accounts of twentieth-century policing are sparse and largely operate with either conservative or radical assumptions. In consequence, we intend only to draw out three broad themes in bringing the picture up to date, and then look at the 'uses' to which policework has been put this century. We shall comment on differences between conservative and radical approaches only where it is necessary to highlight interpretive differences; but, for the most part, there is substantial agreement about what the observable trends and changes are. The three broad themes we shall focus on are centralization, specialization and professionalization. They are not of course unrelated, and we hope in what follows to draw out the interconnections, especially the key thread connecting them all, namely the concept of 'efficiency' (value for money).

The 'New' Drive for Organizational Efficiency – Centralization and Standardization

The argument that bureaucratization has a dynamic of its own clearly has merit (so long as we avoid seeing such a dynamic as inevitable) as the development of twentieth-century policing illustrates. Two key elements of bureaucratization – centralization and standardization – are clearly linked to that of efficiency: the impetus towards centralizing power is effected so that standardized practices, in the interests of rational administration or 'efficiency', may more easily be introduced. Both elements are observable in the twentieth-century development in policework. Take, for example, standardization. Police forces today are more alike than different, given almost any criterion you care to mention: 'strengths' (numbers of officers), police/population ratios, modes of operation, departmental structure, degree of specialization, rank structure and so on. By way of illustration, the majority of forces (28 out of 43) currently have strengths in the same broad range of 1000–3000 (Whitaker, 1979, p. 173; Critchley, 1978, p. 299; HMCIC, 1985, Appendix 7) and the variation in police/population ratios has dramatically reduced. In 1856 the ratios varied between 1 : 11,491 in Rutland at one extreme to 1:393 in Liverpool at the other (Critchley, 1978, p. 123). By 1984 the ratios outside London only varied between 1 : 326 and 1 : 562, though the inclusion of London extends the range a little in the case of the Metropolitan Police District (1 : 266) and a lot in the case of the City of London which, with few regular inhabitants, has a clearly anomalous ratio of 1 : 8 (HMCIC, 1985, Appendix 7).

The achievement of this far greater uniformity has only been possible through the parallel growth of the power and influence of the 'centre', more specifically, the Home Office. The powers granted to the Home Office in the nineteenth century (inspection, withholding grant aid, etc.) laid the basis for future developments. The First World War and the police strikes of 1918 and 1919 jointly provided the key catalyzing events which led to 'the mutation of the Victorian police system' (Critchley, 1978, p. 183), the gradual replacement of 'the total want of system that characterized the disparate police forces of the nineteenth century by a federal structure of local forces, each of which forms part of a greater whole and employs recognisably similar techniques and policies in serving national as well as local interests' (ibid.).

What the war provided was a new perception of the need to co-ordinate the operations of chief constables under central leadership. This led to regular meetings between representatives of chief constables and the Home Office and the origins of a new role for the Home Office: 'as a general clearing house for the exchange of ideas and experience' (Newsam, 1954, p. 40), a sounding board for new ideas, and an experimental tester and disseminator of best ideas and practices.

The abortive police strikes led to the setting up of the Desborough Committee in March 1919, and then to the Police Act of the same year based largely on the committee's recommendations. Basically the Act 'introduced the new concept of a centrally guided and largely uniform system of local police forces' (Critchley, 1978, p. 194). Specifically, it standardized pay and conditions of service, including discipline, under the the control of the Home Secretary, established a Police Council as a central consultative and advisory body to examine proposed regulations, and set up a police department in the Home Office. Perhaps it should also be added that the same Act had other provisions which distanced the police from the public being policed in various ways. For example, the Act made it illegal for police officers to form a union and for anyone to induce an officer to strike, it established the Police Federation but prohibited it from associating with 'outside' associations such as trade unions, and Desborough's recommendations on pay finally severed the historical link that had always tied constables' pay to that of agricultural labourers or unskilled workers. Henceforth, as Critchley (1978, p. 192) put it, 'the constable was to be a semi-professional man'.

Between the wars, the new Police Department became increasingly influential in matters of training and the provision of specialist services to the police. For example, the period witnessed the setting up, under Home Office direction, of the Police College, District Police Training Centres, forensic science laboratories and wireless depots. Immediately after the Second World War, the Police Act of 1946 gave the Home Secretary new powers to compel amalgamations of small forces – those serving populations below 100,000. The 1964 Act set the seal on these many developments. In providing 'the Home Secretary with new powers, a strengthened inspectorate and formal recognition of his erstwhile *de facto* control over influential matters like training and the provision of scientific and technological services to the police' (Jefferson and Grimshaw, 1984, p. 17), it confirmed and bore witness to the degree of centralized power within the system, the complementary 'independent' powers of chief constables notwithstanding (to which we return on pages 158–61 below). It was also the instrument for *furthering* the process of centralization and uniformity. The enlarged inspectorate and the Home Secretary's new powers to compel amalgamations were used together to produce the post-1964 amalgamations – by persuasion where possible, by compulsion where necessary. The result was a drastic reduction in the number of forces: from 126 in 1964 to the current total of 43 (cf. Jefferson, 1987, p. 17).

Perhaps one of the most instructive recent examples of how the new centrally directed system works to standardize practices is the way in which Unit Beat Policing (UBP) became the norm of British policing. Problems of staffing, poor morale, low productivity and loss of public contact in the 1960s led to the Home Office handing the problem over to the new police Advisory Board. It set up three working parties on manpower, equipment and operational efficiency and management, out of which came the description of a Home Office initiated experiment, the UBP scheme. The Home Office gave the scheme its financial blessing in the form of panda cars and two-way radios. Very soon, as we now know, what had been an idea on the

Home Office drawing-board had been transformed into universal police patrol practice (cf. Critchley, 1978, pp. 307–8; Jefferson, 1987, p. 17).

More recently, and controversially, there is the example of the use of the National Reporting Centre in the miners' strike of 1984–5. The role of the centre was to co-ordinate the deployment of officers around the country to help meet the police requests for aid in the mining areas in what was effectively the biggest exercise in mutual aid ever mounted (cf. Kettle, 1985; Spencer, 1985a). Whether or not the centre acted outside its official brief as a central co-ordinating agency to direct operations under the ultimate control of the Home Secretary, as some would claim, it is not necessary for us to decide. For the plain fact is that the highly visible part of the operation – the central co-ordination of deployments – is sufficient to demonstrate our present point, namely that policing in the 1980s is a highly standardized and centrally influenced activity – a point not incompatible with the independent powers of 'direction and control' of chief constables.

'Centralization and uniformity owed much to the justifying criterion of "efficiency" ' (Jefferson, 1987, p. 17). And not surprisingly efficiency forms a *leitmotiv* running through the whole centralizing enterprise, from the early powers granted the Home Secretary to withhold grant aid to 'inefficient' forces, to the specific inclusion of 'management and efficiency' as criteria by which the inspectorate were to judge forces (in 1890; previously the criteria had been only numbers and discipline) and finally, to the 1964 Act which required the Home Secretary to use his powers so as 'to promote the efficiency of the police'. Each new centralizing thrust is justified, in line with bureaucratic logic, on the grounds of increasing efficiency. And it is here we encounter the rational core of the conservative argument that an evolutionary bureaucratic impulse lay behind the 'rationalizing' process so apparently active across a whole range of institutions in the nineteenth century. (It should also be added that the logic of capitalism also has 'efficiency' at or near its centre, this time at the service of profit maximization rather than rational administration as such. However, we cannot explore here the relationships between these two 'logics'.) Conservative accounts are on to something when they stress this aspect of the development of police in the nineteenth century.

But it is important to stress, against the conservative accounts, that such a bureaucratic logic is never uncontested. At each step of the way, as the history of police reform testifies, an alternative argument is clearly discernible in the debate; and it always affected the 'reform' outcome in some way or other, producing some sort of compromise between the 'centralizers' and their opponents. Indeed, it is possible to

read the history of police reform as a series of (at least partial) *defeats* for
the centralizers as first the early reformers and more recently Dr
Goodhart in his dissenting contribution to the Royal Commission on
Police of 1962 came up against the powerful and enduring ideology of
the rights of 'free born Britons' to be free of the snooping intrusion of
a 'continental-style' central state police. The outcome each time has
favoured the logic of 'locality' against the more 'efficient' and rational
logic of a National Police force, even if the practical, cumulative effect
of successive compromises has been, as we have seen, a sort of
creeping centralization. Even so, the fact that this creeping centralization has produced, in effect, a *de facto* National Police Service when
required, as the policing of the miners' strike 1984–5 demonstrated,
should not obscure the *de jure* position of locally based 'independent'
chief constables, since this too has very important effects. What this
demonstrates, against the conservative account, is that the bureaucratic impulse is not teleological – a process whose end is given in its
beginning – but an ideology supported and opposed by more or less
powerful groups with particular interests to protect. The outcome of
such a power struggle is not pre-given, even if it can sometimes be
predicted. But it is the recognition of this underlying element that
constitutes the strength of radical accounts alert to the bureaucratic
factor. The bureaucratic logic of 'efficiency' behind centralization is
also behind our second theme – specialization. For specialization is
one of the core features of 'rational administration'.

Specialization

Accounts of the development of specialization in policework have
tended to focus on the development of centralized specialist functional
departments, especially the CID and Special Branch. Lesser attention
has been given to the much later development of, say, traffic departments. Though we know something of the details of the establishment
of these departments, based largely on the Metropolitan Police
District (MPD), interpretive emphases remain somewhat divided.

Whatever the motives underlying the development of specialized
departments to deal specifically with the detection of crime (as
opposed to prevention which was at the heart of the rhetoric informing the New Police), there were problems of legitimacy to be
overcome. The three ancestors of the new detective – the thief-taker,
the informer and the *agent provocateur* – had not endowed the function
with much public support. Thus there is no doubt that early
suspicions of a state secret police inhibited the growth of a state-

sponsored, non-uniformed thief-taking role (Critchley, 1978, p. 160) – a view only reinforced by the Popay incident in 1833, when a police sergeant acted as an *agent provocateur* in infiltrating the National Political Union. The detective section established at Scotland Yard was thus kept very small (Stead, 1977). And even after the Fenian bombing campaign started in 1867, suspicion of detectives was still such that the MPD Commissioner could write in 1869 of the 'greatest suspicion and jealousy' felt by 'the majority of Englishmen' towards a detective system which he felt was 'entirely foreign to the habits and feelings of the nation' (quoted in Critchley, 1978, p. 161). Neverthe- less, the appearance of Irish terrorism was doubtless the jolt needed to overcome public resistance since, in the same year, 1869, a detective force covering the whole of the Metropolitan area was established (Moylan, 1934). It is probably also true that public concern about garotting in the 1860s and the general perception that violent street crimes were on the increase as a result of the substitution of penal servitude and ticket-of-leave (a form of parole) for transportation, contributed to the dissolution of public resistance to the detective idea.

A corruption scandal (by no means the last) followed in 1877 when 'three out of four chief inspectors in the detective branch . . were found guilty at the Old Bailey on charges of corruption' (Critchley, 1978, p. 161). And the reorganization, for it was in the following year, 1878, that the MPD Criminal Investigation Department was started with 250 men.

Within six years it had grown to 800 and had established, in 1884, a Special Irish Branch to counter Irish terrorism, which later became known simply as the Special Branch. Provincial forces gradually followed the MPD example and established separate detective departments, though not all had done so by the end of the nineteenth century. Piecemeal attempts at co-operation were attempted, such as the criminal record office established at Scotland Yard in 1871 which became a resource for all forces. But it was really not until the interwar period, after the committee on detective work and procedures had produced its monumental five-volume report in 1938, that the basis was laid for a national system of detective work and for 'all that has come since' (Critchley, 1978, p. 210): the application of science and technology to the detection of crime, systematic training courses for detectives, the systematic collection and dissemination of informa- tion about criminals, and so on.

In the postwar period the principle of specialization has been increasingly adopted. Traffic, juveniles, community relations and finally public order have all become additional functional specializations. The CID itself underwent further specialization. Specialist crime squads to deal with particular crime problems such as fraud, drugs, 'serious crimes' and so on were set up, sometimes on a temporary basis to deal with a particular 'outbreak' of crime, but in many instances they have achieved an institutional permanence. Few large modern forces can be without some such permanent crime squads. But specialization has not been confined to particular forces operating alone; indeed the point of specialization, the more efficient use of scarce resources, has always implied inter-force co-operation and, to that extent, has been intimately connected with the centralizing impulses. The first fraud squad, established in 1945, was a joint venture uniting the Metropolitan and City Police Forces, for example; and forces affected by the first motorway (M1) co-operated in the setting up of traffic squads to cover the motorway. These co-operative developments have continued to develop, as motorways have multiplied and 'criminals' and demonstrators have become more mobile. Some of these have become national exercises in co-operation, under Home Office direction.

A national network of Regional Crime Squads was set up in the 1960s to deal with organized, professional crime and, in 1972, two National Intelligence Units were set up, one to co-ordinate information on drug users, the other information on immigrants. More recently, the establishment of the National Reporting Centre to co-ordinate applications for mutual aid for large-scale public order events, together with the requirement that all forces have identical units of officers similarly trained to send on such occasions (Police Support Units or PSUs), has meant that, as we suggested earlier, effectively a National Riot Squad exists in all but name. And of course the Police National Computer, established in 1974, gives every police officer in the country almost instant access, via a 'walkie-talkie', to records of convicted persons, stolen and 'suspicious' vehicles, fingerprints, wanted or missing persons and other like information.

If few would dispute the broad thrust and factual details of the foregoing, the meaning of such developments is seen somewhat differently from different perspectives. Conservative historians, in line with their view of beneficient progress, tend to view bureaucratic developments like specialization as unproblematic. Since such developments are both desirable and inevitable, there is little to find problematic. Thus 'the quest for efficiency' (Critchley, 1978, pp. 255–8) is not seen as problematic in itself, even though certain parties with vested interest in the old ways of doing things may intermittently hold up progress. 'The quest for efficiency' also becomes, in such accounts, the central if not exclusive motivator of change.

Radical historians, by contrast, stress the *use* to which such developments are, or can be, put. The development of plain-clothes detective work, combined with new and improved forms of record keeping, were not undertaken simply with a view to improving 'efficiency' as such – but in order more efficiently to infiltrate, watch and monitor target individuals and groups. And while suspected 'criminals' were part of this targeting, equally so were the political radicals and militant trade unionists and other oppositional elements. Thus Scraton, talking of the early formation of the CID, says that 'plain clothes work opened up a new form of policing' and that 'surveillance techniques, which included the infiltration of target groups, suggested a qualitative shift in police intervention' (Scraton, 1986, pp. 36–7). Bunyan (1977), talking of the period from 1964 onwards, mentions the developments like Regional Crime Squads, the National Drugs Intelligence Unit and National Immigration Intelligence Unit, and similarly emphasizes the 'qualitative' shift these developments entail. The massive extension of keeping records on people not convicted of any crime Bunyan evocatively calls 'pre-emptive policing'. Both these radical historical accounts, commenting on early and late specializations, effectively reassert against the bureaucratic logic of 'efficiency' the *underlying* functional logic of 'policework under capitalism' – its role in dealing with working-class crime and dissent that an iniquitous and unjust system necessarily produces.

What is needed is not a conservative account which emphasizes only the 'logic of bureaucracy' and its effects, nor a radical one which reduces such a 'logic' to the functional requirements of policework under capitalism. Rather, what is needed is an account which is sensitive to both issues and the complex way they are connected. This does mean taking seriously the effects of specialization, for example, and in particular those that are not intended, but without losing sight of their relationship to core functions of policework. For, to focus *only* on the unintended effects is to risk jumping straight from the conservative logic of bureaucracy to an 'illogic of bureaucracy' approach. Tempting though that may be at times, given the ironic humour to be gleaned from a history of reforms 'gone wrong', the more important question is how such unintended effects impact upon core aspects of the policework role.

By unintended effects we have in mind some of the following. One of the effects of establishing a specialist squad is to stimulate artificially a demand for its continuing existence. This can happen either through the squad simply uncovering more of the particular crime problem than was originally thought to exist, or through an enthusiastic squad creating the crime problem by converting previously tolerated practices on the borders of illegality into crimes. The spiral of amplification involved here where, to justify continuing in existence, squads have continually to produce that which they are (ironically) established to eliminate, does point to an important inertial tendency at work – a point some chief constables, trying to deal with 'squad mentality', are becoming aware of. When such unintended effects are combined with particular organizational processes, further unintended effects become visible. For example, where specialist squads become an important route to promotion, the effect is, effectively, to downgrade 'core' routine tasks, like patrol work. The result is that these tasks are left to the youngest, the least experienced, the least skilled or the least promotable (cf. Kinsey, 1985a, p. 105). If these tasks are seen, simultaneously, as the most difficult and the most important – a truism of police patrolwork to which all chief constables would assent – the unintended irony is complete as the 'efficiency' of specialization produces the far more damaging 'inefficiency' of ordinary police work. Such a process has indeed taken place, as Jones (1980) has demonstrated.

The problems of upgrading specialist tasks can be further compounded in a number of ways. The special training involved, the separation from other aspects of policework, the camaraderie developed, the constant dealing with only a small, specific part of policework, all contribute to the feelings of superiority that can accompany the development of a specialized expertise – the adoption of elite status. The emergence of 'crack' squads can lead not only to interdepartmental jealousies and rivalries but, more importantly, can lead to a 'superior' approach to the public. Some would argue that Special Patrol Groups have indeed taken their 'special' tag too seriously – a point not lost on Sir Kenneth Newman, a former MPD Commissioner, who during his period of office (1982–7) recently reorganized such work in the MPD.

Statistics have been a further source of unintended effects. Once crime statistics were required to be recorded by all forces after 1856, 'in the interest of efficiency', not surprisingly they became an important, since tangible, indicator of productivity. In connection with the specialization effect, the statistics effect produced a particularly potent dysfunctional brew. Once justifications for continuing existence became reducible to numbers of crimes uncovered, solved, etc., the temptation to massage figures in the interests of productivity becomes very great. We now know that the opportunities for such massaging are enormous, given that crime statistics reflect the processes by which they are constructed rather than are real level of crime (cf. Box, 1981, chs 3, 6; Bottomley and Pease, 1986). We also know that this is even more the case in those 'proactive' crime areas where police control both the reporting and the recording stage. The result is that those squads operating in proactive, 'victimless' crime areas (drugs, vice, gambling, etc.) have enormous freedom to define the nature of the crime problem and their own level of productivity. Given such a situation, it becomes impossible to determine the 'real' state of play in these areas.

Temptation to massage the figures is not the only temptation open to detectives, which is to say that another unintended effect of CID work, especially crime squad work, is corruption. There are several reasons why the crime detection role has achieved its pre-eminent position in the occupational status hierarchy, but one reason is the practical *freedom* it gives detectives – to control their working hours, to decide how to fill them, to wear their own clothes, to enter pubs, to mix with the criminal underworld, to cultivate informants, and so on. Mixing unobtrusively with the criminal world has all kinds of un-intended consequences: it increases the opportunities for criminal dealings, it supplies neutralizing justifications for so doing (Matza and Sykes, 1957), and generally blurs the boundaries between the two worlds. These consequences are all compounded in proactive, 'victimless' crime areas. Unsurprisingly, therefore, police corruption scandals have tended to be associated with the CID and, more specifically, with the proactive crime squads (cf. Honeycombe, 1975).

Unintended consequences are not confined to crime detection work but can be seen also in connection with the Unit Beat system and with Community Relations policing. In the former case, the irony is that one of the origins of the system was an alleged loss of contact with the public due to a shortage of personnel. The resulting application of science and technology (i.e. cars and radios) which produced the Unit Beat system has subsequently been widely criticized for producing 'fire-brigade' policing, as panda cars dash from one crime-event to another and, in their haste to reduce 'response-time', end up also reducing public contact. In a similar vein, the establishment of Com-munity Relations Departments to take community relations with ethnic minorities and other disadvantaged groups more seriously, has had the ironic effect of making those not in the department take community concerns less seriously – *because* the department exists to take care of 'that sort of thing'.

So it is that the quest to correct an inefficiency sometimes produces others. But specialization not only has unintended effects of this sort. It is also one of the key planks of professionalization. Specialist functions produce specialist expertise. This specialist expertise is one important component of the professionalizing project, our next and final 'update' theme,

Professionalization and 'Independence'

Without entering the debate about whether there is any intrinsic difference between the work of 'professionals' and of 'non-professionals', it is factually true that 'professionalization' is about increasing control of the terms and conditions of work (cf. Johnson, 1972). 'Real' professionals are groups of workers who have achieved a high degree of self-determination; in the work they do, the conditions under which they operate, and in the management and disciplining of their own deviants.

In this sense, the history of modern policework is also about the achievement of a degree of professionalization. The story of this achievement is the story of how the bureaucratic tendencies already identified, and developments in science and technology, built on the independent foundation of the office of constable to produce 'the professionals'. It is an unsteady foundation, as we shall see, which is why the image of the professional jostles uneasily with less flattering images, and perhaps why Critchley settles (see page 72 above) for the idea of 'semi-professional'.

The conservative view of the growing professionalization of policework is a conventional one of an occupational group growing in status and thereby *earning* their occupational autonomy. After Rowan and Mayne had laid down the high standards expected of the new police, and drummed out those incapable of matching them in those early difficult years, the police through tact, good sense and minimum force won over a hitherto hostile public: they became 'expert street negotiators'. The application of science and technology added new kinds of expertise, thereby enhancing professional status.

The radical view is a story of how constables, once the menial of the justices and then, in the towns, of the Watch Committees, progressively freed themselves from their masters' control (Brogden, 1982). A propitious combination of circumstances in the twentieth century helped. These included a series of legal disputes about the status of constable at the time of the growth of a bid for professional status by a range of occupational groups. The successful exploitation of these legal disputes gave birth to the spurious doctrine of constabulary independence, the idea that constables, responsible for upholding the law, should be accountable *only* to the law (cf. Marshall, 1965;

Lustgarten, 1986). This freed chief constables from the directives of their erstwhile political masters; and it also provided an independent power basis from which to exploit the new doctrine of 'professionalism'. Together with the bureaucratic elements already referred to – not least having the ear of the Home Office, and the amalgamations which gradually left only relatively large police force areas – the combination was a potent one for the emergence of a new breed, the 'professional' cop.

The problem with the conservative thesis is its gullibility. It is too ready to believe the rhetoric of police 'professionalism'. The problem with the radical one is its cynicism. It is too dismissive of the doctrine of constabulary independence. While it is true that Watch Committees did have greater control over chief constables in the nineteenth century, this was a consequence of three factors: 'the greater specific powers then possessed by watch committees; the lesser specific powers enjoyed by the Home Office; and crucially, given the ambiguity of these powers, the immediate politics of the situation' (Jefferson and Grimshaw, 1984, p. 44). In other words, the fact that Watch Committees tended to win in disputes with chief constables did not alter the legal position which remained ambiguous – a point borne out in part by the fact that there *were* disputes at all. The clarification of the legal position in the twentieth century, in so far as it is clear even now, has consistently favoured the 'independent' interpretation (ibid., pp. 51–8). Given this interpretation, the foundation for the building of an occupational autonomy is far from spurious. This foundation – a *unique* independence – appears to provide a solid base for a bid for professional status. The fact that it is not, requires an explanation. But first we need to turn to the second element in the professionalizing project – science and technology. If 'efficiency' means centralization and specialization it also, and above all, means the introduction of scientific criteria: 'the introduction of set, neutral and universal criteria according to which efficiency . . . can be most effectively measured and evaluated' (Jefferson, 1987, p. 16). The professionalization of policework implies 'the use of scientific management and evaluation methods' as well as 'the wide ranging application of scientific and technological advances' (ibid.), which 'opened up the possibility of introducing . . . new methods of policing on a wide scale' (Critchley, 1978, p. 314). And it is clear that such introductions have been widespread. No area of modern policework remains untouched by such professionalization, most visibly in the ubiquitous panda car and walkie-talkie, most sophisticatedly in the highly computerized command and control communication systems increasingly becoming the norm, and most terrifyingly in the

ever expanding technology of riot-control equipment. The new
initiatives in Human and Racial Awareness Training mentioned
above on pages 18–19 also represent examples of this application of
science – social science. The consequence, some would argue, is a
transformation out of all recognition of policing as we know it.

One interesting example of the scientific approach in action can be
traced in the area of police establishment. Here there has been a relentless pursuit of the holy grail of a scientific means of establishing a
force's personnel requirement. Attempts have focused on producing
a precisely weighted and quantified equation, using population,
recorded crimes, street mileage, rateable value and other factors, by
which the optimal establishment for each force can be precisely
calculated.

However, just as the above project has always foundered on the
rock of the ultimately qualitative subjective judgements involved in
choosing and weighting factors, so, ultimately, does the scientifically
based professionalizing project come up against the real bedrock of
modern policework, namely 'common sense'. The independent
office of constable effectively grants the constable discretion over
legal decision-making. Where the law is unclear or ambiguous,
officers must fall back on something to guide their actions and the
doctrine of independence precludes looking for political direction.
The 'something' they fall back on, in the absence of adequate policy
direction – itself a consequence of the independence doctrine (a point
to which we return later) – is, not surprisingly in the circumstances,
their own occupationally structured, learned, subcultural 'common
sense'.

Put another way, the basis of 'operational' policework is ultimately
a subjective common sense; the objective 'scientific' discourse is much
more applicable to the organization and administration of the force,
and to equipment, than the operations themselves. Thus it is that the
real 'professional' experts in the new management disciplines of public
administration, operational research and computer technology are
the civilian support staff. Even though these work under the direction
of a police officer (ultimately of course the chief constable), the source
of their professionalism, their expertise, lies outside policing. The
obverse of this is that the real source of a police officer's *operating*
professionalism is a subculturally defined 'common sense'. And that
is altogether more volatile than 'science', though in its own way
usually all too depressingly predictable in outcome. It is the routine
use of this 'common sense' in situations requiring something rather
more flexible and developed that has been at the back of nearly all the
recent examples of controversial policing. Nevertheless, if indepen-

dence gives the chief constable his 'operational' freedom, it is the
scientific discourse he must master if he is to take on the concomitant
professionalism of the Home Office in arguing for more resources or
supporting new ways of working. To the extent that he is able to
master both – the discourse of common sense required to make him a
'coppers' copper', and 'scientific discourse' required in dialogue with
the Home Office – his professional power is correspondingly
augmented.

As the above hopefully makes clear, these developments are all
closely linked: the shift of power towards the centre, the emergence of
ever more uniform police practices, growing specialization, and the
increasing application of science and technology to every area of
policework. The growing interest in policing by objectives (see pages
27–8 above), clearly fits in here. The thread connecting them all,
justifying each new development, as we have also argued, is the
concept of 'efficiency'. It is a concept that has been taken too seriously
in two senses: by conservative historians in failing to question the goal
of increased 'efficiency', the *uses* to which faster, more co-ordinated,
better equipped policework are being put; more generally by all those
who mistake 'efficient' for 'effective' policework, the latter a concept
which clearly does have to take into account the uses as well as the
methods of policing. It is of course this latter failure that accounts for
some of the unintended effects: the efficiency of 'decreased response
times' simultaneously producing the *in*effectiveness of 'reduced
public contact time'. We shall return to this important other issue of
the uses to which policework in the twentieth century have been put,
in order to round out our update. But first we should conclude this
section with how these linked developments – centralization,
standardization, specialization and scientization – have affected the
respective powers of the principal parties responsible for policework,
namely chief constables, the Home Secretary and police authorities.

Some would argue that centralization has meant a transference of
power from chief constables to the Home Secretary. This would be a
mistaken view. Quite apart from the effects of the 1964 Police Act in
more clearly recognizing a chief constable's operational discretion
(see pages 159–60 below), some of the effects of 'centralization' have
obviously strengthened the power of the chief constables. Amalgamations have resulted in bigger forces – fewer chief constables, but each
controlling larger areas, more officers and more resources generally.
Centralization has also involved bringing together chief constables
regularly to discuss shared problems – a process of co-ordination
which has clearly strengthened their collective power as a group. For
example, such meetings led to the formation of the very powerful

body representing chief constables, their deputies and assistants, namely the Association of Chief Police Officers (ACPO) (Brogden, 1982).

Increased resources have enabled individual forces to match the 'professional' expertise of the Home Office. They can justifiably afford to employ all sorts of experts – researchers, planners, management consultants, computer technologists, etc. – to devise and evaluate schemes, both those originating internally, and those proposed by the Home Office. This means that chief constables do not operate as subordinates in an unequal debate, but as equals. Each 'side' is supported by its own personal advisers, who debate the issues using the language and justifications of a neutral 'science'.

Thus centralization has meant not only more power to the centre, but also more power to local chiefs as well. It has acted, therefore, to augment the powers granted to both the Home Office and the chief constables under the new Act. As for the police authorities, they have been clear losers in this 'battle of the giants'. Unable to claim, like chief constables, an 'independent' responsibility for law enforcement, nor to benefit from professionalization, they have had no basis other than their democratic credentials as elected representatives (and that has foundered on the myth that policework is 'above politics') from which to mount an effective response to centralization. The result has been that the 1964 Act ratified the effective status quo by taking away the existing powers of borough Watch Committees to appoint, promote and discipline all ranks below assistant chief constables, and insisting that all police authorities should comprise one-third non-elected magistrates. Subsequent battles between police authorities and chief constables (cf. Simey, 1985), valiant through they have been, only bear out this depressing interpretation (see pages 169–70 below).

The Old 'Uses' of Operational Policing

It is easy to be dazzled by the new, by change, by science and technology, and to be overtaken by the quest for efficiency. But it is important not to be. That is why it is essential to end this update by asking: What is *really* new about policing in the twentieth century?; has the social *function* of policework changed?

If a member of the public was asked today what was the primary function of policework, s/he would probably answer 'serious crime', by which, if pressed, s/he would understand crime committed by organized professionals. There is no doubt that this is one important strand of twentieth-century policework, which has grown since the nineteenth century. The transformation of the 'dangerous classes' into the 'labouring classes' was effected, as we suggested earlier, partly by structural changes in the working class and partly by changes in the mode of policework – from confrontation to negotiation. The result was not only 'grudging acceptance' of a police presence in working-class communities but, in line with the new respectability, the driving of a wedge between the people and 'criminals'. In this way, the ground was prepared for the emergence of the full-time professional criminal, living on the margins of working-class society, operating secretly, socializing largely with criminal associates. Not that the boundaries were ever watertight, nor that the relations between 'criminals' and their community of origin were (are) other than complex (cf. Hebdige, 1974). Nevertheless, the changes were such as effectively to constitute the professional criminal as part of a class apart from ordinary, working people, at least in the popular imagination. From the police side, such a development laid the basis for an important contemporary and pervasive image of policework: the hardboiled detective in relentless pursuit of dangerous and ruthless criminals on behalf of society (and rarely even thanked for his/her troubles).

Phil Cohen (1979) dates the changed relationship between police and community as a product of the interwar years. His evidence was based on Islington. Elsewhere, the precise dating of this change undoubtedly varied, in line with local differences in transformations in the labour market, and so on. Consequently, we should expect variation in the timing of the 'gap' opening up between criminals and the 'responsible' elements in the community. This may also help explain why dating the precise moment when certain kinds of criminal activities first emerged or changed their character is not easy, and will explain why our discussion of changes must be very general.

If the period prior to the 'pacification' of the working-class city had been marked by a blurring of the boundaries between the amateur and the professional criminal, it was also marked by a form of crime McIntosh has called 'craft-based' (McIntosh, 1971). It 'is characterised by small-scale thieving from many different sources and it relies heavily on learned techniques such as pick-pocketing or burglary' (Scraton, 1986, p. 67). And, just as the subsequent period has been marked by the emergence of organized, professional crime, it has also been marked by a shift to 'project-based' crime (McIntosh, 1971): crime 'characterised by large-scale thieving from well-developed and highly protected corporate bodies' (ibid.). This change is a reminder that the historical changes produced by the development of industrialization have had an impact, not surprisingly, on the technology of crime.

The important 'transitional moment' was probably the interwar period, and was most marked in the big cities like London, Glasgow and Liverpool. Here organized 'gangs' of professional criminals were emerging centred on activities like prostitution and vice rings, gambling and bookmaking, and protection rackets (cf. Albini, 1975; Gladstone-Smith, 1970). The war, with its flourishing black market, undoubtedly opened up new opportunities for organized crime and postwar rationing ensured the continuance of such opportunities (Lucas, 1969, p. 35; McConnell, 1969, p. 60; Meehan, 1978, p. 32).

The emergence of project-based crime seemed to coincide with the 'break-up' of London's criminal underworld in the mid-1950s, with the retirement of its erstwhile self-appointed kings: Jack 'spot' Comer and Billy Hill. As a 'loose federation of existing gangs' (Pearson, 1973) attempted to sort out control, a 'new generation' of gangs appeared (Payne, 1973): more 'freelance', less willing to deal with other gangs and the police, and more violent. The Kray twins from the East End and the Richardson brothers from South London best epitomized this new era of organized crime. And the 'commando type armed robbery' (Mack, 1975), which 'emerged during the late 1950s on a regular basis' (Scraton, 1986, p. 68), most dramatically exemplifies the new 'project-based' crimes so characteristic of the new era. The Great Train Robery of 1963, a daring, highly organized and violent robbery of a London mail train which netted two and a half million pounds, was but the most audacious (and lucrative) early example of such new-style robberies.

These were but the more violent and visible examples of the new organized crime era. More traditional, underworld areas like gambling and vice continued to evolve and develop. The 1960 Gaming, Betting and Lotteries Act was an 'unprecedented stimulus . . . to British crime and gangsterism', according to Hebdige (1974, p. 80). Certain forms of lower-class deviance were shifted from visibility on the street to the relative invisibility of the club or office. It is probably safe to suggest too that certain postwar changes in attitudes and technology have contributed significantly to organized trafficking in drugs and pornography.

Yet, despite these changes, it seems unlikely that organized crime ever took on generally the characteristics of syndicate crime, which requires, according to Albini (1975), an organization which provides illicit goods and services on a continuous basis, as well as the use of force, intimidation and threats, and 'the gaining of protection from the legal structure to ensure immunity from the law' (quoted in

Scraton, 1986, p. 67) – though Albini (1975) 'did find evidence of syndicated crime . . . in pornography, drugs traffic and money lending' (Scraton, 1986, p. 67).

These developments produced changes in the organization of policework. Just as there is an intimate connection between technological development and crime, so there is an intimate connection between the technology of crime and the technology of crime control. Which comes first – who leads in the technology stakes – is debatable (and probably variable); but about their interconnection there can be no doubt. So just as the emergence of violent armed robberies led to the use by the private security industry of armoured transport for cash and valuables (Draper, 1978, p. 20), they also led to the formation of more specialist squads to deal with them.

More generally, the growth of organized crime practised by highly skilled professionals made information, the life-blood of detective work, hard to come by. This put a premium on the painstaking surveillance of targeted 'known' suspects to build up dossiers to assist the difficult task of securing evidence that might lead to conviction; and on the cultivation of informants. Since the stakes were high and the pressures to secure convictions mounting, the temptation to cut corners increased correspondingly. Examples of such corner cutting, as subsequent purges, corruption scandals and investigations have revealed, included all those practies long associated with detective work, but writ large: the ignoring of lesser crimes (of informants) in pursuit of more serious ones; the use of informants to set up crimes and thus entrap targeted suspects; the 'fitting up' of those known to be 'at' it but against whom evidence is slim (cf. Ball, Chester and Perrott, 1979; Cox, Shirley and Short, 1977; Robertson, 1976). The increasing use of the 'supergrass', which led to the setting up of the ill-fated Operation Countryman in 1978, encapsulated all these practices: known criminals who could themselves have been tried on very serious charges were being granted near immunity for their own offences, a practice involving both police and courts, in return for shopping other known criminals, suspected of certain offences against whom there was no other evidence but the word of someone with a vested interest in coming up with some names. The dangers of the 'fit up' in these secretive, murky, complicated deals, the dubious morality involved in overlooking sometimes even numerous serious offences in the prospect of clearing up an ever greater number of similar offences, all but obliterated the mythical line, between the 'straight' world and the underworld, that 'the blues' protect.

But if the 'war' against organized professional crime is new to the twentieth century, and increasingly dominates media and police self-imagery, it absorbs only a small amount of police resources, personnel and time. For the most part, policing retains its more traditional foci and function: order maintenance, which effectively boils down to policing working-class culture and crime, and conflict and dissent more generally. By way of illustration, we will take first the question of crime and culture, and then that of conflict and dissent.

Policing Working-Class Culture and Crime

Concern with the general activities of the working-class young, especially those thought to lead on to or be associated with crime, is a feature of the nineteenth century generally, from the early report by the Society for Investigating the Causes of the Alarming Increase of Juvenile Delinquency in the Metropolis (1815), through the mid-century industrial and reformatory schools 'child-saving' movement spearheaded by the philanthropic Mary Carpenter, to the late-century imposition of compulsory schooling and 'organized' leisure pursuits such as youth clubs and the Boys Brigade.

But it was the intersection of the more focused police attention on the 'rough' working class, consequent upon changes in both the class structure and police tactics, together with the discovery of adolescence as a naturally wayward time, which produced the 'modern' twentieth-century notion of the typical juvenile delinquent: lower working-class male, uninterested in school or organized youth provision (or, if older, jobless or in and out of work), spending a lot of his time 'hanging around' in the similarly bored company of a 'gang' of mates. It is such 'undersocialized, unclubbable' youngsters (cf. Morse, 1965) that increasingly come to dominate police time and attention.

One of the effects of the growing respectability of the working class generally was to highlight the activities of the 'rough'. The ironic effect of this *decline* in 'unrespectable' activities was an *increase* in 'crime' as previously tolerated pursuits became subject to official attention. This, for example, is how Gillis explains the apparent rise in juvenile crime between 1890 and 1910. The concern with controlling the leisure time of working-class youth led to 'a new willingness to prosecute on the part of the police and courts. After 1900, juveniles were increasingly arrested for gambling, loitering, playing on public or private property and malicious mischief' (Gillis, 1975, p. 102). 'Forms of activity that had formerly been ignored increasingly came to be perceived as indicative of a new social problem' (Muncie, 1986, p. 19). This attack on working-class youth culture echoed the more general nineteenth-century criminalization of working-class life. 'From the 1900s onwards, successive legislation sought to prohibit another source of family income – that of juvenile street trading.' The result was that many 'were forced to turn to other illegal activities to compensate for their dispossessed earnings and to supplement the family budget' (Muncie, 1986, p. 20).

The consequence of these changes was to place adolescents into two opposed camps – the delinquent and the organized:

> The model adolescent therefore became the organized youth, dependent but secure from temptation, while the independent and precocious young were stigmatized as delinquent. (Gillis, 1975, p. 97)

And it was no doubt from the 'independent and precocious' young that 'gangs' originated. Since the emergence of youth gangs parallel the emergence of professional crime, their precise moment of appearance is not easy to ascertain and is probably similarly variable. But, there is no doubt that during their heyday in the interwar period they became a focus of police attention: partly because street confrontations between rival gangs obviously presented problems of order; partly because of their associated criminal activities, which Scraton (1986, p. 61) talks of as being 'breaking and entering, theft and small-scale protection'; and also, no doubt, partly because gang-based activity was thought to be a direct apprenticeship for a life of professional crime. This idea of an apprenticeship to crime is not borne out by the work of Mays, 1975, and Mayo, 1969, which is not to deny that the same conditions that produced gangs (poverty and overcrowding) produced professional criminals, so that the former produced an *indirect* apprenticeship for the latter (cf. Boyle, 1977).

This police concern with youth gangs, not only what they do but what they might do, continues in police interaction with the postwar equivalent of gangs: the succession of visible youth subcultures from the teddy boys, mods, rockers and skinheads through to the stylistic apocalypse of the punk phenomenon. While the class composition of such groups is less clear, especially from the middle-class inspired hippie movement onwards (a factor compounded by the way race and gender have interacted with such subcultures), the point is that in police, media and popular demonology such groups are symbolically 'rough' since potentially delinquent: they are, in Stan Cohen's terms, modern 'folk devils' who stimulate an over-reaction, or 'moral panic' (Cohen, 1973, p. 9) because they appear to pose a threat, intentionally or otherwise, to society's normative boundaries. Such boundaries, we know with benefit of historical hindsight, are not 'society's' but those of 'respectable' (male) society, imposed to distinguish itself from the 'rough', those left behind by structural change and the best attempts of nineteenth-century middle-class philanthropists at 'reform'.

But, it would not be right to end this section without mentioning the latest and most fearsome 'folk-devil' – black youth. Whether within a deviant youth subculture or not, black youth as a category are, in this historical moment, the archetypal 'rough' group, as a result of both their economic exploitation and cultural oppression. Their economic plight – their poverty and their multiple disadvantages, including very high levels of unemployment – makes them susceptible to the sorts of survival strategies, including involvement in certain forms of crime, that are historically associated with chronic economic insecurity. And, as with other groups living on the margins in the past, such strategies render them liable to regular police surveillance and attention. Their cultural predicament – their subjection to the harsh realities of a white racism that has colonized their past, oppresses their present, and offers them 'no future' – ensures that their own 'cultural solutions' are very different from those of their oppressors. And, once again, as with previous groups living by different and marginalized values, it brings them up against the official guardians of dominant ones, namely, the police.

To be routinely subject to police surveillance and attention as an individual because one is presumed to 'belong' to a group presumed to be 'criminally inclined', is to be a victim of the process of criminalization. To be routinely subject to more police surveillance and attention as a group than any other single group in society is to be a victim of discriminatory policing. Together such over-attention is experienced as 'unjust harassment'. Not coincidentally, such unjust harassment was both an underlying cause and the trigger of all the urban riots of the 1980s, the 'worst-case' outcome of what policing a whole way of life can lead to, under certain conditions. (In Chapter 6 we return to this issue in more detail.)

However, it is worth citing here a comment by former MPD Commissioner, Sir Kenneth Newman. Although not framed in the same way as the above, the ideas are not dissimilar:

Throughout London there are locations where unemployed youth – often black youths – congregate; where the sale and purchase of drugs, the exchange of stolen property and illegal drinking and gaming is not uncommon (*sic*). The youths regard these locations as their territory. Police are viewed as intruders, the symbol of authority – largely white authority – in a society that is responsible for all their grievances about unemployment, prejudice and discrimination. They equate closely with the criminal 'rookeries' of Dickensian London . . . If allowed to continue, locations with these characteristics assume symbolic importance – a negative symbolism of the inability of the police to maintain order. Their existence encourages law breaking elsewhere, affects public perceptions of police effectiveness, heightens fear of crime and reinforces the phenomenon of urban decay. (Quoted in Gilroy and Sim, 1985, pp. 48–9)

Policing Industrial Conflict and Political Dissent

Policing industrial conflict and political dissent from the late nineteenth century on, in the interests of 'order', remains a core policing task, and a continuous one. The big demonstrations of the unemployed in the 1880s heralded a very turbulent period up to and beyond the First World War – a period when labour unrest and the resulting strikes coincided with the more general growth of trade unionism, the threat of 'socialism' posed by the newly formed Labour Party, and feminism posed by the suffragettes. All these developments were fiercely resisted by the male propertied classes. The general strike of 1926 represented both the high point and the turning point of this agitation – and was followed by the depression, and the twin developments of mass unemployment and fascism: developments which provoked the hunger marches on the one hand, and street confrontations between the fascists and their opponents on the other.

After the Second World War, the late 1950s and early 1960s saw the emergence of CND and non-violent civil disobedience, and the late 1960s huge protests against the war in Vietnam. During the 1970s, the revived fascist challenge in the form of provocative demonstrations and meetings by the National Front in immigrant areas was determinedly met by the youthful Anti-Nazi League. And, on the industrial front, the period after the historic miners' strike of 1972, which successfully closed the gates at Saltley Coke Depot and precipitated a general election which brought down a government, witnessed a series of increasingly lengthy and bitter industrial conflicts culminating in yet another miners' strike, that of 1984–5. But before that, and after, came the mass civil disorder of the urban riots or uprisings, undoubtedly the most significant series of public order events this century. Less dramatic, but persistent, were the problems of order being presented by the civil and criminal disobedience of the peacewomen at Greenham and elsewhere.

The conservative thesis concerning the police role in such twentieth-century order-maintenance parallels their view of policing the working-class community more generally; namely that structural change and more pacific police techniques led to acceptance. In the field of public order, the argument is that the achievement of key elements of a democratic polity such as the right to vote, and organizations such as trade unions and the Labour Party to represent previously unenfranchised interests, reduced both the need for a violent struggle to achieve them, and for aggressive policing.

The radical view inverts this conventional wisdom and points to the continuities between the repression of disorder then and now. The same history is reread from the underside, to uncover the enduring repressive core at the heart of the policing of conflict and dissent.

The truth, as usual, fits exactly with neither view, though it draws on both. It is no doubt true that there has been a degree of pacification with the passage of time, evidenced both by the largely non-violent nature of most contemporary public order policing and by a change in the typical tactics used. Geary, analysing the policing of industrial disputes, summarizes the change as a movement from the potentially lethal 'shooting and stoning' characteristic of the early century, situations where armed military support to the police might shoot a volley to disperse stone throwing pickets, to the altogether more ritualistic 'pushing and shoving' of the postwar period, by both sides. But it is also true that such pacification is neither automatic nor necessarily irreversible, as the aggressive paramilitary policing of stone throwing pickets and demonstrators which appeared in the aftermath of Saltley bears witness. In other words, changes in police tactics are a contingent not a necessary consequence of certain economic, political and social conditions. And if such conditions worsen and social conflicts intensify, the preferred mode of policing by consent may 'have' to give way to more coercive forms. In this regard, it is worth noting that Geary's own thesis is taken somewhat by surprise by the re-emergence of violently policed industrial conflicts in the 1970s, a result we suggest of his latent evolutionism.

The fact that pacification is altogether more contingent should remind us of the strength of the radical view: the idea that the order-maintenance function of the police is necessarily coercive and in a divided society some groups must finish up having another's definition of order imposed upon them. Such imposition may be resisted passively or actively – but it will not be welcomed. Thus it is that the experience of those on the receiving end of police violence, whenever such violence occurs and whether it is typical or not, is remarkably similar. Thus the experiences of early strikers and pro-testers, of suffragettes, hunger marchers, anti-fascist demonstrators and so on, are not dissimilar, taking account of technological change, from those of the CND protestor, the Anti-Nazi League demon-strator, the Warrington picket, the 'peace convoy' travellers, and so on. So, even if things have become generally more pacific, the similarity of the experiences of those subject to police violence confirms the radical's view about the social function of policing order. Seen from above, things appear to be changing, progressively, for the better: seen from below, everything stays the same. A crack on the head from a police officer's truncheon feels much the same now as it always did.

Summary

What we have been arguing in this thematic look at policework in the twentieth century is the need to take seriously both the continuities and the discontinuities that are clearly evident. The discontinuities we explored through the theme of *efficiency*: the way in which centraliza-tion, specialization, professionalization and the application of 'science and technology' provided a 'rationalizing' input which had a series of independent and often unintended effects. Conservative writers, we argued, have over-emphasized this aspect and have tended to be blinded by it, and so have failed to see the continuities also in evidence. These continuities we explored through the *uses* to which such new developments were still put, uses given by the enduring nature of the police mandate to 'uphold the law', an 'independent' mandate which, we argued, the newer notions of efficiency could never completely override, especially in the field of police operations. Such uses retained at their core the traditional focus on working–class culture and criminality, industrial conflicts and political dissent. And if conservative writers failed to see this partiality, radical writers tended to be blinded by it, unable to recognize the discontinuities: the input of important new elements.

Against this Tweedledum/Tweeledee series of inversions, we have emphasized throughout the need for sensitivity to both new and old elements in their interpretation. It is time now to draw together the features of this approach in order to make clear how such an approach differs from both conservative and radical approaches and, as impor-tantly, the 'history as accident' approach; one which has not been in evidence in twentieth-century accounts, and so has not figured in ours.

The crucial question amounts to this; how can we construct an approach which recognizes *both* the class-based nature of policework *and* the sorts of autonomous developments – centralization, professionalization, and so on – that have no necessary connection with class? The important starting point is to remember that the police have a mandate not to suppress the poor but to uphold the law. In other words, whatever class bias is evident in policing practice is an *effect* of their work in upholding the law, is *mediated* through law enforcement. Starting with law, two things of central significance emerge: (1) criminal law is skewed against the powerless; (2) there is enormous *discretion* in upholding the law at all levels. From the beginning, the laws from which police officers derived their municipal powers were skewed towards the suppression of lower-class life. The legislation which framed policework stemmed from bourgeois moral entrepreneurs – from temperance leagues to associations for the suppression of vice – and focused on readily visible proclivities. Law enforcement then meant putting into operation a medley of statutes whose purpose was normative – to remoralize the poor. Much of this hotch-potch of petty legislation was codified in Britain during the first half of the nineteenth century (although some, such as an Act which prohibited all Sunday labour except 'works of charity or necessity', dated from as early as the reign of Charles II). The statutes over vagrancy, and over street trading and hawking, were targeted, even if indirectly, at street leisure and the street economy. For example, the Small Tenements Act, 1838, required the police to help landlords evict tenants. The first food adulteration legislation penalized the stallholder in his or her competition with the ratepaying small shopkeeper. The host of offences created by the Towns Police Clauses Act, 1847, allowed the police to control lower-class life in all its nooks and crannies. Such legislation was not only class-based but also patriarchal – most obviously in the Contagious Diseases Act, 1864–9, which gave police officers omnibus powers to harass, detain and humiliate women on the grounds that they might be venereal and hence a risk to unsuspecting men. Victorian public order legislation provided the essential enabling weaponry for police control over the lower classes and, in so far as they spent time on the streets, youth and women. Statutes were designed, through the instrument of the New Police, to regulate what national and local elites regarded as the disorderly edges of society. This still remains broadly the case today.

However, perhaps more significant is the question of discretion. This operates at two levels. The chief constable, through his [all chief constables currently are men] independent responsibility for upholding the law, has to make decisions of policy about how to distribute his resources so best to fulfil his mandate, given that he cannot possibly know about all infringements nor deal with all those he does know about. This discretion as to the selection of priorities, it should be added, is his alone – the notion of 'independence' *requires* that he does not seek *political* direction for fear that this would subvert his 'impartiality'. The chief constable's discretion extends beyond the selective targeting of offences to *how* questions: questions of squad formation, numbers required for particular operations, the sort of equipment thought appropriate, foot or car patrols, and so on.

Constables too operate with considerable discretion. This is especially true of some offences. Those public order offences, for example, which require the constable to decide whether the behaviour in question is likely, in his or her subjective judgement, to lead to a breach of the peace, are highly discretionary. Other offences – failure to display an excise licence for example – are not discretionary. Though the constable may ignore such an offence, or offer up an unofficial warning to the offender, such a discretionary approach is not vested in the law: in this instance the *legal offence* is quite objective and non-discretionary. Between these two extremes there are a range of legal situations which are more or less discretionary.

The effects of such a skewed and discretionary legal starting point can be similarly viewed from two levels, chief constable and constable. The chief constable's discretion as to what to focus upon and how, means that the general shape of the force, its degree of functional specialization, its priorities and operating philosophy, are set by the chief constable, either directly or through his delegated authority. Thus the degree of centralization, specialization, professionalization and the level of scientific and technological sophistication – and whatever unintended effects flow from these – all ultimately flow from the chief's use of his discretionary legal mandate, subject of course to the central influence of the Home Office which clearly feeds into his decision-making process. Organizational developments then flow from the chief constable's legal mandate.

The constable's discretion means that in particular situations s/he is required to make subjective judgements as to whether an offence has been or is about to be committed. Such subjective judgements need to be made quickly, and economically, which means by reference to a common stock of already existing knowledge. The source of such 'recipe' knowledge is, of course, police 'common sense': that series of subculturally based interpretations of typical legal situations that are developed on the streets and passed on through all the processes of informal socialization.

It still needs to be asked why both organizational and subcultural 'solutions' to the problem of discretion should point in the same direction, namely towards controlling the poor. The answer is, of course, that such solutions satisfy, simultaneously, the demands of both the organization and the occupational culture for a regular volume of relatively easy and trouble-free transactions to process, in the interests of 'efficiency'. In other words, the demands of 'efficiency' and the thrust of much criminal law both point towards the same end: the control of the least powerful. Thus the present occupational culture of police work (as outlined in Chapter 3) grew historically on the Victorian street, assisted by the low visibility of policework on the street (as far as their superiors were concerned), as well as the camaraderie engendered through confrontations. In dealing with real or putative 'troublemakers' or 'suspicious persons', patrol officers quickly learned to concentrate on those low status groups who excited the least general public sympathy and the most distrust, strata which had the least power to combat police harassment. The pickings were easy and the catch satisfied the demands and prejudices of the respectable citizenry. In this mediated way, the deployment of a legal discretion in the interests of organizational 'efficiency' and occupational 'ease', the structural focus on low status groups became an inextricable part of occupational common sense. It should also be possible now to see the essential complementarity between microsociological and macrosociological approaches conceived in this way; how wider social processes inevitably leave their (mediated) traces in the small-scale, particular instance.

The principal tactics in newly formed police forces was to employ their discretion to make large numbers of arrests for such minor offences as drunkenness or disorderly conduct. Exhorted by their superiors to demonstrate 'value for money', street patrols found their own answer. The creation of police forces across England and Wales led to a significant expansion in the number of public order arrests (Emsley, 1983). The tabulation of these 'body counts' was also a convenient way of measuring effort in doing a job, a task which in reality defied precise evaluation. It was quickly discovered too in the larger cities that in making such arrests, or indeed any arrest, a personal force reputation for toughness was a decided asset. Officers themselves justified brutality in terms of the dangers of their working environment. The result was that the rank and file developed their own code, one which emphasized toughness, tolerance of the deviant and corrupt behaviour of colleagues, and a spirit of emotional cohesion and mutual support born out of a shared experience and principally a common enemy (Johnson, 1979).

Although there is a marked lack of academic studies of Victorian street life, fictional and biographical accounts – from Charles Dickens to Jack London, from Mayhew to Trollope – suggest a continuing cultural division between the police and lower-class street people. Since the moral thrust behind much early Victorian legislation was towards controlling the visible proclivities of the lower classes, their leisure pursuits, in the bars, brothels and gambling houses, and since the idea of modern policework involved preventive patrol (of the streets), this ensured that the two could not avoid meeting.

It is worth emphasizing the centrality of such cultural pursuits to working-class life generally. Stedman Jones (1977) has suggested that there are two false and romanticized views of working-class recreation in the nineteenth century: either that leisure activity should be seen as a soporific, as the opium of a people which detracted from their political momentum; or that those pastimes have been portrayed as the site on which working-class solidarity was forged – the battle for trade union rights was won over the playing cards of the saloon bar. Rather Stedman Jones argues, leisure should be seen as an appendage of work, a necessary and inextricably linked component of the working day.

In the lower-class areas of the expanding and overcrowded Victorian municipalities, bars were often the only important and accessible communal centres, dance-halls the focus of social relations, and gambling 'dens' one of few possible sites of adult recreation. The saloon bars acted as a kind of service centre – often providing banking, postal and employment services. For example, in Liverpool, a major seaport, the services of the street – from beerhouse to brothel to secondhand-clothes shop to fence to pawnshop – were almost inevitable adjuncts of a patriarchal low-wage casual economy. Street life, encompassing both the varieties of street trading as well as that located in the adjacent buildings, was produced by the economies of the Victorian cities that required pools of accessible, cheap and disposable labour, but refused to pay that labour more than a subsistence wage (Brogden, 1982).

Police patrol practices encountered that economy head-on. Preventive policing entailed continued interventions in the disciplining and attempted subordination of those institutions of the poor. Policing the city in effect meant regulating the street economy which serviced the lower social strata in the interests of the primary economy. Modern policework was street work and street work inevitably meant persistent individualized confrontations with the participants in street recreation and in the secondary economy. If such street activities, whether the secondary economy of the pawnshop or street pedlar or cheap ale in the unlicensed beerhouse, undercut the primary economy of city business or were seen by manufacturers and merchants as detracting from the useful toil of the new labour force leaving them unfit for the waged economy, from the point of view of the police organizations it provided a relatively easy harvest which could be 'efficiently' reaped.

But the consonance between the broad thrust of much of this early legislation and the use of policework discretion goes beyond a happy coincidence of police patrolling those same public spaces regularly used by the lower classes who, in the interests of 'efficiency', presented the most accessible and 'processable' pool to fish. Since the unifying feature of the new legislation was its normative character it is hardly surprising that police, whose job it was to uphold such laws, used their discretion in accordance with this legal intent: in accordance with the perceived threat to the cultural norms, the values, the ways of living, of the urban middle classes. Thus, that occupational culture became linked with aspects of the culture of the respectable male working class and petty bourgeoisie in agreeing on the need to suppress and harass the lower strata, those outside the notion of 'public propriety' (Phil Cohen, 1979, p. 124). Popular stereotypes, purveyed by folk ballad as much as by the new educational system, inculcated through a Samuel Smiles self-help ideology, constructed a common pathological view of those at the bottom of the social spectrum. Victorians of all classes, congruent with the emerging police occupational culture, came to perceive a distinction between the respectables and the 'roughs', that is, between the employed classes and the casually employed poor, the latter apparently divorced from the discipline of the work place and from organized religion.

But this 'distinction' was not achieved without first 'resistance', and then the negotiating of a compromise solution, as Cohen's seminal account of the policing of lower-class youth and street traders in Islington reveals (Cohen, 1979). After the initial period, when the Metropolitan Police impersonally clamped down on most forms of working-class leisure in the street habitat, a clamp-down which produced resistance initially, an effective compromise was achieved. This compromise was necessary because of the resistance; it was possible because the leisure-time pursuits and street activities of the urban poor affronted not only the urban middle classes, but also the increasingly structurally segregated 'respectable' working-class residents. Consequently, an alliance between the respectable male working class and police, founded on a consensual notion of a patriarchal 'public propriety', emerged. In this quite specific 'class-based' form, the rational core of the consensually based evolutionary accounts can be retained. Those outside this notion, the young and the costermongers (street sellers) became targeted (as did the respectables, when they posed a threat to industrial, political or social order in the event of strikes, demonstrations or general unrest). Policing thus acquired some form of consent from those groups who agree on a moral target for symbolic and actual repression. Similar accounts of the singling-out of minority groups appears in various American studies – Schneider's (1980) account of the policing of young male itinerants in Detroit focuses on the 'bachelor subculture' which disturbed local cultural mores. In England, Weinberger (1981) talks of policework in Birmingham being directed at the outcast Irish minority whose mores might be deemed unsettling to the native English. The policing target formed an economically useful and disposable labour pool, but their threat to established social values was deemed dangerous to the city's social order.

Evidence of this action against such 'floating' male populations, necessary to production at certain seasonal times but also seen as socially disruptive, appears in several other studies such as Jones's (1982, pp. 178–209) account of police harassment of seasonal workers and unemployed vagrants generally on the tramping round of Victorian England. Again, American studies provide more detailed accounts (Harring, 1983; Johnson, 1979), with one such tramp, Jack London, recounting vivid personal experiences of police practice. For Fogelson (1977), policework was essentially an attempt by the indigenous elites to maintain a form of moral control over the recent immigrant minority. Class control then was exercised by the disciplining of leisure pursuits, in the bars, brothels, and gambling houses of lower-class society.

In short, the combination of the legal framework of enforcement focused upon the lower social strata, an organization committed to the preventive patrolling of streets and other public spaces and an emergent occupational culture concerned with developing relatively 'trouble-free' transactions, resulted in the stigmatizing and criminalizing of those social groups with limited power, high visibility, and which embodied the popular stereotypes of the dominant culture. Lee has called powerless, low status groups 'police property': 'a category becomes police property when the dominant powers of society (in the economy, polity, etc.) leave the problems of social control of that category to the police' (Lee, 1981, pp. 53–4).

At the outset of our long journey through these policework histories, we justified it by suggesting that a historical perspective can help test current ideas and help sift out significant from more superficial charges. Our contribution to the latter endeavour has been to contrast the genuinely new centralizing, specializing and professionalizing quest for organizational 'efficiency' with the relatively unchanging targets of operational policework. The identification of these enduring targets – Lee's 'police property' – can now provide the 'retrospective test' for the next chapter, which looks at the present relationship between policework and a socially divided society.

Suggestions for Further Reading   (Chapters 4 and 5)

Brogden, M. (1982), *The Police: Autonomy and Consent* (London: Academic Press).
Bunyan, T. (1977), *The Political Police in Britain* (London: Quartet Books).
Critchley, T. A. (1978), *A History of Police in England and Wales*, 2nd edn (London: Constable).
Emsley, C. (1983), *Policing and its Context, 1750–1870* (London: Macmillan).
Monkkonen, E. H. (1981), *Police in Urban America 1860–1920* (Cambridge University Press).
Radzinowicz, L. (1955), *A History of English Criminal Law, Vol. 3* (London: Stevens).

6 Policing Social Divisions:

Age, Gender, Race and Class

Introduction

Our historical examination clearly highlighted the importance of social divisions in understanding policework. In particular, it showed a broad class bias in police attention, albeit one mediated in particular ways. Without an understanding of this historical backcloth – the enduring role of the police in relation to the powerless – it is quite easy to be distracted by what in practice they may happen to spend most of their time doing, the 'mundane daily round': sitting in an (im)mobile patrol car on the highway, perambulating down the street in casual conversation with a colleague, acting as a walking/talking A-to-Z to city strangers, clearing up the human debris of a road accident, completing a crime report form, and so on. But this sketch of the profane reality of policework – waiting, watching, serving, form filling, etc. – can obscure what the history chapter has so relentlessly revealed: the bias in police attention towards particular powerless groups, Lee's 'police property' (Lee, 1981). To shed light on *this* question, how such attention operates currently, we need to attend to the social patterning of police attention (something Chapter 3, with its microsociological focus, could not deal with adequately) – to the systematic biases evident in the pattern of police attention to groups of citizens, both as victims and offenders. The pattern of such bias will provide the key to understanding how policework relates to the wider structure of society – its role in relation to society's social divisions – in ways which attention to the most obviously visible and time-consuming feature of policework, the mundane, uncontroversial routine matters, cannot.

An important clue to the pattern of this bias can be found in the recent focus of media accounts of controversial policing operations. The British inner city riots of 1981 and 1985, for example, directed attention to the relationship between the police and young (especially black) people. The notorious television documentary on police practices in cases of rape (BBC1, 18 January 1982) underlined the curious relationship between a predominantly male police force and that half of the population that happens to be female. The twelve-month miners' strike of 1984–5, with its nightly dramatic visual renderings of picket-line confrontations on the television news, depicted policing in confrontation with a major section of the industrial working class. Finally, there are the episodic conflicts between the police and young people (Pearson, 1983) – whether they be the mods and rockers of the 1960s, the skinheads of the late 1970s, bands of young football supporters in the present day, or simply street-corner youths at any time in the history of urban-industrial capitalist society. These four categories – race, sex, class and age – happen to be the major social divisions of inequality in our society: to be young, to be black, to be female, to be working class, are all different though related ways of being socially disadvantaged, relatively powerless and of low status in our society. It is our intention in what follows to take a closer look at the current evidence on the policing of these social divisions, and to see how well this withstands the retrospective historical test of Chapters 4 and 5.

As we saw in Chapter 2, it is important to distinguish at the outset between police *attitudes* and *behaviour*. Just because police officers utter prejudices (negative preconceptions of individuals or groups) in speech, this does not of itself demonstrate that their practices will be discriminatory (unjustly targeting individuals or groups). The rhetoric of police prejudice may speak louder than police discrimination in practice. So we must recognize that the raucous nature of some aspects of the police culture is not necessarily the same thing as documenting police discrimination in public encounters, and in arrest and prosecution decisions. Moreover, *different* treatment of social groups is not necessarily the same thing as *discriminatory* treatment. The former may result, quite legitimately, from different levels of offending between groups. However, as we shall see there is plenty of evidence of all three – prejudice, differentiation and discrimination – as the following sections make clear. We start with age.

Age Divisions and Policework

We have seen how, historically, the category 'troublesome youth' emerged out of the structural changes in the working class which produced the 'respectable/rough' division, and the concomitant discovery of adolescence as a 'dangerous' time. In the contemporary post-Second World War period, 'troublesome youth' has become even more visible, and more problematic: partly because the crime problem, statistically, has increasingly become the problem of delinquency; and partly because the massive visibility of youth, one result of the consumer boom of the 1950s and 1960s and the commercial creation of 'the teenager', has become a symbol of the new – what has been called a *'metaphor* for social change' (Smith, Blackwell and Immirzi, 1975, p. 242, italics in original) – with all the fears and anxieties that such a break with tradition, especially in a conservative nation, portends. The combined result has been an at times obsessional concern, in the media and in official pronouncements, with 'the youth problem'. However, we must not overlook the fact that statistically, and in the popular imagination, the problem of youth is massively the problem of young *men*. We deal separately below with the question of the importance of sex/gender divisions and police-work, but must note here that all references to youth in this and the next section essentially reference *male* youth.

If the statistical involvement of youth in crime provides the justification for police attention to them, it would appear to be the *image* of 'deviant' youth as *potential* trouble, or symbolic threat to authority, that structures much of police thinking and practice in this area. This is not to deny the statistical reality of juvenile delinquency. As Muncie (1984, pp. 58–9) reminds us, the peak age for male offending appears to coincide with the final year of compulsory schooling, and 20 per cent of all recorded indictable offences were committed (in 1981) by juveniles age 14–17. Expanding the age range a little reveals that 10–21-year-olds commit most recorded thefts (57 per cent), robberies (60 per cent), criminal damage (66 per cent), burglaries (70 per cent), and most recorded crime overall (54 per cent). This is not true of sexual and violent offences, which are largely committed by the over-21s. (Figures are based on persons found guilty of, or cautioned for, indictable offences in England and Wales for 1981; quoted in Muncie, 1984, p. 60.) Since most recorded, indictable crime (which excludes the bulk of motoring offences) is non-violent property crime, with sexual and violent offences a comparative rarity statistically, it is clearly justified, in statistical terms, to regard the recorded crime problem as essentially a youthful one, even if more petty and mundane than the media imagery of 'vicious young criminals' would have us believe. The question of youth robbery may seem anomalous, since it is formally speaking a violent offence. We think, however, that it is an ambiguous category, and liable to be confused with the non-violent, 'theft from the person' category (as Blom-Cooper and Drabble, 1982, have argued). Moreover, there is evidence from self-report studies of a positive relationship between self-reported offending and adversarial contacts with police (cf.

Riley, 1984, p. 19; Southgate and Ekblom, 1984, p. 18). This means that police suspicions and stopping behaviour, however much based on 'hunch', can point to statistics for justification.

When the statistical crime picture is fleshed out, the statistical 'normality' is revealed as culturally normal too. For example, four major British research studies of juvenile delinquency, two conducted in Liverpool (Mays, 1954; Parker, 1974) and two in the East End of London (Willmott, 1966; Downes, 1966), all drew attention to the taken-for-granted cultural normality of petty theft and other forms of minor delinquency like 'joyriding', as well as to its transitory and relatively insignificant status in the lives of the male adolescents studied. The association with leisure was also brought out – either 'for laughs' to combat boredom, as with joyriding, vandalism, etc., or to help buy 'excitement', 'kicks', etc., as with theft.

The cultural normality of petty theft, etc., is not confined to studies of basically working-class youth, routinely engaged in petty delinquency. For, not only have crime victimization studies begun to reveal officially the huge extent of unreported and unrecorded crime, and hence the general normality of much crime, but self-report studies specifically of schoolboys (cf. Belson, 1975) have revealed that childhood stealing is so commonplace that 'it is probable that all youth qualify for the label of "juvenile delinquent"' (Muncie, 1984, p. 61). Against such a background – the ubiquity of youthful delinquency – the statistical 'overinvolvement' of youth in much crime seems less a justification for the 'overpolicing' of youth crime and more a reason for under-reacting, in the safe knowledge that crime for most is not a 'way' but a 'stage' of life, one that will be shortly outgrown (cf. Rutherford, 1986), the more easily if less of a record, with its accompanying stigma, has been picked up on the way. Yet the evidence suggests that police do not adopt this realistic view.

The reason they do not is partly because of the other image of youth: youth as the deviant and rebellious harbinger of moral decline and the loss of social authority. This other image is a composite of 'violence' (exemplified in football hooliganism, the 'mod-rocker' seafront clashes and the 'paki-bashing' skinhead youth), of cultural rebellion (exemplified in the symbolic 'resistance through rituals' of the succession of youth subcultural 'styles' from the teddy boys to the punks (Hall and Jefferson, 1976), and the hedonistic pursuit of 'sex and drugs and rock and roll'), and of political radicalism (exemplified by the youthful early CND movement, the New Left, the politicization of the counter-culture and student protest). Arguably, the image has grown more threatening as the 'weekend' pursuit of sex and drugs and rock and roll began to inform a whole way of life, from the hippy movement onwards, and as some groups and styles – black rastas, hippy protestors, anarcho-punks, for example – appeared to exemplify all deviant images, the violent, the culturally subversive and the politically dissident, simultaneously.

It is this threatening and deviant image as much as the mundane reality of youth crime which accounts for the historical continuity of such police tactics as 'moving on' young people on the streets – always a major feature of police beatwork. From the inception of paid policework to the present day, young people hanging round the street corner have been the ready target of police patrolling practice. In the early days of the New Police, moving on young males (together with costermongers) soon became an established feature of the beat patrol. The preoccupation of young males on the street – from games of pitch-and-toss to idling time on the street corner – was constructed as one target of policework from the outset.

Cohen's account of youth–police relations on the streets of Islington during the later nineteenth and early twentieth century graphically demonstrates the feud-like relationship that can develop between police patrols and groups of young people. And Pearson's (1983) account essentially confirms this. Here two nonagenarian, ex-Liverpool officers confirm (from their perspective) the essential normality of their 'move on' practice with kids on streets between the wars:

> They'd usually break-up as they saw you coming. They'd soon wander off – you'd have to give some kids a whack with your glove – with a couple of marbles in. (taped interview)

Part of the 'move on' practice is related to the police need, as they see it, to be physically in control of the streets 'in the interests of order'. But, much urban juvenile leisure, informed by a rather different sense of 'order' which stresses the search for laughs, excitement and kicks, is also street-based. Consequently, normal street leisure can often mean conflict with the police:

> The boys see trouble as something connected purely with the police . . . At no stage do they perceive it as *doing* wrong, or break-ing rules . . . What wrongs are they doing if they just walk around the streets and the police harass them? The reasons for the harass-ment lie with the police, and NOT inside any rule that the boys are breaking, since for the boys the streets are a 'natural' meeting place. (Corrigan, 1979, p. 139, italics in original)

The problem for police posed by Corrigan's 'Smash Street Kids', was not *what* they were doing, but their *absence* of activity. Just walking round the streets 'doing nothing', or 'simply hanging around', felt innocent enough to the youths themselves. But, to a police force imbued with the virtues of useful toil, and its corollary – 'the devil finds work for idle hands' – such unstructured, unsupervised and essentially 'disorganized' inactivity is always vaguely suspect, since potentially threatening. 'Doing nothing' is all too close, from a police viewpoint, to 'loitering with intent' – especially if you 'belong' to a group, male youth, with a 'known' propensity for crime.

Much more threatening of course is 'doing nothing' on a mass-scale – which is largely how the mods and rockers saw their seaside gatherings in the early 1960s (cf. Cohen, 1973). But once young people have been targeted for special attention, as clearly happened with the mods and rockers, the tendency to take pre-emptive or deterrent action – to prevent the potential becoming the actual – escalates. And when these punitive measures are undertaken with the collaboration of the court, the disjunction between the young person's sense of 'order' and that of 'the authorities' is likely to be complete.

> by Easter, 1965 the magistrates in Brighton were employing the highly dubious practice of remanding young people in custody as a form of extra-legal punishment. Bail was refused not on the merits of the individual case but as a matter of principle – the ostensible reason given by the magistrates for remand as being to enable the police to make enquiries, was not in fact the reason given in court when bail was opposed. The police opposed bail on the grounds that if the boys were allowed to go free justice would not be done and the public would not be protected. On the flimsiest of evidence a boy, who by the police's own account had done nothing more than refuse to 'move along', would be certified as an 'unruly person', refused bail and remanded in custody in an adult prison – in some cases for up to three weeks. (Cohen, 1971, p. 232)

Of course, it is not only 'doing nothing' that 'invites' police attention and activity in such settings. The major Black–Reiss observational study of police–public encounters in the USA concluded that the main factor in determining negative outcomes was not, as might have been expected, race but 'disrespect', though they also found (a point to which we return below on page 136) that black people showed disrespect more often. And, as we know, young people are most likely to display the characteristics – of 'cheek' and apparent lack of respect – which result in an abrasive relationship. The classic confirmation of this view lies in an early North American study:

> in the opinion of . . . patrolmen themselves the demeanour of apprehended juveniles was a major determinant of their decisions for 50–60 per cent of the juvenile cases they processed. (Piliavin and Briar, 1964, p. 169)

And those who 'did not manifest what were considered to be appropriate signs of respect tended to receive the more severe dispositions' (ibid.). The overall result, as Phil Cohen so neatly summarizes it,

> has been to narrow the scenario of law and order down to a battle between two rival gangs, both composed of young, single working-class males, each seeking territorial control over the class habitat – but with this difference, that one mob has the full weight of the state behind it, the other only themselves and their mates to fall back on. (Cohen, 1979, p. 135)

Once such conflicts have become endemic, an internally amplifying and self-fulfilling dynamic is set up. In Parker's Liverpool inner city study (1974), as in Gill's (1977) similar Birkenhead ethnography, such a spiralling of conflict may be institutionalized as a feud between police officers and young people, with the continuing dispute taking precedence over any specific concern by the police with 'crime'.

For Gill, a major labelling effect took place. 'Luke Street', a depressed area of Birkenhead, initially regarded as troublesome by the media for reasons unconnected with crime, led to police officers defining local youths as potential criminals. A mutual and self-reinforcing labelling process occurs. Hence a local police constable giving evidence in court, 'When you see a gang of youths in that area, it usually means trouble'. Similarly, from one Birkenhead youth, 'The coppers come round here looking for trouble' (Gill, 1977, p. 122).

Against such a background, it is not surprising that more youngsters than the older age groups have unfavourable attitudes towards policework – a fact borne out by both ethnographic studies and surveys. At their most extreme, such attitudes can be highly antagonistic, with police violence – or rather the threat of it – a taken-for-granted feature of police–youth interaction:

> The police enjoy it – it is their afternoon out. They are like skinheads, they enjoy knocking people about. They only join to knock people about. They join a mob, only it is a legal mob. 'alf of them

was like the snidey kid at school, who can't say fuck all and grasses 'em up but when he joins them, has a right to march up and down. It's like a private army. (Daniel and McGuire (eds), 1972, p. 101)

More generally, Belson's (1975) findings on the differences between adults and young people in terms of attitudes to the police are representative of the research studies. In that survey for the Metropolitan Police, the ratings of young persons were consistently less favourable than those of the adult sample. The difference was greatest for perceptions of the police as 'bullying', and was also high for 'rudeness' and 'tendency to be frightening'. Young people were two to three times as likely as adults to suggest that the police used too much force when arresting people, hushed up complaints against them, and forced their way into homes without a warrant. Generally, young people signified that the police were more likely to act in an unfavourable way to their age group. Conversely, in the same survey, the police officers questioned thought that juveniles in particular and young people generally were far more likely than most other sections of the population to create problems for the police. Unsurprisingly, in view of our sketch of police–youth relations, such attitudes were related to the experience of negative encounters. As the two British crime surveys reveal, young people have a relatively high number of 'adversarial encounters' (encounters 'in which the person is treated as an offender or suspect' Smith, 1986, p. 2). For example, one in five (one in four in the 14–15 age cohort) of the young people asked in the first survey had been stopped and questioned by the police in the street. The teenagers had also been asked whether they thought that the police locally treated young people fairly. Only a minority – one-sixth – responded negatively. But the most useful predictor of that latter attitude was the recent experience of having been stopped and questioned:

> Those who had been stopped and searched within the last year were the most likely to hold unfavourable views. Moreover, while those who had been stopped in the last 12 months were more likely to say that police treatment of young people was unfair, this effect was more pronounced for those apparently not involved in offending. It seems that what may be seen as unjustified intervention by the police may have a marked adverse effect on attitudes towards the police. (Riley, 1984, p. 19–20)

And, once again, David Smith's PSI study confirms this finding:

The number of adversarial encounters, and the proportion of all encounters that are adversarial, is much higher among younger than among older people and among men than among women, so it is particularly high among young men. These differences in the pattern of contact are accompanied by equally large differences in views about the police, especially in the incidence of highly critical views indicating hostility. (Smith, 1986, p. 2)

Given the high rate of youth unemployment, Smith's further finding that 'unemployed men tend strongly to have adversarial . . . encounters with the police and to be more hostile to them than other groups' (ibid.) offers another indirect form of confirmation.

It might be argued that all the foregoing represents only one (repressive) side of the story, the other constituted by policework in schools, youth clubs and in cautioning rather than prosecuting juveniles. This, of course, is a much more recent side of the story and has, as yet, to be fully told. But the sight of police officers in schools, not just as police officers delivering technically based talks about road safety and 'not taking sweets from a stanger', but in some instances as 'teachers' introducing and leading general discussions about crime, law and order, and also in youth clubs, sometimes in a full-time capacity, is becoming increasingly commonplace. So is the decision to caution. But if routine policing of youth constitutes the 'hard' repressive side, there are decidedly mixed views about this new 'soft' ideological side.

Take police involvement in youth work, which might be seen broadly as work with 'potential offenders' or 'pre-delinquents' – until they can be 'usefully engaged in productive leisure'. Local police forces have developed complex leisure schemes which seek to determine and structure the non-school time of young people. Intervention at source, prior to any deviant action, has justified many police-sponsored Duke of Edinburgh Award schemes and their less accredited alternatives. Twenty years ago, inner city youth fleeing the patrolling constable might seek refuge in the neighbourhood youth club. Now, they may meet the constable on the club doorstep in the guise of a youth worker or a Police Liaison Officer. Likewise, police involvement in schools might be seen in a similarly 'pre-emptive' fashion – as an attempt through sessions on law, policing, crime and so on to teach 'law-abidingness'.

For traditionalists such work might either be seen as diverting police from their 'real' task of catching criminals and maintaining the peace, or benignly: as a 'good' thing which obviously requires support. For those of a more critical or radical cast of mind, such

involvement presents two problems. The first is the opportunity such
occasions appear to present for police generally to extend the net of
surveillance and intelligence, or to find out more about particular
young people who may be suspected of particular crimes. In extreme
form, such a viewpoint can suspect all such police initiatives of being
part of an intelligence gathering conspiracy. The second problem,
which is connected with the first, is the terms under which police enter
schools or youth clubs, and who 'controls' the exercise. From this
perspective, the critical issue is not whether the police enter such
arenas or not, but the establishment of a proper and accountable
framework for such decision-making so that the terms and conditions
of police entry can be discussed and agreed and guidelines drawn up.
Implicit within this approach is a recognition that the primary
motivation for police involvement is ideological and not intelligence
gathering; to win hearts and minds, not find offenders. This being so,
the issue becomes one of ensuring education, not ideology, is in
command – that police contributions to either school or youthwork
programmes are properly subordinated to the goals of those institutions, not those of the police institution. (For a critical discussion of
those issues, see Advisory Committee on Police in Schools, 1986.)

   Cautioning raises slightly different issues. When arrested, young
first offenders have, since the Children and Young Persons Act 1969,
increasingly been dealt with by the system of police cautioning (rather
than through the judicial process). Between 1968 and 1974 cautions of
juveniles rose from 'under 34,000 to over 101,000' (Home Office,
1984, p. 3). By 1980 this had risen to 104,000 (Muncie, 1984, p. 157).
Between 25 per cent and 65 per cent of all young males who came to
the attention of the police in 1982 in England and Wales were
cautioned (Laycock and Tarling, 1985, p. 26). Formally, the intention
is to keep young people out of court to avoid any labelling effect and
thus frustrate the development of a criminal career. In that sense it is an
embodiment of the 'welfarist' philosophy lodged (partly) in the
Children and Young Persons Act 1969, the Act which gave the
caution its first legal recognition. And, ostensibly, its apparent
humane intent looks to be laudable.

   However, there are two particular problems that critics perceive.
One is the possibility of 'net-widening' (Stan Cohen, 1979), that is the
use of the caution in situations where formerly no further action
would be taken. Although the police must have sufficient evidence of
guilt, and the juvenile must also admit to it, the lesser safeguards
involved, including the temptation to admit the offence simply to get
'it' over with, make net-widening an endemic potentiality. Ditchfield
(1976) demonstrated this was happening in the early days, though the

official belief is that this no longer applies. The second problem is that of safeguards. Effectively, by accepting a caution, the argument runs that the traditional safeguards against wrongful conviction that are available to adults are, to all practical intents, unavailable to many young people. The police, as the cautioning institution, assume the four separate functions of arresting, prosecuting, judging, and sentencing. Young suspects, of course, have the option of facing trial instead of accepting a caution. But the stressful exigencies of that process discourage all but a few young people from proceeding along that path, where there is the option. Inequality in relation to the traditional safeguards is an inevitable feature of the unequal bargaining power of the police–juvenile participants in the cautioning decision. Because police handling of juveniles without regard to the safeguards of due process has become a major feature of the justice process of England and Wales (Pratt, 1986), many have argued for a swingback to a 'justice' model, for all its imperfections, for juveniles (cf. Taylor, Lacey and Bracken, 1980; Morris, A. *et al.*, 1980).

Summary and Conclusion

Where then does this leave the policing of the 'generation gap'? Is the treatment youth receives at the hands of the police commensurate with their offending behaviour, such that any evidence of *different* treatment can be attributed to different levels of criminal activity? Or is police treatment of youth *discriminatory*? Do police, in other words, subject youth to levels of attention over and above what can be justified by their levels of offending? We have tried in the foregoing to overview the available evidence. This has come from a variety of sources and, where research-based, has been produced using a variety of methodologies – from qualitative, participant–observation ethnographic studies to quantitative, statistically based surveys and analyses. And, for those who demand strictly verifiable answers, the questions we pose at the outset must remain open.

Our own general answer runs like this. Taken overall, there is evidence of differential *and* discriminatory treatment of young people. The evidence that young people get *different* treatment is massive and overwhelming – statistical and observational studies both consistently point to the great number of adversarial contacts between police and youth. Some of that extra attention is justified. Young males commit most of the officially recorded crime, and those that are stopped 'on suspicion' are more likely, on their own admission, to have been a recent offender (which is not to say they were doing anything wrong when they were stopped). But there is also strong evidence of discriminatory treatment: from the consistent statistical findings that adversarial contacts produce both a low 'strike rate' ('the proportion of stops that lead to the detection of an offence' – about 1 in 12 in London, PSI, 1983, Vol. 1, p. 311) and hostility, to the more ethnographic accounts all pointing towards police 'over-suspiciousness' of youth. Nor should this dual finding, of differentiation and discrimination, surprise us. In the absence of strong counter-tendencies, such as vociferous public concern, once a group has been statistically identified as criminal, and satisfies other criteria such as low status and relative powerlessness, the resulting police 'overattention', begins to produce the sorts of results that justify the original over-attention. This then leads to continued overattention, and so on. In short, a self-fulfilling prophecy is always likely in such situations. However, there is a prior element of discrimination hidden within the apparent objectivity of the statistics. Although youth are over-involved in the official statistics, this is partly because the official statistics, and certainly the police-defined, proactively produced offences, consist of what, from a range of deviant behaviours, has been selected for criminalization. In other words, youth suffer a *double discrimination*: the offences that they tend to be involved in (minor disorderly acts, mundane property offences, fighting, etc.) are subject to police 'overattention' in the first place; and the results of this over-attention provide the justification for yet more attention, with all the potential for amplification this entails. It is this double discrimination which enables us finally to conclude that the social division of age is unjustly overpoliced, and that 'troublesome' youth constitute one category of 'police property'. The 'retrospective test' of this conclu-sion supplied in Chapters 4 and 5 serves further to confirm it.

Sex/Gender Divisions and Policework

Introduction: Sexual Divisions, Gender Divisions

Sexual divisions refer to the biological distinction between the male and the female of the species. Despite the fact that all of us possess both male and female characteristics, and despite the existence of the 'mixed-sex' hermaphrodite, and the 'confused-sex' man or woman who desires or has a sex-change operation, to deny a sex-based biologically different starting point for men and women is to fly in the face of a very material and concrete reality. Gender divisions, by contrast, refer to the socially constructed differences that have been built upon these natural differences between men and women – 'masculinity' and 'femininity', for example. Thus, whilst men and women cannot escape their *biological destiny* prescribed by their *sex* (i.e. as male or female), it is a question of *biography, not biology*, that determines how constrained they are by notions of masculinity or femininity, how well they have been able to resist the social blandishments of behaviour deemed appropriate to their sex, i.e. the *social destiny* prescribed by *gender*.

The first thing that stands out in thinking about sexual divisions and policework is that policework massively involves men: male officers policing other, usually young, males. Since, officially, there is a huge discrepancy in offender rates – 'official statistics for those in the peak-offending 14–16 group show a male–female ratio of about 6:1 for indictable offences (Criminal statistics, 1984)' (Riley, 1986, p. 34) – this is, no doubt, the basis for all the other sex-based differences: stops, arrests, charges, convictions and so on. However, what we also know is that the offending ratio, using self-report studies, is much less, at around 2:1 or even lower, and for some 'specific types of offence (for example, damaging school property or stealing from family or relatives), the sex ratio in self-report studies is close to 1:1' (Riley, 1986, p. 34). More importantly still, when these much smaller differences are examined in relation to *opportunity*, the difference disappears. Thus, 'given equal opportunities, sex differences in crime participation by young people – as offenders or victims – are minimal' (Riley, 1986, p. 38).

What these findings mean is that though the official crime picture stresses the importance of sexual divisions, the 'reality' of crime is largely a function of gender divisions. Because girls and women have been historically confined to the 'private' sphere, with their entry into the public sphere – the world of men – strictly controlled by men, as fathers, husbands, boy-friends, etc., the opportunity of participating in those kinds of crime that have become the staple of police attention, has been, and is, much less. But 'given equal opportunity', that is to say, given a situation in which teenage girls have managed to escape the closer supervision parents traditionally reserve for their female offspring (in conformity with gender expectations), their offending rates parallel their male peers.

So, it is a *gender-based* division that ensures that official statistics make crime appear to be a sex-based phenomenon, and orientate police activities accordingly. But, if this is one fundamental effect of gender, there remain others. And since, for reasons just made clear, our discussion of other social divisions has been (or will be) predominantly about men – *young* men, *black* men, *working class* men – our primary concern here will be to explore the effect of gender on women, as police officers, as police suspects and as victims of crime.

However, before turning to the question of gender and women, we should not leave this section without a short discussion on the way gender affects a particular group of men and women, namely homosexual or 'gay' men and women. Unfortunately, the evidence we have here is largely anecdotal, but it all points in the same direction: towards an experience of policework which strongly suggests the equation of 'gayness' with deviance, and the consequent 'rough' treatment of which all groups consigned to the status of 'police property' complain.

The deviant status of 'gays' stems from their failure to conform to a core feature of gender-based expectations concerning appropriate sexuality, namely heterosexuality. Though the law does not officially recognize lesbianism, the label 'lesbian', like that of 'slag' or 'whore', is sufficiently delegitimizing (i.e. places those so labelled outside the only legitimate characteristic and behaviour – the 'feminine') to 'justify' the 'rough' treatment of women so labelled. And it really matters little whether we are talking of groups of self-confessed lesbians, or 'protesting' women who have been simply called lesbian (an accusation of which arrested women sometimes complain). It is the term 'lesbian' that is sufficient to rob the offending woman of 'respectable' status and place her into the 'rough' category of 'police property'.

Gay men suffer a similar fate, but, in addition, the law makes some homosexual activities illegal; for example, the laws against 'importuning' and against sexual activities between consenting adults who happen to be under 21. Partially illegal then, and wholly deviant, homosexual men can suffer a triple fate: the unpredictable capriciousness of police activity against importuning; the vindictiveness of the use of the laws to variously 'entrap' homosexuals; and the general 'pariah' treatment reserved for members of deviant groups.

The ideological claim underpinning the attitude of 'abhorrence' is that homosexuality is a crime 'against *nature*'. The real offence, however, is quite the opposite: homosexuality is an offence against the *social* construction of a gendered sexuality that equates normal masculinity and femininity with heterosexuality. While gay men, by their 'refusal' to conform to the 'normal' image of masculinity, effectively have their sexuality policed, *all* women, as we shall see in the next sextion, have their sexuality policed through the gender-based notion of 'femininity'.

Gender Divisions, Women and Policework

There are three ways in which the impact of gender on women will be discussed in relation to policework: first by examining the way in which women police officers experience their role; secondly, by examining the way in which police officers deal with female offenders; and thirdly by looking at their treatment of female victims of crime. Each will be examined in turn. But first a brief historical sketch, since this will assist the later discussion.

The history of women as police officers is marked by a concern to deploy such officers in the supervision of female prisoners and to handle female suspects. In 1883 the Metropolitan Police appointed two women to supervise female convicts, but it was not until later, 1914, that the Women Police Volunteers were formed. From this grew, in 1918 in the MPD, the Women's Police Service (Benn, 1985, p. 133). Later, in 1924, a government departmental committee investigated the employment of police women and recommended that policewomen be properly declared constables, recognizing their particular usefulness in the case of sex offences and with female offenders. It was left to local police committees as to how this recommendation was to be acted upon, that is to decide the exact duties to be performed by policewomen. The tendency was for separate policewomen's departments to be established, with their own training, hierarchy, and promotion prospects, primarily concerned with duties pertaining to women and children. This was the case until the Sex Discrimination Act of 1975, which enforced the integration of these separate departments into the body of the police force. (See the Sex Discrimination Act, 1975, section 17.)

This potted history of the position of women in the police force highlights a number of features relevant to their current status. First, the initial role conceived for policewomen was seen very much as an extension of the traditional female gender role; that is they were seen as possessing the caring qualities necessary to handle other women and children, particularly in the case of sex offences. Secondly, they were seen very much as performing a complementary role to the policeman, but not as equally able to do a policeman's job. Thirdly, the potential involvement of policewomen in a more general police role as a consequence of the Sex Discrimination Act has had a comparatively short history, and thus it might be expected that some resistance to this relatively new role of policewomen still exists within the police force as a whole. Indeed the changes imposed by the Sex Discrimination Act provoked a considerable debate at the time as to what the role of policewomen should be, a debate which still remains unresolved despite the formal legislation, as shall be seen.

Gender and Women Police Officers

The relatively short history of policewomen, the small percentage of women who joined the police force, and their specialized role prior to 1975, help explain, at least in part, the predominance of the macho police subculture (Chapter 3). Indeed the historical emergence of that culture occurred largely in the absence of women. The years since 1975 have however seen little impact on the cult of masculinity among police officers, the cult well documented by the PSI studies (1983) and Jones (1987), among others. This cult of masculinity is however overlaid by organizational features with respect to the deployment and promotional opportunities of female officers which places them on the receiving end of a double-edged sexist sword. The precise impact of this requires fuller explanation.

The police subculture, placing a high value on masculinity, carries with it notions of male superiority when it comes to handling violent situations. It was this issue which provoked a strong reaction to the implementation of the Sex Discrimination Act of 1975, as a Superintendent Hawkins is recorded as saying at the Police Superintendents' Association Conference, 1977:

> We cannot do without women in the force but I think the job of a police officer, certainly in 1978, is one which calls for what the male has to offer by way of strength and it is grossly unfair to encourage young slips of girls to join the police force and expect them to go out on the streets to deal with the public disorder we find today.

The argument which suggests that females are less capable than males of handling situations of disorder is given a further chivalrous dimension ('chivalry' constituting sexism's other edge) in that many police officers believe that in such circumstances they are faced with the dilemma of whether to deal with the public disorder or protect the female officer! This attitude is not necessarily borne out by the evidence nor by policewomen's own accounts of handling violent situations. Sherman (1975) reports the pacifying effects of a policewoman's presence, and Stretch quotes the following anecdotal comment, albeit one that involves a policewoman exploiting her femininity in a sexist fashion:

> Drunks might be quite happy to wear my hat, give me a kiss and cuddle and go home. (Stretch, 1981, p. 12)

Policewoman also generate fewer complaints. (Whitaker, 1982, p. 119).

The study by Jones (1987), dealing with this in greater detail, points to the predominance, even among young male officers, of the need to protect policewomen; and it still provides the backdrop of discussions between the Police Federation, the Metropolitan Police and the Equal Opportunities Commission over the integration of women into public order policing (*Guardian*, 21 April 1987). The attaching of stereotypical qualities to female members of the police force constrains policewomen to either accept the stereotype and retain their femininity in the eyes of their colleagues or to question it and cast doubt on the feminine qualities. As some recent work indicates:

> The difference is that when a man displays a physical weakness, the tendency is for colleagues to regard it as an individual failing. On the other hand, if a woman does not contribute equally in a fight, for example, her characteristics are transferred to all policewomen . . . The policewoman is in a predicament as to how to act, however, because if she does 'prove' herself in brawls she is, in the opinion of some policemen, contradicting their ideas of acceptable feminine behaviour. (Bryant, Dunkerley and Kelland, 1985, pp. 239–40)

This predicament leads to strategies of making out in the police force open to policewomen, which have been described by Ehrlich-Martin (1980). While this study is based on American material, the study by Jones (1987) points to the relevance of these strategies in understanding the ways in which policewomen in her sample made out in the force. Ehrlich-Martin identified POLICEwomen, those who embrace the male culture as their own, and policeWOMEN, those who see themselves fulfilling the more traditional expectations associated with the role of policewomen, the service role. The identification and the existence of such strategies for policewomen must throw into doubt the presumption that a more equitable balance for the sexes within the police force and the deployment of women to deal with female victims of crime will automatically produce a different if not better handling of such victims (Kinsey, 1985a, p. 105). Questions of female representation in the force and deployment must, however, lead to a consideration of the institutionalized basis of the treatment of female police officers.

Despite increased applications from women to join the police force after the 1975 legislation (female probationers in the Metropolitan Police doubled from 11 per cent to 22 per cent by 1977 though currently the figure for woman PCs is still only 10 per cent, London Strategic Policy Unit, 1986, p. 2) women still form the minority of police officers (9.2 per cent according to Benn, 1985, p. 134) and within that minority they rarely move higher than the rank of constable. In 1984 some 93 per cent of all women police officers were constables as compared with 73 per cent of all male officers, and in that year while women accounted for 9 per cent of the total police force they provided only 3 per cent of sergeants, 2 per cent of inspectors, and 1 per cent of superintendents (*Policing*, editorial, 1985). The management explanation for this poor representation of female police officers is couched in terms of the high drop-out rate of female officers from the force. The average length of service for a WPC is five years, at which point many young female officers leave the force to start a family. The demands of shift work, it is argued, make it difficult for them to contemplate continuing a career in the police force and a family. (Though many nurses, for example, seem to overcome this difficulty.) Consequently, the police force loses a considerable proportion of expensively trained expertise just at the point at which they become eligible to sit promotional examinations.

The explanation for the under representation of women in the higher ranks is not quite so simple, however. Kinsey's survey of police officers on Merseyside revealed that of those eligible to sit promotion exams, 5 per cent of the men did so but only 1.45 per cent of the women (Kinsey, 1985a, p. 27). This suggests that all other things being equal women are much less prepared to sit the examination in any case. This of course may well be the result of a managerial self-fulfilling prophecy; women leave to have babies therefore it is not worth promoting them; women, seeing that few women get promoted are not motivated to try. In addition, career policewomen offend the male subcultural stereotype of women. Consequently the decision to step on the career ladder involves taking on the institutionalized sexism of management *and* the informal culture of their peers. The overall effect is a male-dominated hierarchy in the police force.

The second issue to be raised at an institutional level is the question of the deployment of female police officers. Kinsey again reports that while 18 per cent of men work in the CID, only 6 per cent of women do, and when one looks at the deployment of officers under 30, 43 per cent of those under 30 on station duty (the least prestigious job in the force) were women (Kinsey, 1985a, p. 28). These figures begin to show the way in which the refusal to see women other than in their stereotypical role, and as likely to leave the force early to take on their 'primary' role, effectively cuts off avenues of career development for policewomen. Thus, while *formally* policewomen are available to do the same policework as men, in practice this is restricted because short service curtails their opportunities to specialize, and for the most part they are still deployed in the traditional policewomen roles.

In many respects the attitudes outlined above towards policewomen and their experience within the police hierarchy are marked, not by their peculiarity but by their normality in a society organized on gender lines. If the force reflects these stereotypical notions with respect to their female colleagues, it seems reasonable (though not necessarily acceptable) to expect that such attitudes carry over to their dealings with female offenders and female victims of crime. In this case the effect of such attitudes is not only compounded by the inherent power dimension to such relationships but by other factors as well. The handling of female offenders will be discussed first of all.

Gender and Female Offenders

Heidensohn argues that:

> The courts and the police process relatively few women as offenders, nevertheless they still seem to stereotype them into a narrow range of feminine roles, such as wife or 'whore'. (Heidensohn, 1985, p. 58)

This wife-whore continuum provides a basis from which to examine police practices with respect to female offenders. An initial starting point would be to ask whether such attitudes result in the police adopting a chivalrous stance in any respect to female offenders, perhaps viewing them as somehow less capable of committing crime because of their femaleness, or perhaps in some way in need of protection. Most of the research examining the notion of chivalry in the handling of female offenders is again North American. To date, the conclusion seems to be that the determining feature of the decision to arrest is the seriousness of the offence rather than gender (Smith and Visher, 1981), and while there might appear to be some favouritism in the initial criminal processing phases towards the older white female, this is lost when the nature of the offence is taken into account (Visher, 1983). This conclusion is also reached by Box (1983) in a much more detailed review of the question of preferential treatment of female offenders of serious crime. Thus while females might not receive as rough treatment as males (Holdaway, 1983), this does not necessarily translate into an overall preferential treatment of female offenders. (There is however some alarming anecdotal evidence emerging of the use of the 'strip search' with some women prisoners, Northern Ireland politicos and peacewomen in particular (NCCL, 1986). This may be functionally equivalent to the rough handling of male prisoners.) The notion of chivalry is however two edged. It not only suggests the possibility of preferential treatment, it also has a protective element to it. For the female juvenile offender (or 'near' offender) this protective label 'for her own good', especially in situations where she might be thought to be at risk of stepping outside of a traditional (constrained) female sexuality to place herself in 'moral danger', is likely from both police and courts. And as Box states, such 'protection' becomes the means by which, effectively, a gender-specific punishment is enacted:

> Thus, rather than concern themselves with dispensing justice, juvenile courts are often transformed into stern parental surrogates who lock up their naughty daughters for behaving in ways which gain scarcely concealed approval when committed by sons. (Box. 1983, p. 170)

Once inside the system, the label 'naughty' can prove self-fulfilling. The story of Diana Christina (Christina and Carlen, 1985, pp. 59–103) is but one shocking, exemplary case in point.

There are of course specific offences which are defined by the legislation in a thoroughly sexist manner, and encourage police officers in their stereotypical responses. The policing of prostitution, from the early Contagious Diseases Acts to the present soliciting offences, reflect this bias. McLeod (1981, p. 65) outlines the problem of 'The Law' for prostitutes. As permanent suspects, prostitutes are always subject to all the width of police discretion – to harass or not, to arrest or not. The legal context in which the police operate with respect to specific pieces of legislation, in this case a legal context which grants the police officer much discretion, makes a real difference to the treatment of female offenders. The continuity of these stereotypical views of women is found when one examines the police handling of female victims of crime, to which we now turn.

Gender and Female Victims of Crime

In general female victims of crime are in receipt of a similar pattern of stereotypical notions of femininity and the need for protection. Elderly female victims are most frequently earmarked by the police as in need of help and support as a result of their victimization or their symbolic status as 'archetypal victim' (Grimshaw and Jefferson, 1987, p. 152). Within this general sympathetic approach towards the elderly, however, the treatment of victims of domestic violence and the treatment of victims of sex offences demand a closer examination.

The intervention, or lack of, by police officers in domestic disputes is framed by the overarching view that:

We are after all dealing with persons bound in marriage, and it is important, for a host of reasons to maintain the unity of the spouses. (ACPO statement quoted by Johnson, 1985, p. 112)

This view is amplified by the police view of the privacy of the domestic domain, and the idea that this is in any case not real police-work (Faragher, 1981). Even when all the conditions are met in which the police could make an arrest, this is rarely done in the case of domestic disputes (Edwards, 1986). If a crime is recorded it is more likely to be identified as some other offence, drunk and disorderly, for example (McCabe and Sutcliffe, 1978). Where women are keen to pursue a prosecution, the police are reluctant to do so, since it is argued that such complaints are frequently withdrawn. Dobash and Dobash (1980, p. 208) report that this only happened in 6 per cent of their cases (and in only 8 per cent of cases in North America). This cumulative unwillingness to act on the part of the police leaves women in this situation highly dissatisfied with the police (Pahl, 1978; Binney, Harkell and Nixon, 1981; London Strategic Policy Unit, 1986). If such an approach reflects a view of women as wives of Heidensohn's continuum, it is one which also emphasizes the privileges of the husband within the private domain.

However, in the case of sex offences, victims are likely to be in receipt of attitudes from the 'whore' end of Heidensohn's spectrum. The failure of women to report sex offences to the police is well documented (Hough and Mayhew, 1983; Kinsey, 1985b; Jones, MacLean and Young, 1986). Benn quoting from a small Wandsworth survey, summarizes the reason women give for not reporting such offences to the police:

> Three quarters of the women interviewed who described incidents of male violence . . . did not report them to the police. The . . . study also noted. . . the 'patronising paternalism' of the police – the long list of do's and don'ts handed out to women, carrying with them an implication of female guilt. Women were told 'not to get upset, not to get things out of proportion , not to go out alone, not to go out at night, to avoid "dangerous areas", not to put themselves at risk'. (Benn, 1985, p. 136)

These police attitudes reflect a victim precipitation view of such incidents, one which sees the victim's behaviour as being responsible for inviting a sexual response. This has been translated in the courts as 'contributory negligence' (see Jeffreys and Radford, 1984; Edwards, 1987), though subsequently repudiated by the Lord Chancellor

(Adler, 1987, p. 2). Thus unless the victim of sexual assault bears all the physical marks of not having 'consented' to such activity, and unless the circumstances of that assault are public, women are likely to find themselves subject to humiliating interrogation (Toner, 1982). This culminates in the police view that most complaints of rape are unjustified (Assistant Commisioner Jennifer Hilton, 1967). Our most substantial piece of research on the processing of rape complaints unhappily demonstrates that police practice is in line with such a view (Chambers and Millar, 1983). It is of course pertinent to indicate that some changes are taking place in the handling of complaints of rape and sexual assault, particularly since the much publicized handling of one such complaint by the Thames Valley Police (BBC 1, 18 January 1982). The Metropolitan Police have been involved in establishing special centres for the handling of such victims by non-police counsellors, with no imperative to report such incidents to the police incumbent on those who come to the centres. It is hoped that such centres will encourage more women to bring their complaints to the attention of the police. Feminists would argue, however, that what is ultimately required is to remove the burden of proof from the victim.

Summary and Conclusion

In reviewing this literature on the treatment of women, as police officers, offenders and victims, the two orienting questions, once again, have centred on *differentiation* and *discrimination*; that is, do women receive different treatment from men, and, if so, is such treatment unjust or discriminatory? There can be no doubt that the treatment of women in all three categories shows clear evidence of different treatment. As police officers the difference was largely institutionalized, prior to the Sex Discrimination Act of 1975, in the form of separate policewomen's departments with different training, duties, etc. And even after the Act, and the enforced disbandment of separate departments, the 'difference' lingers on: there are far fewer women, they are underrepresented in senior and in prestigious positions, and tend to be deployed away from the 'trouble spots' and towards the 'caring' end of the spectrum of police duties. As offenders, women's different opportunity structure ensures their underinvolvement in the kinds of activities that routinely occupy police attention, and hence ensures a commensurate freedom from police attention. When they do come to attention they may benefit from a lesser likelihood of rough treatment (though this benefit may be outweighed for some by a greater likelihood of the indignity of a strip search). On the other hand, certain activities of teenage girls – those thought to place them in 'moral danger' – will be subject to over-policing, as a consequence of the benevolent paternalism informing police and court actions. And, as victims, women suffer the dual fate of a mythology of male protection, which makes the elderly female victim the symbol of all victims, and the reality of an attitude towards actual female victims of male violence – the beaten wife, the raped girl friend, etc. – which ranges from the indifferent to the hostile.

The justification for this different treatment resides in the alleged differences between men and women, differences which require the weaker female sex to be 'protected' in various ways. Thus, it is male 'protectiveness' that keeps women police officers from the potential violence of the picket line, and then confines them generally to sub-ordinate roles. It is male 'protectiveness' that keeps women from the public spaces which are the province of 'male' crime, and then 'protectively' polices their moral life 'for their own good'. And it is male 'protectiveness' of female honour that sings the praises of female virtue, and then lamentably fails to protect it in practice since, by a supreme irony, lost virtue signals 'whore' – and 'whores' have forfeited the right to protection.

Is such different, 'protective' treatment just? If you start from a position that the differences between the sexes are natural, then male 'protection' of the 'weaker' sex appears just. We started by arguing that such an approach confuses natural, biological, sexual differences with socially constructed, gender-based ones. From this position, female 'weakness' stems from the socially constructed idea of 'femininity', not any natural difference between the sexes, and male 'protectiveness' from the equally socially constructed notion of 'masculinity'. Situating 'weakness' and 'femininity' in the social not the natural world allows us to understand the dichotomous wife/whore view of women: 'whores' are women who stand outside the weak/feminine space allotted them. Similarly, socially situating 'protectiveness' and 'masculinity' allows us to understand the punitive edge to the protective sword: those who stand outside the allotted space (whores, lesbians, the illegitimate rape victim, etc.) shall be punished not protected. From this position the different treatment accorded women is clearly an example of unjust discrimination.

Racial Divisions and Policework

Few commentators would dissent from the idea that relations
between police and the black communities, especially black youth,
are problematic, and most would agree that such relations had an
important part to play in fomenting the inner city riots of the 1980s.
Indeed, many would support Reiner's observation that the 'contribution' of policing was *doubly* important 'as both a background
condition and the immediate trigger' (Reiner, 1985b, p. 151; see also
Benyon, 1986, p. 3). The nature of the problem, seen from the
perspective of the black communities and documented in a series of
publications from Joe Hunte's 1966 pamphlet, *Nigger Hunting in
England*, onwards (see also, for example, Institute of Race Relations,
1979 and 1987, Lambeth Council Working Party, 1981), can be stated
simply: '*overheavy policing* of suspected black offences, and . . . *under
policing* of black victimisation, particularly in cases of racist attack'
(Reiner, 1985b, p. 152, italics added). The police case can be stated
equally simply: they would claim that communities get the level of
policing (as suspects or victims) that 'professional' judgement deems
appropriate.

So where does the truth lie? Research evidence from both sides of
the Atlantic gained from analyses of police statistics, surveys of
people's experiences of, and attitudes to, policing, and observationally
based studies of police behaviour on the beat and in the station, can be
found to support all the allegations of black communities, and indeed
much does so. On the other hand, some evidence has been read in
ways which support police claims. And some evidence, for various
reasons, is clearly inconclusive and therefore open to multiple interpretations.

These differences need not be a cause either for despair or cynicism:
no body of social research conducted at different times, in different
places, for different purposes and with different methodologies can
expect to achieve a unanimity of findings, much less agreement as to
what particular findings *mean*. What we intend to do, therefore, in
picking our way through the research is to summarize the consensus
where this obtains and the debate where conflicting interpretations
are the order of the day. The latter involves two principal axes around
which different interpretations hinge and which will therefore
provide the foci of our discussions of the debate.

(1)   The centrality of *race* as a determinant of police behaviour, as
      opposed to other factors known to have significance in police–
      public encounters, such as age, class, demeanour, etc.

(2)   Whether *different* treatment is necessarily *discriminatory*.

We end by offering our own 'resolution' of the debate.

The terminology in the research literature is not wholly consistent. Sometimes there is a clear distinction drawn between Asians and Afro-Caribbeans (or West Indians). At other times black is used – both as a synonym for Afro-Caribbean (though not always explicitly) and/or as a general term referencing both ethnic groups. Other non-white ethnic groups tend to be either ignored or assimilated within one of the other categories. We can only follow this terminology, but will try to highlight the different experience of Asians where we can. Finally, the adopted format will involve a move from 'attitudes' to 'behaviour'. Under 'attitudes' we shall consider the attitudes of black officers to their fellow officers, of police officers generally to ethnic minorities, and then of ethnic minorities to the police. Under 'behaviour' we shall consider 'blacks' first as 'offenders', and then as 'victims'. The latter will include the question of 'complaints against the police'.

Attitudes

Black Officers' Attitudes and Racism

One black former police officer recently had this to say about his time in the police.

> I joined the Merseyside police in 1982, yet my experience is typical of . . . that of many other black police officers . . . I cringe at the thought of ever letting my son, now aged five, join the police force. The police force is one of the most blatant forms of racism I have ever had to encounter. I still view my ex-colleagues with suspicion because of their anti-black, anti-working class views. The intensity of racism that I experienced caused me to view all white persons as my enemy. Thankfully, my views have now changed and I can now view black and white on their individual personalities, but I must admit it was not easy and I had to seek psychiatric treatment. I had enough racist experiences whilst serving as a police officer to fill the paper. (Letter from Glen Small, *Guardian*, 31 May 1986)

The experience of racism underlying such a viewpoint is not untypical, as Wilson, Holdaway and Spencer (1984) reveal in their account of the experiences of West Indian officers in Britain. Necessarily such a viewpoint is based on very small numbers since in London, for example, in 1983, less than 1 per cent of officers came from Afro-Caribbean or Asian parentage. In the City of London force, out of 774 officers only one was a member of an ethnic minority (Parliamentary Answer, 31 March 1986). (This had risen to 'just over 1 per cent' by April 1987, *Guardian*, 20 April 1987). The situation in the country as a whole is similar. In 1982 there were only 326 black officers in the whole of England and Wales (0.3 per cent). And even after extensive recruitment campaigns in the aftermath of Scarman, the figure in 1985 was still low at 726, or under 1 per cent of the total (Benyon, 1986, p. 57).

Other Officers' Attitudes and Racism

The racist attitudes of police officers and the reluctance of black people to join the police are doubtless related. Though there is no survey data on the attitudes of British police towards ethnic minorities, all the major studies concur that negative, stereotypical, prejudiced and hostile attitudes to blacks are rife amongst police officers, a finding in line with North American research. There is then an extraordinary consensus stretching across four decades and two continents, from the early work of Westley (only published over twenty years later as Westley, 1970) in the USA, through the 'middle period' work of people like Skolnick (1966) and Lambert (1970) to the latest findings of the Policy Studies Institute (PSI) study on policing in London (PSI, 1983). 'Lazy', 'easy-going', 'simple', 'troublesome', 'disrespectful', 'unco-operative', 'violent', 'criminal', and 'anti-police' are some of the recurrent epithets used to describe blacks that these studies reveal, with Asians, where distinctions are drawn, seen 'as no great problem, but liars if suspected of wrong doing' (Southgate, 1982, quoted in Benyon, 1986, p. 55). And young West Indians, if they are singled out, are seen as the most difficult group.

Police cadets too have been found to exhibit similar racial prejudice and hostility. A shocking series of extracts from essays by police cadets at the police training college in Hendon, made public in 1982, gave a glimpse of the problem (*Policing London*, no. 4, November, 'Police racism in the making'). But possibly the most revealing example of the sheer 'taken-for-grantedness' of racist language within the force was the extraordinary gaffe committed by a police community relations officer speaking at the 1984 Police Federation conference. Apparently blithely unaware of what he was saying, he referred publicly to 'our coloured brethren or nig nogs'. Although the Police Federation quickly repudiated the remark and the officer concerned offered first his apologies and then his resignation, the

remark lingers on as a dramatic reminder of the pervasive problem of
racist attitudes, assumptions and talk within the police.

We have already touched on the question of where attitudes come
from in Chapter 2; on whether the force attracts peculiarly 'conservative and authoritarian' personalities, or individuals simply reflecting
the 'normal' prejudices of the social groups from which they are
drawn; or whether recruits are socialized into their attitudes through
contact with the occupational subculture and/or the 'reality-shock' of
street encounters. We do not wish to retrace that ground here, but
simply note that aspects of that 'debate', implicitly anyway, are
discernible in this literature. Skolnick (1966), for example, thought
that the racial prejudice he found amongst police officers was similar
to comparable non-police groups, and Bayley and Mendelsohn
(1969) saw the police as only slightly more prejudiced than the wider
community (see Reiner, 1985b, p. 160). We should also remind
readers that these explanations of the origins of attitudes are not all
mutually exclusive: as Reiner says of the British evidence, in a conclusion which we would endorse, police prejudice is probably 'a
reflection of the racism prevalent in British society and the social
groups from which the police are drawn, *as well* as the situations in
which many police–black encounters occur (themselves the product
of racism within Britain)' (Reiner, 1985b, p. 161, italics added).
Moreover, it is also buttressed by the macho, conservative values of
the police occupational culture (cf. Holdaway, 1983, pp. 70–1).

Black Attitudes to the Police

These hostile police attitudes are mirrored in the well-documented
black antipathy to the police. Once again, across studies conducted on
both sides of the Atlantic, and through time, the picture painted
remains substantially the same: blacks are more hostile to the police
than other groups, and more critical of police performance. However, the fact of this greater hostility does not necessarily mean that a
majority of black people are hostile, nor that all aspects of policing are
equally subject to crticism. Reiner, for example, summarizing the
North American evidence, suggests that 'by the late 1970s it seems
that a clear majority of black Americans had a positive image of the
police, and complained of too little policing' (Reiner, 1985b, p. 160).
It is a conclusion that finds something of an echo in the recent British
PSI study which stated that the hostile views of West Indians 'by no
means amount to a complete rejection of the system' (PSI, 1983,
Vol. 4, p. 332).

The really marked difference appears to them to be less between blacks and whites and more between *young* blacks and others. For, both in North America and Britain, young blacks are noticeably more hostile. In North America, 'hostility is concentrated among those low-income or unemployed young black males who are the special targets of heavy policing' (from Walker, 1983, quoted in Reiner, 1985b, pp. 160–1). And, in Britain, the PSI highlighted the difference in concluding that 'the lack of confidence in the police among young West Indians can only be described as disastrous' (PSI, 1983, Vol. 1, p. 326), a result of their much greater likelihood of believing that 'the police regularly engaged in abuse of powers and excessive force, and that they fabricate evidence' (Reiner, 1985b, p. 173). One consequence of this black youth antipathy is, as the following study conducted during the 1970s revealed, a marked, though unsurprising, reluctance to join the police. Comparable black and white male samples were asked if they had ever considered a career in the police force (MIL Research Ltd, 1979). Only 9 per cent of the West Indian (16–24 year-olds) answered in the affirmative as compared with 23 per cent of the total respondent population. A comparable question on whether they would consider a career in the Armed Services revealed a much greater similarity between West Indians and others (34 per cent and 38 per cent). On a variety of indicators, West Indian youths demonstrated a more marked lack of interest in joining the police compared with other 16–24 year-olds, and emphasized the hostility that would be potentially forthcoming from family and friends if they did. If they did join they would prefer to work in an area where they were not known. And they were only half as likely to ask the police for assistance. In sum, the study concludes the 'West Indians do not share the arms' length respect other 16–24 year-olds feel for the police . . . and are more likely to see the police as discriminating against any identifiable minority' (MIL Research Ltd, 1979, pp. xv–xvi).

We should also note that, generally, Asians emerge as less critical than West Indians (other than with regard to racial attacks), though more so than whites. For example, the PSI study found that 'among those aged 15–24' (PSI, 1983, Vol. 1, p. 246) 55 per cent of Asians (compared to 68 per cent of West Indians and 39 per cent of whites) 'feel the police do not treat all groups equally' (Reiner, 1985b, p. 173).

Once again, we do not wish to engage with the question of the origin of these attitudes other than to remind readers that the relationship between attitudes and behaviour is complex. By the same token, there is some discussion as to how closely attitudes parallel their direct experience of police oppression. The fact that hostility is most concentrated among the young unemployed and heavily policed ghetto males might suggest a *direct* connection between their hostile attitudes and their experiences of oppressive policing; and indeed the PSI study certainly found a positive relationship between contact (of any kind!) with the police and critical views of them (PSI, 1983, Vol. 1, p. 326). On the other hand, the PSI data also revealed that 'for the most part' personal experience could not explain 'the hostility to the police among West Indian Londoners'. The conclusion is then drawn that West Indian youth hostility stems from the police's symbolic role: 'they seem like the most obvious symbol and representative of an oppressive white authority' (Smith, 1986, p. 11). This latter finding suggests that it is *indirectly* acquired hostility which leads to encounters with police being negatively evaluated. It should, however, be added that neither explanation is necessarily exclusive: direct experience might harden and amplify an existing indirectly acquired hostility.

Behaviour

One indication that the relationship between prejudicial attitudes and discriminatory behaviour is not straightforward is the finding of the PSI study, based on their observational research, 'that police officers tend to be hostile to black people in general terms, and certainly indulge in much racialist talk, but often have friendly and relaxed relations with individual black people in specific instances' (PSI, 1983, Vol. 4, p.334). This issue clearly has a bearing on whether it is race, or some other factor, which is the critical determinant of police encounters with black people. But, before we can address that, and the related issue of discrimination, we need first to outline what the research evidence reveals about police actions towards blacks as suspects – evidence drawn from statistical, survey and observational research. In doing that, we shall deal with each stage of the process in turn: stop and search; arrests; prosecution.

Blacks as 'Offenders'

(a) 'STOP AND SEARCH'

The North American evidence is unequivocal: 'the police stop and question young, low-income, ethnic minority males more frequently than any other group' (Reiner, 1985b, p. 157). Boydstun's (1975) field study, for example, produced the following figures from San Diego: '100% of people stopped were male, 66% black or Mexican American and almost 2/3 juveniles' (quoted in Reiner, 1985b, p. 157). The picture in Britain is only slightly less unanimous, with Willis (1983), Field and Southgate (1982), the British Crime Survey (Southgate and Ekblom, 1984), the PSI (1983) and even the Metropolitan Police (in its evidence to Scarman on stops in Lambeth) providing evidence of disproportionate stopping of blacks, and especially of young black males, and only Tuck and Southgate's (1981) Moss Side study out of line in this respect. Though the young were still more likely to be stopped, the proportions for West Indians and whites of whatever age were similar. Probably the most dramatic illustration of the disproportionate stopping of young black males is brought out in the PSI figures. They demonstrate first of all the importance of age: 'younger people were much more likely to be stopped than older people, by a factor of about 11 to 1 in terms of the proportion of people stopped or about 30 to 1 in terms of the mean number of stops per person' (PSI, 1983, Vol. 1, p. 95), and then of ethnicity:

> the difference between West Indians and white people is not very striking (24 percent for West Indians, 17 percent for white people). However, the mean number of stops is nearly three times as high among West Indians as among white people . . . largely because those West Indians who are stopped tend to be stopped repeatedly. (ibid.)

The overall effect and 'the most important finding is that young males are very likely to be stopped, especially if they are West Indian. Sixty three percent of young West Indian men and 44 percent of young white men have been stopped in a twelve-month period, and among those who have been stopped at all the West Indians have been stopped about four times and the whites about 2½ times on average over the same period' (ibid. p. 101).

We return later to the question of different findings, such as the Moss Side one, when we look at competing interpretations. For the moment we draw attention to two things in concluding; the comparatively low stop rate among Asians (cf. PSI, 1983, Vol. 1, pp. 96, 98) and 'Swamp 81'. For though 'Swamp 81' – the 'flooding' of Brixton with officers instructed to use their 'stop and search' powers in an effort to combat burglary and robbery in the week prior to the 1981 Brixton riots – was not so intended, it inadvertently provided a confirmation of 'disproportionate' stopping. Of 943 stops, two-thirds of those stopped were aged under 21, and over one-half were black. It most certainly was, as Scarman (1982) suggested, 'a serious mistake' (para. 4.76). But is was not, in terms of who was being stopped, other than 'routine policing'.

(b) ARRESTS

The pattern for arrests follows that for stops. The study of the MPD statistics for 1975 conducted by Stevens and Willis (1979), found that the arrest rate for Afro-Caribbeans 'was higher than that for whites and Asians for every category of offence' (Benyon, 1986, p. 17). However, when the varying age profiles of the different ethnic groups are controlled, blacks are mainly overrepresented in 4 categories: assault, robbery, 'other violent theft', and 'other indictable offences' (Reiner, 1985b, p. 166; Asians, it should be added, are underrepresented in all categories except assault). Since at least one of these categories, 'other violent theft', allows 'considerable scope for selective perception' (Stevens and Willis, 1979, p. 41; and arguably its near neighbour 'robbery' as the work of Blom-Cooper and Drabble, 1982, would suggest), and since the black arrest rate for the highly discretionary offence of sus was 14 or 15 times the white rate (an important factor in its eventual abolition), the question of discrimination as an element in these disproportionate arrest figures is obviously posed. These 1975 figures, it should be added, were replicated in 1983, when an even greater overrepresentation of Afro-Caribbeans was shown, the 'robbery and other violent theft' (42 per cent), assault and burglary (20 per cent of each) being particularly high (Home Office Statistics, quoted in Walker, 1987, p. 40). The PSI results endorse this picture generally for young West Indians (15–24 age group), though not for the older generation. Further confirmation came in the form of Scotland Yard's revelation to the Select Committee on Race Relations, 1976–7, that 12 per cent of those arrested for indictable crime in 1975 were Afro-Caribbean. In both cases, these findings were reinforced by figures based on victim identification (in the minority of cases where these were available), with, again, 'robbery' and 'other violent theft' being particularly heavily overrepresented. The general overrepresentation of West Indian offenders according to victim identification was also found in Tuck and Southgate's (1981) Manchester study. However, it is worth stressing that all the data on *arrests* refer solely to London.

North American studies also show blacks are disproportionately arrested (cf. Black and Reiss, 1967; Lundman, Sykes and Clark, 1978). As to 'uncivil treatment', there is some disagreement. Skolnick (1966) suggests this is routine treatment for 'negroes'; Reiss (1971, p. 14), by contrast, that police 'did not treat negroes uncivilly more often than whites'. Similarly with physical abuse. While the Black–Reiss study concluded that whites fared worse than 'negroes', the figures for police killings of citizens, which reveal blacks hugely disproportionately liable to be a victim, suggest the opposite conclusion –

though, as Reiner (1985, p. 159) says, 'it should be noted that since some notorious shooting incidents in 1977 policy and training have been tightened with a significant drop in police shootings'.

(c) PROSECUTION

The little evidence we have on prosecution generally follows that on stops and arrests, with Afro-Caribbeans again receiving differential treatment. Landau's two studies on the processing of juvenile offenders by the Metropolitan Police illustrates this. His first showed that for particular offences – crimes of violence, burglary and a range of public order offences – Afro-Caribbean juveniles were more likely to be charged immediately (an outcome regarded as the harshest) than referred to the juvenile bureau for a decision about whether to caution (Landau, 1981). His later study (with Nathan) about such decisions by the bureau similarly found Afro-Caribbeans more likely to be charged 'except for "traffic and other offences" ' (Landau and Nathan, 1983, p. 142). Farrington and Bennett's (1981) similar work, on the other hand, does not support these findings. Examining the cautioning decisions on 907 juveniles referred to a single juvenile liaison bureau in the MPD, they found no significant difference between the cautioning rates of 'whites' and 'non-whites'. However, differences between this and the Landau and Nathan study may well account for this apparently contradictory finding. As Monica Walker (1987) points out, the Farrington and Bennett study included 'almost as many Asians as West Indians' in its non-white category, was 'conducted 5 years earlier' and 'dealt only with those aged under 15' (Walker, 1987, p. 50). Certainly the study by Batta, Mawby, and McCulloch (1978) in Bradford found Pakistanis significantly more likely to be cautioned (76 per cent) than Indians (51 per cent) and non-Asians (50 per cent). But, unfortunately, the data were not analysed in relation to offence type nor were the figures for the small number of West Indians involved analysed separately, thus making it difficult to use the data to shed light on relative cautioning rates.

Further evidence of 'disproportionate' charging can be found in Cain and Sadigh's study of 269 cases in a South London magistrate's court during 1978–9. They found that 'West Indians . . . appear before the court charged with victimless crimes, as a result that is of pro-active policing, far more frequently than white defendants' (Cain and Sadigh, 1982, p. 87). However, the same study also showed that blacks were also disproportionately prosecuted for other 'reactive' offences, a point not made by the authors but pointed out by Reiner (1985b, p. 169).

Blacks as Victims

(a) RACIAL ATTACKS

If over-heavy policing constitutes one side of the coin of black complaints, under-protection constitutes the flipside. And nowhere is this more keenly felt than in the area of racial attacks. Though Asians are generally less critical of police than Afro-Caribbeans, this probably does not hold true when it comes to police handling of racial attacks. The extent of racial attacks has been documented in a number of studies which reveal that

> the incidence of unprovoked attacks, especially on Asian people, appears to have increased considerably since 1976. During this period Asian shops have been attacked, Asians' houses damaged and burned and a number of Asian people murdered. Peter Fryer [1984] reports that 31 black people were murdered by racists between 1976 and 1981, and a report by the Bethnal Green and Stepney Trades Council [1978] documented over one hundred racial attacks between 1976 and 1978 in Tower Hamlets alone. (Benyon, 1986, p. 46)

Despite this catalogue of horror, it was not until 1981 that a Home Office study produced official statistical confirmation. This found that for all racially motivated incidents (including insults, harassment, etc., as well as offences), Asians were 50 times and blacks 37 times as likely to be victims as whites. Even without the insults and other non-offences, the figures for offences only revealed a huge disproportion, with Asians having 44 times and blacks 20 times the white rate. Subsequent documentation continues to add to the catalogue of horror (cf. Klug, 1982; GLC, 1984), and to remain critical of the police response: 'officers were alleged to be hostile to or disinterested in the experiences of black victims' (GLC, 1984, p. 18).

But the further complaint is that such 'hostility and disinterest' is not simply passive. On the contrary, the objection is that any moves towards community self-defence in the light of such attacks are directly penalized, or general 'calls for assistance' are turned into occasions to check passports and immigration status: 'fishing expeditions' for illegal immigrants. The penalization of community self-defence has produced, for example, a number of trials of Asian youths – the Bradford 12 (1982), the Newham 8 (1983), the Newham 7 (1985) – as well as clashes with the police, such as when Asians sought to defend their community from unwanted racists in Southall in 1979, on the occasion of the National Front holding an election meeting, and in 1981, when 300 skinheads attended an 'Oi' concert. Although the trials proved largely (but by no means wholly) successful in arguing the case that 'self-defence is no offence', the fact remains that the youths concerned were in the dock on a variety of very serious charges up to and including 'affray' and 'conspiracy to cause grievous bodily harm' (for making petrol bombs). Examples of turning complaints or other contacts with the police into passport checks can be found in Benyon (1986, p. 51) and Gordon (1983, p. 37). More generally, the scale and manner of passport raids and checks since the Immigration Act 1971, some being quite major operations involving dozens of officers, has been extensively documented in Gordon (1981) and more summarily in Gordon (1983, pp. 35–8).

It should be said, by way of a conclusion, that the former MPD Commissioner, Sir Kenneth Newman, said in his January 1985 report that racial attacks would be added to his list of special priorities. It remains to be seen how much difference this will make. The concern and the attacks certainly continue – as evidenced by the horrifying arson attack in Ilford, in July 1985, which killed the pregnant Mrs Shamiva Kassan and her three young children (see also *Observer*, 22 November 1987, pp. 49–50). And there is the question of whether the present structure of accountability allows other than ultimately discretionary policy-making in operational areas (a point we return to in more detail in Chapter 7).

(b) COMPLAINTS AGAINST THE POLICE

If blacks *feel* over criminalized and underprotected, they would also claim to lack adequate redress through the complaints machinery. This is not a complaint confined to blacks, of course, but in line with the pattern outlined above, 'blacks are more likely to make formal complaints, but less likely to have these upheld' (Reiner, 1985b, p. 170). The early study by Box and Russell (1975) found too few complaints from blacks in its sample to analyse statistically, though they predicted that race would be a 'discrediting factor'. And the Home Office study conducted on Moss Side in 1981 (Tuck and Southgate, 1981) found that twice as many West Indians as whites (16 per cent to 8 per cent) had 'ever wished to complain', though none had. But the most comprehensive analysis, a Home Office study of complaints against the Metropolitan Police during the 1970s (Stevens and Willis, 1981), found 'that blacks (particularly young blacks) and older Asians make proportionately more complaints than whites per head of population' (p. 31), that blacks are more likely to make serious complaints, yet 'the black substantiation rate was considerably lower than that for whites' (ibid., p. 19). It should of course be remembered that in both cases the percentage substantiated is small – 1979, first quarter: 1.5 per cent blacks, 3.6 per cent Asians, 4.6 cent whites (ibid., p. 16). Since blacks were more likely to be under arrest at the time of the complaint, or have a 'record' – both 'discrediting' factors – this may account for the lower substantiation rate. Taken together with the PSI (1983) finding (Vol. 1, pp. 269–72) that West Indians are *less* likely to complain than either whites or Asians, these findings understate the disparity in rates.

Before turning to look at competing interpretations of the data, it might be useful to summarize the broad consensus of the foregoing. To do so we can do no better than quote from Benyon, summarizing his own review of the literature:

> The data show that black people are stopped and searched, and arrested, far more frequently that other people, and were far more likely to be charged with being a 'suspected person' before the relevant section of the Vagrancy Act 1824 was repealed. Many young black people feel they have been 'hunted irrespective of their innocence or guilt' (Scarman, 1981, para. 4.22). There are also numerous allegations of racial abuse, harassment and assault by the police, but only a few of these, such as the case of the Whites [a couple who received substantial damages against the police], have ever been proved. Although the number of formal complaints against the police has risen, few of these are substantiated either. (Benyon, 1986, p. 53)

Interpreting the Data: Competing Accounts

We mentioned earlier there were two axes around which competing interpretations swivel. We can re-pose these now in the form of two questions: (1) Is *race* the real issue? (2) Is *different* treatment the same as *discriminatory* treatment?

(1) *Is Race the Real Issue?*

This question can be subdivided to explore (a) whether the key determinant is structural or situational and (b) if structural, which structural feature is central – age, race, class. Taking (a) first, Reiner makes the point that whereas the statistical studies reveal the 'disproportional' patterns which clearly suggest discrimination at work, the observational studies on both sides of the Atlantic 'suggest that police handling of blacks is largely to be explained by situational (where the encounter occurs, what sparked it, complainants' wishes etc.) and interactional variables (i.e. co-operativeness of citizens), rather than any observable element of discrimination' (Reiner, 1985b, p. 171). Thus, although the Black–Reiss observational study in the United States confirmed the disproportionate rate of black arrests, they put this down not to race but to 'the greater rate at which blacks show disrespect for police' (Reiner, 1985b, p. 157), and to their greater likelihood of being involved in incidents when complainants (usually black) demanded arrest. Though a later study replicated these findings, it also found that the disrepect could have been a *consequence* of the officers' behaviour in about half the cases (Sykes, Fox and Clark, 1976); and a re-analysis of the Black–Reiss data showed that when complainant preferences are controlled for, blacks were still disproportionately arrested (Sherman, 1980; see also Smith and Visher, 1981). These subsequent studies suggest then that not all of the difference in arrest rates can be accounted for by interactional or situational factors, even if much can be. But the Black–Reiss observations find support in the work of Holdaway who argues that policing blacks is essentially 'normal policing', that is policing which is determined by the subcultural values of action, control, excitement, etc. However, he does concede that if blacks are subject to normal policing *more often* this could make for a qualitative change in police–black relations (James, 1979, p. 82).

The question of 'demeanour', i.e. whether blacks are regarded as more disrespectful, may also have been a factor in the Landau cautioning studies. A decision that a caution is the preferable course of action requires three elements: conviction on the part of the police that such a course is the most appropriate; and admission of guilt by the juvenile and a willingness to accept a caution; and a similar willingness on the part of the juvenile's parent(s). If black juveniles are seen generally as a worse risk because of a perceived disrespectful 'stroppiness', or if they or their parents are less willing to accept a caution, this will affect adversely their cautioning rate. Since the Landau studies had no information of this sort, it must remain open whether racial discrimination as such was in play here, or any or all of these other 'interactional' features.

For all who admit the presence, whether weak or strong, of structural features, there remains issue (b), which structural feature is the key determinant. Put another way, since structures rarely operate in isolation, the question is, in any given situation, what is the element of purely *racial*, as opposed to other kinds of discrimination (on grounds of age or class, for example)? The PSI study talked of 'four characteristics that are strongly related to the likelihood of being stopped: age, sex, ethnic group and ownership or use of a vehicle' (1983, Vol. 1, p. 94). The first three of these characteristics constitute structural features. We have already commented upon the importance of age and how, on every dimension, black *youth* are at the sharp end, faring worst. We have also seen that sometimes, when age is controlled for, there is little difference between the treatment of blacks and whites. Of similar importance is sex. As the PSI study says of stops, 'men are much more likely to be stopped than women' (1983, Vol. 1, p. 95), a finding which applies at all other stages of the criminal justice process, and is confirmed by all studies of whatever kind. But both of these – age and sex – are relatively easy to control for statistically, so that the degree to which 'race' is operative in particular situations can be relatively precisely calibrated. Not so with class, which is in any case much harder to control for since it is notoriously difficult to define, let alone measure. The result is that most studies conveniently overlook it, as does the PSI, though where analysis is conducted using class-related factors (such as unemployment and type of jobs), it emerges as a relevant structural characteristic. (For examples, see below.)

It is this aspect that may account for the apparently aberrant findings of the Moss Side 'stops' study – the only one, it must be remembered (see page 130 above), not to find disproportionate stops of blacks. Monica Walker makes the point that these results were obtained from small homogeneous areas within Manchester, whereas the figures for all the other studies were based on much larger more heterogeneous areas in London. This means, effectively, that the Manchester figures have been controlled for class, but not so the London figures. So the 'racial' differences in stop rates found in London could be the result of class, were it to be controlled for, since, when in the Manchester study this is done, the 'racial' difference disappears. It is a criticism Monica Walker makes more generally; thus, the higher arrest rates found for blacks in London may be a consequence of their social-class position. Since offenders come disproportionately from manual workers, the unemployed and the socially deprived, and since black people are overrepresented in these categories, then 'for London as a whole it is not surprising that black people have a higher arrest and offender rates' (Walker, 1987, p. 43). She makes the point, for example, that the PSI study found that the unemployed are more likely to be stopped than those in work and that unskilled manual workers were twice as likely to be stopped in a vehicle as professional and managerial workers. So, she concludes, 'a more detailed analysis, controlling for these [class] factors, would enable a more valid comparison to be made between the black and white groups' (Walker, 1987, p. 49). This failure to control for social class is a point she also makes about the Landau cautioning studies.

If it is so that blacks are discriminated against more because of their age and class than their ethnicity, they are still *more* discriminated against because they are, as a group, more youthful and more working class. But, it seems unlikely that there is not a racial factor over and above a class factor at work. For, whereas being middle class can place a white person above certain kinds of police suspicion, being black can be sufficient to *lower* even the most 'respectable' and middle class into the 'suspicious' category. To put it more graphically, middle-class Nigerian students or diplomats are still more often 'mistakenly' stopped/arrested, etc. than their white counterparts. The overall result is that if a pure racial factor is difficult to disentangle, this is partly because (working) class and race are tightly connected, even if often wrongly, in the 'suspicious' eyes of white police officers.

(2) *Is Different Treatment the Same as Discriminatory Treatment?*

If we accept then that race to some extent, either directly or indirectly, is a factor in policing, the question still remains, is the different 'over-policing' of blacks a product of *discrimination* (i.e. unfair), or a product of the different 'over-offending' behaviour of blacks, and therefore *appropriate* to the circumstances. The traditional line, supported broadly by the police where it is not actively initiated by them, is that black crime levels, as evidenced by figures for arrests, prosecutions and supported by victim identification where available, are disproportionately high and therefore *require* disproportionate attention. In short, disproportionate police attention is justified by disproportionate black offending, for which all the available statistical evidence provides objective justification.

There is, of course, as we have seen, evidence for this view. Apart from the MPD's own statistics, the Stevens and Willis arrest figures suggest a higher rate of black offending. And careful though they are to discuss the range of factors affecting the higher arrest rate, they are forced to conclude that at least part of it has to be attributed to more offending behaviour. Monica Walker calculates that, if offender rates were equal, black people would have to be 4½ times more likely to be arrested for burglary, and 14 times more likely for robbery, than whites (Walker, 1987, p. 40). If these figures are regarded as 'implausible', at least part of the higher arrest rate has to be a function of higher offending. The notion that part anyway of the higher arrest rate has to be related to higher offending behaviour is shared by the PSI (1983), and both Reiner (1985b) and Benyon (1986), after their careful overviews of the available evidence. But the case has been put most strongly and controversially by Lea and Young in a series of articles and stated fully in their book, *What is to be done about Law and Order?*, written on behalf of the socialist society. Their argument, in brief, talks of black deprivation leading to higher offending, of police stereotyping leading to a 'ready' response to such offending, and of the two processes reinforcing each other in the form of a 'vicious circle' (Lea and Young, 1984, pp. 166–7).

Opposition to this case, but in particular to the idea that the higher black arrest rate is connected with a higher rate of offending, has come most vociferously from the Institute of Race Relations (cf. Bridges, 1983a and 1983b; Gilroy, 1982; Gutzmore, 1983). Refusing to 'haggle' over the official crime statistics, the upshot apparently is to regard the higher black crime figures as *simply* the result of police prejudice.

To see the question thus starkly is, as Benyon (1986, p. 24) says, 'unusual'. And indeed, most of those whose work we have been reviewing opt for an explanation which sees police behaviour as partly discriminatory and partly a response to higher black crime rates. Thus Stevens and Willis suggest that the higher arrest rates for blacks can be explained by a combination of 'intrinsic' and 'extrinsic' factors. The former include indices of deprivation and greater offending behaviour; the latter things like more time spent on the streets, greater visibility, and police stereotyping. The PSI interpretation broadly follows this mixture of deprivation, offending and stereotyping. Even Scotland Yard mention the disproportionate youth and social deprivation of West Indians making their higher offending unsurprising – though, not surprisingly, they do not regard policy stereotyping as a factor. Reiner's 'mixed' interpretation couches itself in structural, historical and cultural terms. Structural processes operate so 'that ethnic minorities figure disproportionately in the young "street" population which has always been the prime focus of police "order maintenance" work', and this may include involvement in 'specific kinds of street crime'. And things are worse in a recession. Police prejudice provides the accentuating 'cultural factors'. The result is a vicious circle of conflict (Reiner, 1985b, pp. 175–6).

Conclusion

How then are we to think of the relation between race, policing and crime? Certainly a singular explanation seems insufficient on the evidence, but so too do those mixed explanations which can sometimes read like a cocktail mixture with, for example, so many parts deprivation, so many parts offending and so many parts stereotyping.

Our processual explanation, incorporating structural and situational features, runs as follows:

1   We do not *know* what the *real* rate of black crime is, nor whether it is on the increase. Take robbery for instance. The British Crime Survey reveals that only 8 per cent of robberies were recorded. If these figures applied to London this would mean that there is a suspect for only 1 in 100 robberies. The comparable figure for burglaries would be 5 in 100 (Walker, 1987, p. 39). This means that *whatever* the arrest figures, and *whatever* the victim identifications, the 'unknown' element is so great, *especially* for those crimes where black 'overrepresentation' is seen as greatest, as to make all estimates strictly conjectural.

2   We should not, however, be *surprised* if the black crime rate is higher, even if we cannot *know* this. This is because of the established link between certain kinds of crime, deprivation and unemployment (cf. Farrington *et al.*, 1986), and the overrepresentation of blacks suffering from deprivation as a consequence of structural racism (cf. Brown, 1984). We should not be surprised either if, during a period of recession such as the present one, whose immediate roots go back at least to the early 1970s, there is an *increase* in certain kinds of 'survival' crime.

3   During a recession, crime can become a symptom of the crisis, amongst the authorities and in the popular imagination. The link between the two is often secured through a 'moral panic', which serves to recast the crisis in terms of 'law and order' and provide convenient 'folk devils' to blame. The moral panic also serves to sensitize both police and the public to the 'folk devil' in question, leading to a possible increase in stereotyping, and in public reporting and police targeting behaviour. This can amplify the relevant statistics, which themselves are used to justify the 'law and order' campaign initiated by the moral panic. All of these features have in fact been associated with the present recession. The 'moral panic' about mugging of 1972–3 led to an increased sensitivity to the folk devil of black youth 'street criminals', 'public concern', police targeting, and the production of legitimating statistics (Hall *et al.*, 1978). The release of racially coded crime statistics from the mid-1970s on by Scotland Yard has clearly been a part of the ideological battle to justify their 'tough' policing of black areas. The most notorious example of this was the release of racially coded figures for 'robbery' and 'other violent theft' suspects in March, 1982. Many saw this as the Metropolitan Police's reply to Scarman (cf. Sim, 1982).

4   A recession also increases the police role in 'order maintenance' in various ways, as greater conflict, industrial, political or social, makes police life generally tougher. This serves to harden police attitudes. Those cast as 'folk devils' become victims not only of targeting, but also of this new hardening of attitudes. The clear evidence of worsening relations between police and black youth during the 1970s serves to confirm this (cf. Institute of Race Relations, 1979).

5   From the perspective of disadvantaged groups, including black youth, crime is liable to become a more necessary part of a survival strategy during a recession. The consistently higher rates of youth unemployment during the present structural recession (from the late 1960s onwards), and the even higher rates for black youth (cf. Brown, 1984, pp. 151–2), make such groups currently amongst the most socially disadvantaged. (On 'survival strategies', see Pryce, 1986.)

6   The attitudes of those most affected by the recession will tend to harden, especially towards those state institutions held to be responsible for the increased difficulties of 'life on the margins'. The most visible of state institutions – such as the police – become symbolic of the heightened oppression, and liable to become hated. The attitudes of black youth to the police provide evidence of this hardening, as do their actions, most obviously in the riots of the 1980s (cf. Hall, 1985; Sivanandan, 1985). This reading also squares with the PSI evidence mentioned earlier (see page 129) that personal experience alone could not account for the degree of hostility to the police found among West Indian Londoners (Smith, 1986, p. 11).

7   The combination of points 3, 4, 5 and 6, brings police and the most disadvantaged and stigmatized groups into constant and increasingly conflictual contact. Black youth increasingly become part of the police problem; and the police increasingly become part of the problem for black youth.

8   At this point the self-fulfilling prophecy, the vicious circle, the amplification of deviance (both police and youth deviance) is set in motion. Police enter encounters expecting trouble and act aggressively to pre-empt it. Black youth similarly expect trouble and create the necessary ('disrespectful') mind set to cope. The resulting 'trouble' demonstrates well how the increased racist oppression of a society in crisis is reproduced, in street level encounters, between the state's agents and a chosen folk devil, in what can be a deadly dynamic of mutual distrust, tension, hostility, and, eventually, hatred.

Class and Policework

We end, finally, with class. In many ways, our job here is reiterative, since class has been present throughout earlier discussions, especially in Chapters 4 and 5 where it was like a backbone without which the chapters could not have been conceived, let alone written. In the sections in this chapter on age and race, class, like male, was largely assumed. In other words, 'deviant youth' largely connoted *working-class* male youth; black youth similarly implied *working-class* male black youth. In other words, part of the police treatment accorded the young and the black is class related. This is something about which there is very little disagreement between commentators of all political and theoretical persuasions. The interactionist labelling theorist Howard Becker has said, 'The middle-class boy is less likely, when picked up by the police, to be taken to the station; less likely when taken to the station to be booked; and it is extremely unlikely that he will be convicted and sentenced' (Becker, 1963, p. 13). Radical researchers on policework of course have all argued that the most important form of police discrimination is that based on social class. Race, sex and age factors may compound this original discrimination, but the class structure, in line with classical marxist theory, is the paramount one.

Despite the centrality given to class, perhaps *because* of its very obviousness and taken-for-granted role in police practice, detailed quantitative studies of the relationships between social class and police practice are largely absent. Yet what we have all points in the same direction, endorses more ethnographic accounts, and both sorts of account 'confirm' the findings of the history chapters. Take *attitudes* for example. Both the PSI studies and the British Crime Survey (BCS) concur that unemployed attitudes to the police are less favourable than those of the employed, and that attitudes are more favourable among those from higher socio-economic groups (PSI, 1983, Vol. 1, pp. 200–1; Southgate and Ekblom, 1984, pp. 23–4.).

From the police side attitudes are also class related, but in a relatively complicated way, on account of the social-class origins of police officers. There is for example no ready deference to the middle-class executive in the superior saloon car, no doubt a consequence of the working-class origins of most police recruits. But, simultaneously, the occupational culture teaches police officers that such an individual is likely to carry more clout if a charge is going to be made. The manual worker is generally treated as less competent in opposing police action, but more likely to be a source of physical resistance. The overall result, however, as Reiner says, is that ultimately 'the social map of the police is differentiated according to the power of particular groups to cause problems for the police' (Reiner, 1985a, p. 109).

The evidence on *offenders* echoes that on attitudes. Thus the PSI and the BCS again concur that unemployed men have more adversarial contacts and the middle classes more 'consumer' contacts (PSI, 1983, Vol. 1, pp. 179–81; Southgate and Ekblom, 1984, p. 19). More specifically, Bennett's investigation of police cautioning of juveniles in the Metropolitan Police District found that

> the police appeared to discriminate against working-class offenders in a manner not entirely explicable in terms of offence seriousness. Children of families where the father had a non-manual occupation had significantly less chance of being summoned to court than a juvenile with a father in a manual occupation, regardless of the severity of the offence committed. (Bennett, 1979, p. 140)

It should perhaps be said that some aspects of Bennett's work, especially the detail of the relationship between social class, area of residence, and other extra-legal variables, has been criticized by Landau (1981).

Once again, the quantitative evidence is supported by ethnographic material. Though the following is not a comparative account of class experience, but a personal account of the experience of one young miner on a picket line at the Markham Main Colliery at Armthorpe in South Yorkshire during the year-long miners' strike of 1984–5, the history of industrial confrontation tells us this is dominantly a class-specific phenomenon. The experience it recalls echoed many similar encounters during the strike, just as it replicated that of many caught up in similar confrontations during the past, as the history chapters reminded us (but see also Gilroy and Sim, 1985):

> there was a big red transit van and we moved back from the police 'cos we didn't want to push them against this van and then this big'un got me from behind and he whipped me out. He told his mate that he was taking this one out, like they normally do. He got me clear of the crowd, then got me by the hair. He dragged me up the road – must have been about forty yards, then he shoves my hand up my back and this police inspector comes up and smacks me straight in the stomach. Then this other character had got me on the floor and got handcuffs on one hand and then on the other – and all I'd asked him was to let me stand up. He punched me on the back of the neck. I asked him to let me stand up. He said 'Shut up you cunt, or you'll get some more'. And when I did eventually get to my feet

he got me into this police van and when I'm sat at the back of the van, I says 'I'm not going anywhere now, you can take these off. You treat us like criminals'. He says, 'Well, that's what you are'. By the time they got us to the lock-up my wrists were twice the normal size, and they were bleeding. (taped interview; but see also Samuel, Bloomfield and Boanas (eds), 1986; Coulter, Miller and Walker, 1984)

The industrial confrontations are the dramatic rendering of the more casual and routine discrimination.

Finally, there is evidence that as *victims* working-class people also receive less police support. In the study by Sparks, Genn and Dodd (1977; see also Kinsey, Lea and Young, 1986) of victimization in London, working-class people could expect to receive a slower police response to incidents and less positive support (though it should not be overlooked that such evidence is complicated by factors like area of residence, gender and ethnicity, especially in relation to reports of racial and domestic attacks). And redress also is harder to come by for working people. Box and Russell's (1975) unique study of the complaints system suggests systematic discrimination against lower and working-class complainants in terms of the seriousness with which the complaint is dealt.

However, it would not be right to end this illustrative overview without a note on motorists and policework. Vehicle stops are 'a major part of all contact between police and public' (Southgate and Ekblom, 1984, p. 16), a finding echoed in the PSI study that 'ownership or use of a vehicle' was one of the 'four characteristics that are strongly related to the likelihood of being stopped' (PSI, 1983, Vol. 1, p. 94). Given levels of car ownership among the middle classes, being stopped in a vehicle is one form of adversarial contact to which the middle classes are susceptible. Moreover, because 'the likelihood of being stopped rose steadily in relation to the amount of driving done', and because the 'highest mileages were recorded by the middle classes and skilled manual workers . . . they were among those most often stopped' (Southgate and Ekblom, 1984, p. 16). Here clearly is a potential source of friction between police and the middle classes. However, even here, being young and poor, and therefore probably driving a more dilapidated car, is to be at high risk of being subject to a vehicle stop (despite the fact of a lower recorded mileage). As the BCS found, vehicle stops were especially common amongst 'young male drivers, those who drove a lot, drank most, spent most time out, or committed most traffic offences' (Southgate and Ekblom 1984, p. 19). Once again, the PSI in a roundabout way, confirmed some of this:

'Our observational work . . . shows that people who are of uncon-
ventional appearance and those who drive Mark II Ford Cortinas are
particularly likely to be stopped' (PSI, 1983, Vol. 1, pp. 94–5).

Summary and Conclusion

It really is not a very radical thing to say in 1987 that the system of
criminal justice, and that obviously includes policework, is class
based. The level of agreement in this is such that it really only requires
illustration, as we have given here – though it ought still to be shocking. Perhaps the most telling example, which can stand by way of
summary and conclusion here, is the comparative treatment of tax
evasion and social security fraud (Price, 1987; Cook, 1987). Tax
evasion costs the country far more than the amount lost through social
security fraud, can only be committed by those earning enough to be
paying income tax, and is relatively unpoliced, to the extent that
Inland Revenue's policy in the main is to go for restitution not
prosecution. Social security frauds cost the country much less, are
largely confined to those poor enough to be in receipt of social security
benefits, and are policed in a much more rigorous way (30 to 40 times
more prosecutions, Price, 1987; quoted in *Guardian*, 9 July 1987, p.2)
with a clear policy to prosecute (until a very recent recommendation,
based on this different treatment from tax evasion, to modify this and
concentrate on persistent offenders committing fraud on a large
scale). This different treatment of white-collar 'crimes of the powerful', despite the occasional exemplary flurry of activity and prosecution,
is repeated, less dramatically perhaps, but persistently, across the
range of crime. And, given the largely class-based nature of industrial
confrontations, the policing of much public order exhibits a similar
class-based focus.

If to state the above is to state the obvious, it should be equally
obvious that those who are young *and* black *and* working class suffer
discriminatory policing on all three counts, and are thus subject to
compound or *cumulative* discrimination. (We leave aside the question of
sex since males and females are *both* discriminated against, though, as
we have seen, in *different* ways). We have tried up until now, so far as
the evidence allows, to separate the discrimination specific to each
category or social division, whilst well aware that, in reality, these
categories tend to occur together thus producing cumulative discrimination. Perhaps, therefore, the time has come to look at the
process from the other side. Instead of looking at these forms of discrimination separately, we should try to focus on all four forms of

social division simultaneously: we should try, in other words, to offer in conclusion a general explanation of the discriminatory relationship between particular groups and strata and policework.

Conclusion

Discrimination and Policework

Bittner's observations on why advantage is taken against particular groups and strata, in his classic study on *The functions of the Police in Modern Society*, provide both a useful starting point, and the basis for our own elaborations (Bittner, 1970, pp. 9–12). For our purposes, his observations can be usefully divided into four. These are:

   (i)   biases in the nature of what has become defined as crime;
   (ii) that police traditionally deal with contexts in which people have least resources to help themselves;
   (iii) biases existing in the wider society are taken up by police and constitute part of their occupational common sense;
   (iv) that, as a consequence of these perceptions and practices, some groups are more readily available for 'culling' than others.

(i)   BIASES IN THE NATURE OF WHAT HAS BECOME DEFINED AS CRIME

These discriminatory perceptions have served effectively to remove certain groups from the police province altogether. Much criminal activity, and the individuals who carry out these offences, therefore fall outside conventional policework. These are typically the white-collar or corporate crimes – ranging from municipal corruption to business fraud. In these cases, other agencies than the police may be involved in dealing with the matter. Inland Revenue Inspectors, for example, have substantial discretionary powers in those cases where the principal accused are the self-employed middle class. Much of what we call crime is, in fact, the conventional behaviour of working-class youth on the street.

These perceptions, and the organizational targeting practices that subsequently develop, are not free-floating but have their basis in the structure of the criminal law itself. For example, the sexist practice of arresting female prostitutes for soliciting yet allowing male clients to walk away freely from such encounters is a product of a legal situation which criminalizes only the activity of one party – the female – in the transaction, something the new 'kerb crawling' offence (Sexual Offences Act, 1985) belatedly and inadequately recognizes (cf.

Matthews, 1986, p. 25). Even in those situations where the criminal law appears to apply to all equally, a closer examination reveals why it is that, in practice, the working class, especially the least advantaged, the young and the black – in short, the relatively powerless – are more 'at risk'. Such a closer examination reveals the existence of legal discretion, a discretion which undercuts the formal rhetoric of equality because it enables the police, in practice, to discriminate against certain groups. Such legal discretion is in evidence in many areas of the criminal law: even, ironically, in those legal areas which constitute the legal safeguards to control such discretion, as McBarnet has tellingly demonstrated.

> Deviation from legality is institutionalized in the law itself. The law does not need to change to remove hamstrings on the police: they exist only in the unrealised rhetoric. (McBarnett, 1978, p. 212)

That such discretion should be used to criminalize the poor and powerless rather than the rich and the powerful should surprise no one. Any organization wanting to maximize outputs and minimize trouble for itself would take a similar line of least resistance.

This discrepancy between legal rhetoric and what actually happens in court is most in evidence in relation to the routine public order charges, such as 'obstruction', 'breach of the peace', 'assaulting a police officer', and so on. Here the discretion is so great that the precise legal charges are effectively euphemisms for police interpretations of the relevant behaviour. In these situations those most at risk are still the powerless, but especially those whose natural habitat is the street and other public social spaces – which means working-class male youth. This use of a legally based public order discretion against working-class youth, when combined with the second explanation of why advantage is taken against particular groups and strata, namely that the police traditionally deal with contexts in which people have least resources to help themselves, produces a concentration of police resources within the ghetto.

(ii) THE POLICE TRADITIONALLY DEAL WITH CONTEXTS IN WHICH PEOPLE HAVE LEAST RESOURCES TO HELP THEMSELVES

Where deprivation is multiple, where housing is bad, where the social outcasts live, where the mentally and physically ill survive in hostels and run-down housing, where social security claimants, deprived lone parents, social and ethnic minorities are clustered – policework (in its agency of last resort guise) is often one of the only remaining regulating and servicing agencies. While the reason for this has to do with the traditional associations between poverty and crime and a breakdown of law and order, the net contemporary result is an increased police activity and surveillance in the downtown area, the ghetto or inner city.

The inner city streets have always provided the main leisure arena for poor working-class male youth. Here they are freed from the restrictive ties of family and latterly of the school and youth service, yet a perennial shortage of cash prevents the routine uptake of commercial leisure provision (cf. Downes, 1966). Thus it is that, historically and in the present, the youthful male poor find themselves the primary inhabitants of that public space which it is the police mandate to keep orderly, their poverty making them problematic, their youthfulness doubly so. Between family and society, 'immaturity', and maturity, and between school and gainful toil, they represent an important site of social reproduction, for the inculcation of normative conceptions of conventional behaviour.

What this historical saga amounts to is a picture whereby male youth suffer from the full weight of police discriminatory practices in the name of the law, since the regulation of the leisure life of working-class youth can count on little disagreement from the wider, articulate social audience. Within this scenario it is unsurprising that unemployed youth – with their greater use of public spaces – and black youth – increasingly concentrated in the poorest city areas – figure prominently. But the issue is not simply demographic, nor a question of power, but also *cultural*. Such groups, together with other categories like prostitutes, drunks, etc., contravene the stereotypical police image of normality – which brings us to the third explanation of police bias.

(iii) CULTURAL BIASES CONCERNING NORMALITY EXISTING IN THE WIDER SOCIETY ARE REFLECTED WITHIN POLICE OCCUPATIONAL COMMON SENSE

Police occupational commonsense collectively constitutes the basis of the subculture whose values we outlined in Chapter 3. Where the primary assumptions of 'normality' consist of a constellation of elements – membership of a nuclear family, a style of life that reflects the glossy television commercial, a male breadwinner, with a stable occupation, belonging to a particular (i.e. white) ethnic group, serviced by a dependent woman – those not conforming to such narrow images are constituted as deviant ('spongers', 'drop outs' and so on). Police discretion is informed by such stereotypical ideas of normality. Those who infringe those images are seen as 'trouble' – to be coerced towards some version of the assumed normal middle-class style of life. If there is such a thing as 'middle Britain', the police occupation reflects those views in its prejudices and practices.

(iv) POLICE PERCEPTIONS AND PRACTICES CUMULATIVELY ENSURE THAT SOME GROUPS ARE MORE READILY AVAILABLE FOR 'CULLING'

There is, clearly, a difference between groups in terms of their accessibility for processing into the criminal statistics. In particular, the traditional reliance on the technique of patrol whether it be in the forms of foot beat, or the more recent mobile unit, has ensured that those areas most visible to police action are those public fora inhabited and traversed by those deviant groups routinely subject to police stereotyping.

Such groups – peopled by working-class youth, ethnic minorities, prostitute women, drunks, hippies, etc., and the multifarious flotsam and jetsam surviving on the margins of an urban post-industrial capitalist society – have in common a degree of powerlessness in relation to the established order. Given this powerlessness, their potential to cause trouble for police is reduced (though even the apparently most powerless, for example black youth can hit back on the streets via the riots – which gives them a certain ability to make trouble for the police). Given the nature of the criminal law, these groups find many of their routine activities on or close to the borders of illegality. Given the nature of police deployment the activities of such groups get more than their fair share of attention. Given the nature of police cultural stereotypes, the activities of such groups are more likely to be negatively evaluated. And given police discretion – what police themselves call the old 'Ways and Means' Act – such negative evaluations can be acted upon. Thus it is that the law, police deployment, cultural stereotyping and police discretion combine to produce a criminalized class – a class evocatively described by one writer as 'police property' (Lee, 1981; see also page 99 above).

It is fitting that this chapter should end as did the history chapters with the notion of 'police property'. As one point of the historical overview was to act as a retrospective testing of the present, this mirror-ending shows that the present does indeed 'pass' the test of the past. We have now travelled a long way from our psychological starting point in Chapter 2, and have gradually situated policework in ever wider social contexts on our journey. Here, based in the broadest possible social context, our summary has highlighted the elements – the law, organizational deployment, routine practices and occupational cultural stereotyping – that collectively produce the pattern of discriminatory police attention that we have detailed throughout this chapter. Now we turn more directly to the *relationship* between these elements and highlight the difficulties of *controlling policework* that these pose. That is the central question underlying the debate on police accountability in the next chapter.

Suggestions for Further Reading

Age Divisions and Policework
Cohen, S. (1973), *Folk Devils and Moral Panics* (London: Paladin).
Muncie, J. (1984), *The Trouble with Kids Today* (London: Hutchinson).

Sex/Gender Divisions and Policework
Hanmer, J., and Maynard, M. (eds) (1987), *Women, Violence and Social Control* (London: Macmillan).
Jones, S. (1987), *Policewomen and Equality* (London: Macmillan).

Racial Divisions and Policework
Benyon, J. (1986), *A Tale of Failure: Race and Policing,* Police Papers in Ethnic Relations, no. 3 (University of Warwick).
Policy Studies Institute (1983), *Police and People in London,* Vols 1–4 (London: PSI).

Class and Policework
Coulter, J., Miller, S., and Walker, M. (1984), *State of Siege* (London: Canary Press).
Fine, B., and Millar, R. (eds) (1985), *Policing the Miners' Strike* (London: Lawrence & Wishart).

General
Bittner, E. (1970), *The Functions of the Police in Modern Society* (Rockville: National Institute of Mental Health, Centre for Studies of Crime and Delinquency).

7 Police Accountability:

The Vexed Question of Control

Introduction

At the end of the last chapter we suggested that the central question underlying the debate on police accountability was that of the relationship between the various elements affecting policework; understanding how the law, the organization and the occupational culture interact to produce 'policework', and therefore what we need to do to produce any changes necessary. But, to get to that question, 'How is accountability to be achieved?', we need to proceed in stages. Specifically, we need to answer three prior questions:

1 What is police accountability?
2 Why is accountability an issue?
3 To whom should the police be accountable?

The format, in addressing these questions, will follow that employed in earlier chapters, namely, outlining the dimensions of the debate by noting the major contrasting positions, and then offering our own 'resolutions'. In this case, given the cumulative nature of the questions, this resolution is postponed until the final section.

What is Police Accountability?

Generally, police accountability refers to the institutional arrangements made to ensure that the police do the job required of them (cf. Jefferson and Grimshaw, 1982, p. 82). Specifically, the crux of the matter 'is the degree of control various political institutions are to have over the police' (Lustgarten, 1986, p. 1, n. 3). Disagreements arise, however, over the meaning of the term 'control'. For *traditionalists*, the term is, effectively, regarded as inappropriate to police work. Political institutions should not 'control' policing in any substantial sense at all, since that is the job of 'law'. Rather, accountability requires that the police, beholden as they are to law, offer only 'after-the-fact explanation' for their operational actions to political authorities (ibid.). This form of accountability Marshall appropriately calls 'explanatory' (Marshall, 1984, p. 119). So the way to ensure the police do their job is *retrospective accounting* – requiring police to offer legally acceptable justifications for their operations after they have been undertaken. This offers, at best, an indirect and, for reasons we shall come to, 'a sharply limited degree of control' (Lustgarten, op. cit.).

For the more *radical*, unhappy with control left to the vagaries of law, 'the fundamental problem . . . is how to control police actions' (Reiner, 1985a, p. 170); how to ensure, in other words, *effective control* over operations. From this perspective, the terms 'accountability' and 'control' are necessarily synonymous, as Margaret Simey, the last chairperson of the now abolished Merseyside Police Committee, has observed (Simey, 1985, p. 18). On this reckoning, political institutions in a democracy must control policework (as they must control all other public services), 'on behalf of the people'. So, ensuring police do their job properly requires 'before-the-fact' or *prospective* control. This clearly offers a much more direct form of control than retrospective accounting, and, according to its advocates a much more effective form. There are *weak* and *strong* versions of this radical position (discussed below on pages 161–3). Retrospective accounting versus prospective control is the key to understanding the different viewpoints on the necessary institutional arrangements. But these arrangements only exist to ensure the police carry out their obligations satisfactorily. These obligations are couched in terms over which, once again, disagreements have arisen, namely, *impartiality, efficiency and consent*.

If the maintenance of order is and always has been the primary police obligation, this 'in concrete terms is carried out by the discretionary invocation of legal powers' (Lustgarten, 1986, p. 161). In short, the fundamental police task is law enforcement. Law enforcement, in a democracy, is expected to be undertaken *impartially*, which means according all citizens equal treatment under the law (Jefferson and Grimshaw, 1984, p. 137); the 'like treatment of like cases' and the rigorous exclusion of all possible bias, whether racial, political or whatever (Lustgarten, 1986, p. 164). Being also a huge public service bureaucracy competing with other service bureaucracies for scarce resources, it is further expected that such impartial law enforcement be undertaken *efficiently*, that is with due regard to questions of waste and extravagance. Being a service within a democracy it is, finally, expected to strive for effectiveness in the eyes of those it serves; in other words, to satisfy the criterion of public acceptability or *consent*. Being a police officer in a democracy, then, entails enforcing the law impartially, in an efficient manner, and with the consent of the public. In so far as there is agreement that this is happening, it can be argued that the obligations of office are being carried out. And, if this is the case, it can be said that the police are accountable. Such agreement however, as we shall see, has not always been in evidence.

Why is Police Accountability an Issue?

Broadly speaking, police accountability becomes an issue when there is public concern that the arrangements for ensuring the police perform satisfactorily any part of their role are not working. Such concern may arise through dissatisfaction with any police action, from the biased use of powers and the wasteful deployment of resources to practices unacceptable to any section of the public: with anything, in short, which threatens to undermine any of their central obligations – impartiality, efficiency and consent. To demonstrate this point we shall review briefly some key moments in this history of public concern, and consider them in relation to these central obligations. Then we shall look at the implications for accountability traditionalists and radicals respectively draw from them.

From the start of modern policing, dissatisfaction with aspects of policing and the accountability arrangements has waxed and waned, but has never disappeared entirely. This dissatisfaction is another way of understanding the resistance to 'modern policing' which we charted in Chapter 4. As we saw, the idea of 'modern policing' was successfully resisted for a long time, as those opposed to the idea anticipated problems. Working-class radicals and their allies feared that policing would be both politically partial, in that only they and their organizations would be 'spied upon'. They also feared that their demonstrations and protests would be provocatively policed in the military fashion common at that time, and their communities aggressively intruded upon. Elements of the ruling bloc, especially the landed gentry, feared both for their power (since the new police office posed a challenge to their established monopoly on the office of justice of the peace, then at the apex of the system) and for their purse (since the new 'police package' obviously represented a new burden on taxes). These fears affected both the arrangements eventually adopted in the Metropolitan Police Act 1829, and the subsequent policies and practices of the new Commissioners. For example, the receiver authorized to levy a police rate had a ceiling of 8*d* imposed, and the shadowy relationship between the first Commissioners and their police authority, the Home Secretary, served to insulate the police from charges of direct political (or partisan) control. And once in office the new Commissioners, with the Home Secretary's approval, used all the instruments at their disposal – recruitment, promotion, discipline, regulations, etc. – to promote a form of policing characterized by legality, rectitude and restraint. In this way, they hoped to allay fears about acceptability and achieve policing by consent – an inspiration that laid the basis for one enduring image of British policing, namely that traditional 'benign bobby' of popular fiction, Dixon of Dock Green (cf. Reiner, 1985a, pp. 49–61).

These concerns about impartiality, and so on, continued to affect the changing constitutional arrangements for the 'governance of police' through the nineteenth century and right up to the present (op. cit., p. 40). In the postwar period, for example, a series of incidents during the 1950s, such as the clashes between the police authorities of Brighton and Nottingham with their respective chief constables, illustrated a number of confusions: about the allocation of power within the existing institutional arrangements; about the difficulty elected representatives had in getting adequate answers to questions asked of the Home Secretary in parliament; and about the precise responsibilities of the Home Secretary. The eventual outcome was a Royal Commission to look at the whole question of the police's constitutional position and how they were to be governed. The commission's report was followed by the Police Act, 1964. This largely established the present position, which we discuss in the next section.

Another key moment in this history of public concern is the present, starting from the mid-1970s. The scale and comprehensiveness of the present public concern parallels that of the early nineteenth century, with the difference that the earlier debate focused on the very idea of a police force, while the present one (now that the idea of police has become taken for granted) is largely confined to questions on the kind of policing. Examples of the kind of issue that have caused concern in the past decade or so include: the use (and abuse) of police powers; corruption; 'styles' of policing; riot-control technology and paramilitarism; computers and surveillance; special 'proactive' squads; police entry into the political arena; firearms; deployment; resources and finance.

On the government side, 'answers' to the problems posed by these and similar issues have been sought in a Royal Commission, public inquiries, new legislation, and a steady stream of advice about the best practices that 'research and development' can devise. The police themselves have variously tried rediscovering old philosophies, applying new technologies and reorganization. And concerned sections of the public, especially in the large cities, have campaigned and protested. In doing so, they have used old structures (like police committees) where they exist, and established new ones (for example, independent inquiries, monitoring groups, and unofficial police committees) where they do not. But, whatever the particular concern, each variously bears upon impartiality, efficiency or consent, or the means to ensure these; and therefore relates to accountability, a conclusion endorsed by Reiner. After reviewing recent trends in British policing to see whether these were tending towards a 'police state', he argues that 'the nub of the "police state" argument is accountability. Centralisation, increased powers, militarisation and police pervasiveness do not amount to a police state if the police are legally and democratically accountable' (Reiner, 1984, pp. 55–6).

But there is never only one meaning attaching to a history as we saw in Chapters 4 and 5. Traditionalists and radicals interpret the facts of these periodic eruptions of concern differently and draw different conclusions as to what, in consequence, needs to be done. Thus if the question of accountability has been a more or less constant feature of modern policing from the beginning (sometimes very visible and the subject of intense debate as in the 1820s and the 1980s, at other times all but invisible), one answer to the question at the head of this section is that police accountability is *inevitably* an issue because of the nature of the policing task. *Any* group mandated to uphold law and order ('handle trouble'), with a monopoly over the use of legal coercion to achieve their ends ('violently if necessary') has an intractable problem of accountability ('can't please all of the people all of the time'). This is regardless of the particular social framework. This is a *traditional* argument, since the implications of this position tend towards the maintenance of the status quo. Because the use of legal violence is inevitable, problems of accountability are equally inevitable – and not necessarily, therefore, a pressing problem, nor necessarily a threat to the principle of impartiality.

Another more *radical* argument starts by asking when, where, and in relation to what groups in particular, do problems of accountability surface. 'When' answers highlight 'crisis', 'where' answers the 'city', and 'in relation to what groups in particular' the 'deprived and the powerless'. Take 'crisis' for example. Both the 1820s and the 1980s can be similarly characterized as periods of crisis. Both periods witnessed profound economic restructuring as technological changes made existing skills redundant and made many unemployed; both were accompanied by heated political argument and disagreement – a discussion that occasionally erupted into open conflicts and fierce resistance; and 'law and order' provided the dominant rhetoric (and practice) for both governments, and their respective sympathizers. In short, the crisis of the earlier period 'occasioned by the birth of an urban–industrial capitalist order' finds its echo in the present crisis, 'the attempt to give birth to a *post* urban–industrialist capitalist order' (Jefferson and Smith, 1985, p. 125, italics in original). It is this that helps explain the simultaneous presence, in both periods, of intense concern with police accountability.

As for 'city', it is generally agreed that policing problems have always been greatest in the city, a point our historical overview clearly endorsed. It was in London, with its radical tradition and unruly reputation, that some of the London magistrates like the Fieldings and Colquhoun, for example, first became concerned about the state of the police. After London, the threat to urban order from Chartism in particular was sufficiently worrying for the Borough Police Act to be passed, giving the towns police forces. Only later did the countryside follow suit.

Today, nothing has changed in that regard. The major incidents that have fuelled the debate about accountability have taken place in the cities, though the policing of the pit villages during the miners' strike 1984–5 demonstrated that problems of police accountability do not stop there. But problems of crime and disorder – the twin staples of modern policework – are predominantly city affairs. They are also, increasingly, inner city affairs, as the riots in 1981 and 1985 in particular made dramatically visible. Swamp 81, a policing strategy designed to deal with a perceived inner-city crime problem, produced the massive public order problem of the 1981 Brixton riots. And crime and public order, jointly, produced the most significant official contribution to the accountability debate, namely, the Scarman Report.

The inner city location of the riots, which were the most significant incidents fuelling the accountability debate, also alerts us to the issue of 'which groups'. In this instance, as in the past, we are talking of the 'deprived and the powerless'. Whether or not the police were instituted to deal primarily with crime or disorder, they were certainly instituted to deal with the powerless, as we demonstrated in Chapters 4, 5 and 6 – Lee's 'police property' (1981, pp. 53–4). While the precise nature of who constitutes this group may change over time – as 'respectables' work their way up from the 'rough', and new 'folk devils' are reallocated to the dustbin of the dangerous classes – its policing remains 'a prime function' (Reiner, 1985a, p. 95).

The riots quintessentially involved such groups – 'a carnival of the dispossessed' as some commentators put it. Currently at the centre of the dispossessed, as we saw in Chapter 6, lie black youth, growing up deprived, alienated and angry – which is why the issue of police–black relations has been central to the current crisis of accountability. Their subjection to dual discrimination at police hands, 'over-rigorous law enforcement on the one hand, and failure to protect on the other', explains in brief why this should be so (Jefferson and Grimshaw, 1984, p. 8).

The radicals' attention to the historical and sociological questions of when, where, and in relation to whom accountability becomes especially problematic, produces not only a concrete history but also a concrete agenda of issues to be addressed in any proposed reforms. 'Solutions' must address these particular issues identified as problematic. It should be added, however, that such an approach does not necessarily deny the more universal features of the police task, of the kind that the traditionalists refer to. Reiner, for example, insists on the importance of both:

> The most fundamental difficulty in analysing and dealing with policing in a capitalist society, is that the police have the inextricably dual function of handling troubles derived from the problems of *any* industrial society *and* from its specifically capitalist form. (Reiner, 1985a, p. 34, italics in original)

The radical argument about why accountability is an issue has a more extreme version which effectively denies that police accountability is a soluble issue at all. Broadly this argument says that given the police's specific role in containing working-class dissent and alienation, all attempts at reform are doomed to failure in the absence of broader changes designed to end the endemic 'slump-boom' cycle of capitalist crises and their political ramifications. Ironically, this *extreme radical* position has the same conservative implications as the traditional argument. Since the problem is intractable, reforms to improve accountability can only be of limited value.

However, just as it is possible to be alert to both the historical and the universal aspects of accountability, it is also possible to see the need for particular changes without necessarily expecting these to conjure 'social harmony from a deeply divided and unjust society' (Downes and Ward, 1986, p. 3). Police reform, in other words, may be *necessary* but not *sufficient* for radical social change.

To summarize: police accountability has been an issue periodically throughout the history of modern policing. The evidence for this is the eruptions of public concern precipitated by biased, inefficient or otherwise unacceptable forms of policing. Traditionalists and extreme radicals, from their different starting points, both regard the problems as intractable: an intractability which is a result of the police's social function, namely the maintenance of order, by violence if necessary. Their differences stem from their different conceptions of order. For traditionalists this is a universal problem for all societies which can never be solved, only ameliorated; for extreme radicals, the maintenance of order in unequal societies is equivalent to class domination. The police requirement to uphold this class order will only end when class domination does. Reform for both thus becomes effectively redundant. Radicals, with their more detailed attention to police history, see problems of police accountability in similarly concrete terms. Since issues of accountability have arisen at particular times (of 'crisis'), in particular places (the city) and in connection with particular groups (the powerless), reform efforts will need to be addressed to these facts.

To Whom Should Be Police be Accountable?

In order to make sense of the arguments as to whom the police should be accountable, we must first outline the present position as simply and uncontroversially as possible. We must also insist at the outset that our concern is solely with that aspect of accountability concerned with the control of those 'operational' issues which have been at the heart of the controversies highlighted here. The centrality of the operational to policing controversies is evident even in those instances which appear to be about non-operational matters. Where a non-operational matter, like finance, for example, has been controversial, it is an operational issue that makes it so. For example, the *financial* question of who was to fund the extensive mutual aid during the miners' strike 1984–5 became controversial because of disagreement over the *operational* question of the numbers of officers needed to police the picket lines (cf. Spencer, 1985a).

In the most general terms, police are accountable to law. This simply means that they are responsible only to the law in fulfilling their legal duty to uphold the law. For the individual constable (and all officers of whatever rank are constables) this duty requires her or him to decide in particular instances whether there has been a legal infraction and to take steps accordingly. The chief constable, being responsible for upholding the law generally in his area (we use the masculine 'his' deliberately since all chief constables are, currently, men), must in addition take steps using the force which is under his 'direction and control' (S 5 (i), Police Act, 1964), to fulfil this broader duty.

Should the constable fail in some part of her/his duty, the instruments available to call her/him to account are:

1   *the discipline code* – the international force regulations, prescribing appropriate action, available to senior officers and recently bolstered by the new codes of practice issued under the Police and Criminal Evidence Act (PACE) 1984;
2   *the courts* – since constables have no special immunity from private actions or tort law (though a chief constable is also liable for the torts of his constables), or from the criminal law (which also provides criminal sanctions for neglect of duty); and since the judiciary have a discretion to exclude evidence that adversely affects the 'fairness of the proceedings' (S 78 PACE, 1984);
3   *the complaints procedure* – which provides for citizen complaints which chief constables must investigate and the Police Complaints Authority oversee.

Should the chief constable fail in some part of his duty, the instruments available to call him to account (in addition to the law) are the police authority and the Home Secretary. Their responsibilities and powers, as well as those of the chief constable, the third element in the tripartite structure of accountability, are largely laid down in the Police Act 1964. (All section numbers given below refer to this Act, unless otherwise stated.)

Police authorities (bodies composed of two-thirds councillors and one-third magistrates in the provinces and, in the Metropolitan Police District (MPD), the Home Secretary acting alone) must, for example, provide an 'adequate and efficient' force (S 4 (A)), keep themselves informed about how complaints are being dealt with, make arrangements for local consultation over policing (S 100, PACE, 1984) and can require the chief constable to submit a written report, they can appoint and discipline senior ranks (chief constable, deputy chief constable, assistant chief constables), and call for the retirement of senior ranks 'in the interests of efficiency' (S 5 (4)). Each of these powers is effectively subject to the Home Secretary's approval: because there are grounds for refusing a request for a report and the Home Secretary is the final arbiter; because he is the appellate authority in discipline cases; and because appointments and retirements are subject to his approval.

The Home Secretary is required to exercise his power 'to promote the efficiency of the police' (S 28) and, in addition to supervising the use by police authorities of (most of) their powers, can:

(a) withhold the central grant (51 per cent) to any force judged inefficient;
(b) require a police authority to call for the retirement of its chief constable 'in the interests of efficiency' (S 29 (1));
(c) demand reports from chief constables (S 30 (1));
(d) institute local inquiries into policing (S 32 (1));
(e) make regulations concerning pay, conditions and discipline (S 33); and concerning the constitution and proceedings of the various bodies representing the interests of members of police forces (S 44 (3));
(f) determine (with Treasury approval) the size of the inspectorate, who must conduct inspection of all forces (except the MPD; though the Met. consented to be inspected towards the end of 1987) and report on their efficiency;
(g) provide and maintain a range of relevant central support and research services;
(h) direct a chief constable to provide mutual aid (S 14 (2)) and determine the allocation of costs in the event of disagreements between the aided and the aiding police authority (S 14 (4)).

To summarize: a constable must enforce the law when particular infractions come to light, and is accountable to the law, supervising officers and a public complaints procedure. A chief constable must take steps to deal generally with law breaking in his area, and is accountable to the law, a police authority and the Home Secretary. A police authority's ability to sanction is ultimately dependent on Home Secretary approval; the latter's instruments of 'control' are financial and removal from office (cf. Spencer, 1985b).

Formally speaking, the requirements of accountability appear to be met. Giving both the constable and his or her chief an *independent* responsibility for their respective law enforcement actions appears to meet the requirement of impartiality, and the law itself is the check against abuses. Other abuses – inefficient or unacceptable actions – can be dealt with by the other checks operative at each level: the individual constable is kept accountable through regulations and instructions outlining efficient and acceptable practices and a vigilant, 'complaining' public; and his or her chief through a local and a central political authority – both, in different ways, representatives of the people, and both, in different ways, responsibile for ensuring 'efficiency' and public acceptability. The three demands – for impartiality, efficiency and consent – have been met; and, crucially, law enforcement decisions at both levels have been insulated from 'interference' by political authorities. Supporters of this system, therefore, welcome this explanatory or retrospective form of accounting since it appears to guarantee (and to be the only system that can guarantee) the *bed rock* of policework: impartial law enforcement.

The fundamental difference between *supporters* and *critics* of the present system concerns the degree to which it is possible to regard the chief constable's role as one of impartial law enforcement. *Supporters* have no problem with the notion, and regard the chief constable as a professional: an expert making informed choices as to the best means to achieve the given (and unproblematic) end of 'upholding the law' (cf. Warren and Tredinnick, 1982). *Critics* point to the *inevitably* selective (or partial) nature of devising a policy of law enforcement to respond to a near infinite amount of crime (much of it unknown) with all too finite resources. Such selectivity makes policies of law enforcement *political* decisions, and a chief constable (an unelected public official) a political decision-maker, determining ends as well as appropriate means. In a democratic polity, critics argue, such decisions belong to elected politicans. In essence, this constitutes the general justification for advocating a new form of accountability – democratic accountability – which will be characterized by prospective control by a local democratic authority over a chief constable's general policies of law enforcement.

This proposed form of accountability has a *weak* and a *strong* version. The *weak* version draws a distinction between 'general policies' – which should be controlled by a democratic body (typically a local police committee shorn of its non-elected magistrate members) – and 'particular operations' (essentially the legal decisions of constables) – which it would be improper to control. As Lustgarten, who is in favour of democratic accountability, forcefully puts it:

> The decision to investigate, arrest and charge a particular suspect must remain wholly a matter for the judgement of the officer in charge of the case and aware of all the relevant facts . . . The requirement of independence in this sphere has little to do with the nature of law or criminal process, and everything to do with the nature of the decision to be taken. Positively, the decision requires objective and honest application of a rule or standard of conduct; negatively, improper consideration such as favouritism, racial or political bias and the like must be rigorously excluded. (Lustgarten, 1986, p. 164)

Later we shall return to an unacknowledged problem with the above. For the moment we can say that the *weak* version would like to see police force policy, including law enforcement policy, under prospective (democratic) control, but retain retrospective (legal) accounting for particular law enforcement decisions which would include the routine legal decisions of constables. Current Labour Party policy, strongly influenced by Jack Straw's two private member's bills (1979 and 1980) which instituted this distinction, essentially still follows this line of reasoning.

The *strong* version of prospective control is based on a substantial erosion of this general policy/particular operations distinction, rightly spotting the confusions this distinction fails to resolve (though, it has to be said, not successfully resolving the problem). Basically, it would want to see prospective democratic control extended to include particular operations, such as decisions about the policing of a particular demonstration (which the weak verson would regard as a legitimate chief constable decision, once general policy had been established).

The 'strong' argument is that simply controlling general policies would still leave important political decisions such as the handling of a riot in the hands of a chief constable. The line marking the 'proper' sphere of police operations is thus redrawn creating a new distinction between particular operations (or 'individual cases'), which police authorities must control, and 'cases relating to individuals', which should remain police decisions (Greater London Council, 1983, pp. 53–4). Achieving this change would require transferring the duty to enforce the law from constables to a democratic police authority, a duty authorities would routinely delegate to the police, and making constables local government officers (not 'independent law officers') employed by the police authority.

To summarize: the *traditionalists* endorse the present position, which removes *all* law enforcement decisions, including general policy ones, from the political arena (in the interests of impartiality) and requires only retrospective accounts to be offered. The *weak democratic* argument wishes to confine the scope of impartial law enforcement to particular operations, and subject general policies in this area to the prospective control of a local elected police authority. The *strong democratic* argument goes even further in insisting that everything but particular legal decisions about particular individuals is the legitimate province of a democratic authority. (We should perhaps just mention here the extreme radical position once more. Since its commitment to any reform strategy is attenuated by its particular revolutionary aspirations, its interventions, governed by opportunistic considerations, are less predictable.) Yet all three approaches are in some way unsatisfactory. The *traditionalist* because its notion of impartiality is highly abstract and unrealistic, especially when applied to the real discretionary world of chief officer decision-making. The 'democrats' are certainly right on this point – his decision-making world is a political one. The *weak version of democratic accountability* rightly recognizes the political nature of the chief constable's law enforcement responsibilities, but fails to recognize the inevitable confusions that would flow from assigning general policies to one form of authority, the democratic, and particular operations to another, the legal. Confusions would arise because their respective responsibilities – to public opinion (in the case of a democratic authority) and to law (in the case of a legal one) – differ (Jefferson and Grimshaw, 1984, p. 152). Put concretely, a policy of making certain offences a low priority in line with public opinion places a constable (with a duty to law) confronted by any such offences in the invidious position of having to decide between the conflicting demands of two different authorities.

However, the *strong democratic* answer does not solve the problem either. For its proposal to hand all legal decisions, except those of a constable in relation to particular individuals, over to a democratic authority, ignores the discretionary aspect of much law enforcement work involving individuals (as do both the previous approaches, incidentally). A chief constable's discretion to construct policies is often echoed in the cases of individuals dealt with by constables, a point that emerged in Chapters 4, 5 and 6. Only in the following instance can the notion of an impartial constable have substance: where there is an obvious conflict between parties, and the law is clear. In all other cases any talk of impartial law enforcement is illusory. The reality is that the police officer necessarily becomes a 'street-corner politician': not, *pace* Lustgarten, the 'objective' dispenser of 'a rule or standard of conduct' (see above, page 161). In other words, the crucial distinction is not that between 'general policies'/'particular operations', nor even 'individual cases'/'cases of individuals', but *all* situations 'where law cannot offer an authoritative guide and where there is, formally speaking, an absence of contention' (Jefferson and Grimshaw, 1984, p. 156). Which means that an elected democratic authority should have a contribution to make *both* at the level of chief constable, for all his decisions, and at the level of constable, for some of her/his decisions.

How is Accountability to be Achieved?

If the real problem of accountability arises in those situations where
neither law nor contending citizens can offer any guidance to police
action, we are effectively talking of that substantial discretion over
decision-making currently vested in the police. The central question,
then, and point of difference, is how police discretion can be controlled. There is first the 'rule-tightening' approach. The traditional
version of rule tightening is effectively that embodied in PACE, 1984.
In so far as there has been an admission by the present government that
accountability is a problem, the response has been new codes of
practice and the increased requirement to justify actions in writing.
The problem is seen as internal, the assumption being that tighter
rules will bring officers into line with force requirements (for impartial,
efficient, consensual policing). It is also assumed that the external legal
framework of accountability is basically sound – though the new
consultation requirement embodied in PACE suggests the need for
chief constables to listen more assiduously to their publics. (The
questions of publics and policing we deal with more fully in Chapter 8.)
This assumption of a basically sound external structure makes it a
traditional or conservative approach.

The radical version of rule tightening locates the problem precisely
at this level of the legal structure of accountability. Specifically, as we
saw in the last section, the assumption is that more prospective control
by elected representatives over the activities of chief constables would
render police more accountable. Essentially this would be achieved
through controlling police discretion by a legal change which would
enable democratic control of policy. Both weak and strong versions
of the radical approach share this faith in rule-tightening, legal-
structural change.

All three versions, the traditional and both the radical ones, share a
similar conception of the organization: a 'machine' with 'faulty' rules,
be they external or internal. Change the rules and behaviour will
change. It is a very traditional and sociologically impoverished notion
of organizations and how they work. It underlies almost all text books on
police management, the most complacent of all genres of writing on
police, and perhaps unsurprisingly given authorship largely by
practitioners. The sources of this conception of the organization are
two-fold – 'Taylorism' with its notion of Scientific Management, and
Weber's work on bureaucracy which led to Classical Management
Theory. 'Taylorism' relied on the separation of conception (the job of
managers) and execution (the job of workers) and the scientific
analysis of all work processes and every task in the interests of achiev-

ing the 'one best way of performance' (Mouzelis, 1967, p. 81). Weber's analysis concentrated on producing, by rational deduction, 'the ideal form of organisational structure, and a set of principles upon which managerial practice could most rationally rest' (Bradley, Walker and Wilkie, 1986, p. 49).

In either case, the issue is identical: to achieve, through empirical 'science' or deductive 'reason', alignment between management-conceived objectives derived from the police mandate ('ends'), and worker-executed performance ('means'). Furthermore, neither ends nor means are regarded as intrinsically problematic. Thus Bunyard (1978, p. 88) commenting on the manifold duties (or 'ends') of the police outlined by the Royal Commission on the Police, 1960, asserts simply that these are 'straightforward and unambiguous'. It is a viewpoint Butler echoes in talking about the means (namely, management):

> a police manager is responsible for motivating, directing and controlling the officers and civilians under his command to achieve results which are determined by the policy of the chief officer. (Butler, 1984, p. 1)

This abstract and overly rational (or undersociological) conception of the organization obtains even where there is a recognition of the resistance of officers to new managerial initiatives (Butler, 1984, pp. 243–55) and an awareness of recurrent management failure. Even the spectacular failure of Unit Beat Policing (UBP) has not placed the approach itself in jeopardy. UBP was the system universally adopted after a 'management' rethink in 1967 (Home Office, 1967). It managed to reduce both public contact and police morale, thereby achieving results the exact opposite of two of its stated goals (Butler, 1984, pp. 19–23). The response to such patent failures has been to argue the need for *more* rationality, principally in the form of a greater emphasis on *measuring* whether goals have or have not been attained. Policing by objectives (PBO), the latest in police management thinking, as we saw in Chapter 2, operationalizes this thinking. It seeks to remedy earlier deficiences through a management strategy which proceeds through a number of steps, from the most general to the highly specific ('policy statement', 'goals', 'objectives', 'action plans' and 'implementation') concluding with PBO's most 'significant innovation', namely the stage of 'evaluation'. This means, essentially, objective measurement (Butler, 1984, pp. 163–7). But the problems of the *approach*, the questions of resistance and of recurrent 'failure', none the less remain.

One response to the inherent problems of these approaches which recognizes that organizations are sociologically more problematic than either Scientific or Classical Management Theory allows, became known as the Human Relations School of Management. This recognized the human relations side of organizations: the existence of 'informal' group processes at work which might operate to subvert the 'formal' rules and the best endeavours of the time-and-motion experts. But even if this approach recognised that the 'means' to achieve the organization's goals were more complex, it shared with its predecessors a belief in positivistic science and in the organization's goals as given, as Bradley, Walker and Wilkie, (1986, p. 51) rightly maintain:

> All these approaches towards a scientifically based practice of management were based upon the same positivist ideal, that, through science, which was a combination of rigorous analysis and empirical observation and experimentation, managers might better succeed in designing and running effective and efficient systems of co-ordinated effort. All these approaches took organisational goals or ends as given.

The centrality of the 'informal' group to understanding an organization at work was also at the heart of the interactionist revolt, as we saw above on pages 30–48. But because of the interactionist emphasis on the relative and the subjective, as against the positivist ideal of the possibility of an absolute and objective science, the 'informal' began to all but submerge the 'formal' management structure and its rules and regulations. Though organizational goals or ends were similarly 'given' (i.e. unexamined) for the interactionists, they became essentially irrelevant since the norms and values of the occupational culture which informed the situational dynamics of street encounters provided the 'organizational reality' of policework. The rest was rhetoric and public relations. But if the interactionists took the informal group more seriously than any previous approach, it shared with all previous approaches a failure of the sociological imagination with regard to management. Since the formal was essentially irrelevant, there was no need to examine management practices and the question of policy. One consequence of this shared blindness was an inability adequately to address the question of the recurrent failure of management initiatives, an issue to which we shall have to return. Another consequence, of immediate relevance to us, was a sceptisim towards 'rule tightening'.

If faith in tightening the formal rules links, in a very unlikely fashion, the reform efforts of PACE, the National Council for Civil Liberties (NCCL) and the GLC, others place their faith in a transformation of the informal culture. The latter, basing themselves largely on observations of the 'police in action', regard the occupational culture, not the rules, as the critical focus of change. In so far as this 'cop culture' approach sees the need to make police more accountable, it is radical. But it is also so in relation to its more 'realistic' conception of the organization. Organizations 'work' through the informal rules members construct to help them 'make it through the day', rather than the official codes which are largely irrelevant window dressing. Observational studies of police officers at work paint a picture of deviance and rule manipulation in the pursuit of ends the informal occupational culture values – excitement, a good chase, the 'capture', and so on. Since existing rules do not control the behaviour of officers, the argument runs, why expect new rules *pace* PACE, or new structures of accountability *pace* the Labour Party, NCCL or the GLC, to fare any differently?

If the decisive focus of change is felt to be the cop culture and not the structure of rules, it can be argued that rule change is not only irrelevant but may even be damaging. This is because people respond better to reward than punishment. Unwanted rule changes, perceived as punishment, may be the more fiercely resisted; better to remotivate officers positively: change the cultural climate by rewarding desired behaviour, as Reiner (1985a, p. 178) has recently argued. From this perspective rule-tightening changes 'will only become effective if they transform and co-opt the informal values of police sub-culture' (Reiner, 1985a, p. 180). Though this approach is based on a closely observed and in some respects radical knowledge of police organizational sociology, it has clear affinities with a more traditional approach which also blames the 'rank and file'. In the case of 'traditionalists', blame attaches to the rank and files less for its deviant antics and more for its lack of education and inadequate training – in short, for its lack of 'professionalism'.

The key question, however, is not whether formal rules should be tightened *or* the cop culture co-opted, but 'the *relationship* between formal rules of law and procedure and the sub-cultural rules which are the guiding principles of police conduct' (Reiner, 1985a, p. 174, italics added). The 'rule tighteners' and the 'cop culturalists' have either failed to address this queston, or done so inadequately, simply asserting the priority of rules or the cop culture respectively. Reiner, for example, is clearly aware of the need to address the question, but he ends assertively prioritizing the importance of the cop culture. His conclusions that 'formal accountability is not the crucial issue', and that 'elected control of police policy-making is neither necessary nor sufficient for accomplishing the goal of a police force whose operations are "democratic" ' (Reiner, 1985a, p. 180) remain essentially unargued and hence unconvincing.

To begin to address this question adequately requires that we first develop what is missing from both sorts of account, namely a more adequate (i.e. concrete) conception of management, and of the key management practice, namely, policy. The rule tighteners have produced very detailed accounts of the formal structures of account-ability, both internal and external, and the cop culturalists have matched this in their observation of the police in action. But neither sort of study has yet produced a comparably detailed account of management *in action*. This is the missing link to understanding the relationship between formal rules of law and the subculture rules, precisely because management's role is, effectively, to attempt successfuly to relate the one (legal rules) to the other (subcultural rules), in practice.

If the cop culturalists and the external rule tighteners are blind to the question of management because of their particular objects of attention, the cop culture and the external legal structure respectively, text books on police management have no such excuse. Yet, with one notable exception, the genre remains, even today, hopelessly idealistic, both in its conception of management and, consequently, in its proposals for reform. Starting from a conception of the ideal and finding present performance wanting when matched against such an ideal, such texts propose strategies to bring the two closer together, latterly through an emphasis on the objective measurement of performance. The model of the organization, as we have seen, derives from Classical Management Theory with its highly formal and rationalistic approach to reconciling means and ends. But, as Bradley, Walker and Wilkie (1986, p. 64 – the one notable exception mentioned earlier) point out, the mechanistic model of organizations 'presumes that organizations, like machines, are more or less appropriately designed so as to achieve a set of functions or objectives which are: (i) unambiguous . . . (ii) mutually compatible . . . (iii) naturally legitimated . . . (iv) uncontentious'. In other words, the possibility of ambiguous, incompatible, illegitimate or contentious police functions is precluded *in advance* in these management text books. This is because they start from an assumption that, even in the absence of reform, a consensus between management, officers and the community is possible, the 'ideal police organization' towards which management efforts are constantly directed, and against which they are peridocially measured (Butler, 1984, p. 134).

In the light of our examination of police history and policing the present social divisions, such consensual underpinnings simply cannot be sustained. The mandate, to enforce the law impartially, efficiently and acceptably, is inherently unstable, the more so in that the necessarily political dimensions are rendered invisible by the present structure of accountability. This compounds the injustice of partial policing by calling it impartial. From *this* starting point, the failures of management, such as the constant emphasis on the centrality of uniformed beat patrolling and community policing and their routine marginalizing in practice (evidenced by the practices of staffing cars first, using specialist experience as the route to promotion, leaving the youngest and least experienced as 'walkers', using resident beat officers as an 'operational reserve', and so on), are better located within a series of incompatible demands. These are the demand for *efficiency* promoting emphasis on reduced response times, productivity, clear up rates and hence motorized responding and specialization; the counter demand for *acceptability* pulling the organization towards highly visible preventive foot patrols and broadly based community police work (cf. Jones and Silverman, 1984).

It is this realistic starting point – ambiguous and incompatible police goals – that is necessary for a concrete conception of management, i.e. one that is alert to the real constraints operating on the process. Though there are many management tasks – training, promotion, supervision, discipline, advice, command, deployment, and so on – these are all subordinate to policy, the internal goal (Butler's 'policy statements') towards which all the efforts of the organization are directed. Traditional police management texts and critical analyses of police accountability alike are agreed about the centrality of policy. They both make similar assumptions about it, namely that policies are management statements intended to guide practice. And even though cop culturalists regard policy as an irrelevance, they none the less operate with similar assumptions about it. However, such a conception remains idealistic unless we define policy in a way that concretely links it to practice, that requires it to specify a practice (and a 'settled' one at that to distinguish it from temporary commands), otherwise *any* statement made by management could conceivably be regarded as policy. The only study yet to have conducted a concrete examination of policy defined it as '*an authoritative statement signifying a settled practice*' (Grimshaw and Jefferson, 1987, p. 204, italics in original). Armed with that definition, and after examining many policy files and attending numerous management meetings and conferences where policy was discussed, the conclusion was drawn that operational policy – that is policy relating to operational matters as distinct from policy relating to administrative matters – was either non-existent or so ambiguous as to be effectively so. This was not the case with administrative policy.

When the question 'why?' is asked, the virtue of starting with the external structure becomes apparent. The legal structure of accountability which makes all officers, as constables *independently* answerable to the law, is *only* compatible with an internal structure which recognizes and respects that independence. Ambiguous or non-existent operational policies do just that.

In the light of this, when we return to the question of 'the relationship between formal rules of law and the subculture rules', we can counterpose to Reiner's assertive prioritization of the cop culture an *argued* alternative – namely, that the key lies with the formal rules, on the grounds that it is the permissiveness of the external structure (the uncontrolled discretion), and the concomitant internal permissiveness (an inevitable consequence of a system of legal accountability which renders operational policy redundant) which creates the *space* for the occupational culture to flourish. Controlling the (external) discretion would leave the (internal) culture with few spaces to flourish. At *that* stage, with the rules tightened, co-optive work on the cop culture, as Reiner suggests, would be important – but as a subordinate not superordinate factor in the process of change.

A similar argument can be made with respect to police committees. A cultural approach might make a similar argument to the cop culturalists, namely that the problem is less structural than cultural. That is to say, it it less the rules that need changing than the composition/culture of the police committee, since 'In the one authority that received extensive study, the members were disproportionately elderly and viewed their work as entirely non-partisan and apolitical'. However, it is very possible that, just as the cop culture flourishes because of the permissive framework, it is the very powerlessness of present police authorities that keep away the young and politically active (Lustgarten, 1986, p. 87). The recent exceptions to this rule, the authorities such as Merseyside and Greater Manchester which were highly active before their abolition, serve only to strengthen the point about structural powerlessness (cf. Simey, 1985; Loveday, 1985).

Summary and Conclusion

Police accountability concerns how policework (fundamentally, 'law enforcement') is to be controlled (rendered impartial, efficient and consensual), whether through the very limited means of retrospective explanation or through the much more direct system of prospective control. It becomes an issue when the public feel controls are not working, which has been a recurring feature of police history. Some (conservatives) regard it, in consequence, as an endemic problem, an inevitable result of the role of legal coercion. For some (extreme radicals), the issue is irrelevant until broader socio-economic change has been effected. Others (radicals), alert to the particularities of its emergence as a problem, particularly at times of crisis, in urban centres, and in relation to the disadvantaged, regard it as an issue possessing historically specific features which can be changed.

At present police of all ranks are formally controlled by law in their law enforcement decisions, a system designed to guarantee their impartiality. If they give dissatisfaction they can be called to account – in the case of the constable through the courts, the discipline code and the complaints procedure; and, in the case of the chief constable, by his police authority and the Home Secretary. Such a system of retrospective accounting appears to some to cover the key issues of impartiality, efficiency and consent, in the best possible way to keep law enforcement impartial. Critics, by contrast, regard impartial law enforcement as inapplicable to the chief constable's role of generally upholding the law, and demand, in the weak version, prospective control of his discretion over operational policy, and, in the strong version, that this be extended to particular operations. Both would exclude from such control the legal decisions of constables dealing with particular cases, for which traditional retrospective accounting is still felt desirable. Each critical position has something to recommend it, the weak because it rightly sees the chief constable's role as political, the strong because it includes particular operational decisions under the same heading. But, neither sees the importance of the political control of the discretion of the constable in those situations where law is unclear or there is no conflict between parties.

The rule-tightening approach to controlling discretion has both traditional and radical supporters, disagreement centring on the need to alter external rules, which represents the radical case, as against internal ones, which traditionalists want. Radicals who also have a radical view of the organization suggest the locus of reforming attention should be the deviant, rule-breaking cop culture. When the relation between the rules and the cop culture is highlighted, either one can be taken to be the fundamentally determining level. The argument for prioritizing rule change, our argument, is that the current permissive structures – external and internal – enable the cop culture to flourish. It follows that rule tightening would disable.

Finally, however, there is the question of 'what kind of policing' a more accountable police force is designed to achieve. The achievement of a reformed framework or 'born again' cop culture provides only means, not ends. In a democracy, these ends have to be the concrete realization of the presently idealistic conception of equality under the law, i.e. they have to be *just*. Our concentration on the 'how' has thus far largely sidelined this question of justice. Given its relevance to the issue of accountability, we mention it here. But, because it has not been a central focus of the debate, and because of its centrality (albeit still largely unrecognized) to other new developments which we consider in Chapter 8, we shall postpone our discussion of it until then.

Suggestions for Further Reading

Jefferson, T., and Grimshaw, R. (1984), *Controlling the Constable* (London: Muller/Cobden Trust).
Lustgarten, L. (1986), *The Governance of Police* (London: Sweet & Maxwell).
Punch, M. (ed.) (1983), *Control in the Police Organization* (Cambridge, Mass.: MIT).

8 *After Scarman:*

Monitoring, Effectiveness and Public Justice

Introduction

In the absence of the kind of structural reforms advocated by the democrats in the previous chapter, the debate about accountability continues. But the jolt given to the debate by the 'riots' and the Scarman Report has led to a range of initiatives – from 'above' and 'below' – which are attempts to grapple with some of the issues raised by the debate. They might be regarded generally as different ways of exploring the question of how, in the absence of radical structural surgery, more effective/legitimate/acceptable policework can be established. We shall therefore outline these developments and evaluate them in terms of their likely success. And we shall end by discussing the idea of *public justice*, arguing for a need to incorporate such a notion into the debate, if the debate on 'effectiveness' ('what kind of policing') is to progress.

Post-Scarman Initiatives

The initiatives which have developed in the wake of the events of 1981 are held together by the commitment to monitoring policework. This monitoring takes a number of different forms. There is first the *internal* monitoring of developments in the training of police officers and in the requirements of the Police and Criminal Evidence (PACE) Act, 1984, legislation. Secondly, there is the *public* monitoring implicit in the formal establishment of police–community liaison committees and in the introduction of lay visitors to police stations. Thirdly, there is *partnership* monitoring intrinsic to the mushrooming growth of neighbourhood watch schemes. Fourthly, there is '*monitoring by crime survey*'. And finally, the *independent* monitoring group has emerged. Each of these will be discussed in turn.

(1) *Internal Monitoring*

Chapter 2 introduced us to the way the discipline of psychology has contributed to a critical evaluation of police officers' training and has led to the emergence of such initiatives as Human Awareness and Race Awareness Training, particularly within the Metropolitan Police. Looking to the formal training process as a means of improving the police officers' skills in community awareness and interaction is not without its difficulties as we saw in that chapter. However, in the context of monitoring, examining the kinds of attitudes and skills the formal training process equips the police officer with, and then looking to what can be done with the formal training process, would seem to be something which all can support. Any attempt to improve the quality of the interaction between the police and the public, by critically examining how a police officer might handle himself or herself in particular situations, must be viewed positively. To date, Bull and Horncastle (1986a) report a degree of success in improving such skills within the Metropolitan Police training. Difficulties arise, however, when too much emphasis is placed on formal training *at the expense* of appreciating that police officers construct their work in a much wider context than interpersonal dynamics. In other words, the impact of training-based initiatives *unaccompanied by other changes* is unlikely to prove more than a marginal contribution to improving police effectiveness.

Internal monitoring, however, has another face. The PACE legislation, in introducing such things as the custody record has demanded that policework be recorded and consequently open to monitoring in a much more detailed and systematic fashion. Strictly speaking, the origins of PACE in the Royal Commission on Criminal Procedure (1981) predate Scarman with the 'monitoring' clauses intended to 'balance' the new powers PACE granted the police. Failure to comply with the legislation may constitute a disciplinary offence for the officers. There is therefore an apparently imperative element to this legislation though it is too early to make an assessment of the way in which this legislation is being implemented. The demand for detailed records, the new codes of practice, and the disciplining features associated with this would suggest that at least the requirements in terms of the paperwork will be met. And the requirement that copies of, for example, written records of a conducted search are available to suspects, their solicitors and the courts suggest the possibility of greater external oversight too. But, for all the new post-PACE accent on recording and tightening, it is hard to be convinced by the traditionalist's optimism that this form of basically *internal* monitoring can prove sufficient to the task of producing effective policing. Rather, we share the radicals' concern that this form of monitoring will prove largely cosmetic, for two basic reasons. First, the constraints still leave considerable *discretionary* leeway in the hands of constables. For example, the requirement to record the details of a search can be set aside if it is impracticable to record these. Secondly, external bodies have no effective *powers* to ensure police conform to the new requirements. It still relies very largely on the internal system of discipline, that is, essentially, on the police monitoring themselves.

(2) *Public Monitoring*

Lord Scarman recommended that 'statutory liaison committees, or other appropriate consultative machinery' be established in every force for the purpose of local police policies being discussed by the local communities affected by them (Scarman, 1982, para, 5.71). He envisaged that these 'should have real powers' (para. 5.69), that they should not 'simply be a statutory talking shop' (ibid.) and that '*any* aspect of public policy should be regarded as a matter for discussion through the machinery, including operational questions' (ibid., italics added). However, since he failed to specify what statutory *powers* the new committees might have to force chief constables to discuss operational policies, since he insisted chief constables should retain their independent *decision-making* over policy, and since he even qualified what might be a fit matter for committee discussion, namely, 'any aspect of police policy . . . other than those [operational questions] which, in the view of the Commander of the District, must remain confidential' (ibid.), it was hard to be optimistic about what such bodies might achieve. For the government, however, such committees offered a 'compromise' on the accountability issue without giving away anything essential (like police independence).

In the subsequent PACE legislation, the kind of consultative arrangements were left, for the most part, to the discretion of the different police authorities. Morgan and Maggs (1985, p. 2), in reviewing the kinds of arrangements which have been made, make the observation that 'formal committees are now almost universally the norm'. These committees have some common features: membership includes representatives from the police, the police authority, constituent councils, and voluntary, statutory and community groups; meetings are held regularly and records kept; each has some sort of constitution; and the proceedings are generally publicly available. While the *openness* of such groups varies (Merseyside, for example, holds comparatively open community forums in which the public can fully participate), as does the level of public *participation*, some form of formal consultative arrangement now exists throughout England and Wales.

It is, of course, early days to evaluate these new arrangements properly. But the early pessimism does not seem unwarranted. Though Morgan and Maggs (1985) took a hopeful line at the outset, seeing these arrangements as an important development in police community liaison, Morgan's (1987) subsequent report is less hopeful. Although the picture is varied, the common signs favour the critical view. The broad findings to date suggest that the committees are dominated by the 'concerned and worthy' middle classes, that the agenda and discussion is very police dominated, and items tend to be mundane, trivial and rarely contentious. And though no opportunities for discussing police policies should be spurned unilaterally, nor prematurely, it is hard to see how middle-class, powerless, police-dominated committees are going to be able to produce effective policing for those 'dispossessed' minorities (the *policed* communities) who bear the brunt of it.

The second element of public monitoring is the introduction of lay visitors to police stations. Lord Scarman drew attention to the benefits to be derived from such a system (paras 7.7 – 7.10), which had previously been highlighted by the Home Affairs Committee in 1981. Indeed, he thought this system might be one of the 'real powers' of the liaison committees. Pilot schemes for lay visiting to police stations were established in 1983 in the Metropolitan Police in Lambeth, and in the provinces in Greater Manchester, the West Midlands, South Yorkshire, Humberside, Leicestershire and Cheshire. The purpose of lay visiting is to

> enable members of the local community to observe, comment and report on the conditions under which persons are detained at police stations and the operation in practice of the statutory and other rules governing their welfare. (Home Office, 1983)

This does *not* include matters concerning the case, bail considerations, investigating or dealing with prisoners' complaints of misconduct or maltreatment. In other words, the *scope* of the monitoring is strictly limited to welfare considerations and general custodial arrangements.

In developing the pilot schemes, all the authorities, with the exception of Cheshire, chose to nominate either 'appropriate persons' to become lay visitors through the police–community consultative committees, or chose non-magistrate members of their police authorities to fulfil this role. Cheshire (followed by Merseyside in 1984) chose to advertise for members of the public to become lay visitors. None, to date, appear to have reached the level of organization of the Lambeth scheme, where they produce independent quarterly reports on their visiting and have made some progress in improving the conditions of people held in custody in their area.

Evaluations of such schemes have been made by Burney (1985) on Lambeth, and Walklate (1986a, 1986b) on Merseyside. Whilst the Home Office states that evaluation of lay visiting schemes is still in progress, Circular 12/1986 'commends' such schemes to other police authorities, in so far as they have

> the potential for promoting public confidence in the work of the police, flowing from a better understanding of what goes on within police stations [as] has already been demonstrated. (Home Office Circular 12/1986)

As with the police–community consultative committees, the traditional assumption is made that the relevant 'public' or community has been adequately identified and involved in the operation of these schemes, is being effectively briefed about their work, and has sufficient *powers* to do their job. Most schemes to date chose to appoint existing representatives of the community to their lay visiting panel. This does not necessarily ensure that the community at large consequently has a

> better understanding of what goes on in police stations. Even in the case of Merseyside, where members of the public were advertised for and appointed as lay visitors, the composition of the initial group was drawn largely from the middle aged, professional/white collar group, who, if they had any first hand experience of the police, had positive experiences. (Walklate, 1986a)

The schemes themselves, therefore, are not generally peopled by representatives of the community for whom police activity can be a problem. Indeed, because the Home Office believes that lay visitors must be credible witnesses both with the community and the police, it suggests that those 'convicted of an offence punishable with imprisonment or detention *may* not be suitable' (HO Circular 12/1986, italics in original). Additionally, whilst the Home Office recommends that the findings of the lay visiting panels be publicly available, these have generally been communicated through the police–community liaison committees. Moreover, the powers of visitors can be effectively circumscribed in a number of ways, as Walklate (1986b) has detailed. However, Burney sees hopeful signs in Lambeth,

> Perhaps the most hopeful sign is the initial success of the drive to recruit young black people onto the panel. Since so many police prisoners in Lambeth are also young and black, their presence has wide implications, not all foreseeable. (Burney, 1985, p. 240)

At the time of writing, Lambeth lay visitors had withdrawn from the scheme 'after the Metropolitan Police decided to stop them speaking to prisoners out of the hearing of officers' (*Guardian*, 11 December 1987, p. 4). Even with more representative lay visitors, well briefed and with sufficient powers to do their work, the contribution of lay visiting to more effective policing, given the limited scope of its activity, is necessarily quite small.

In each of these public monitoring initiatives the question has been raised concerning whose community is being represented in these processes and whose voice is being heard. For those sections of the community actively involved in and represented in these developments, some measure of increased information and reassurance concerning police activity may be achieved. Whether this also means that the police are now really more accountable to these sections of the community than they were before the introduction of such measures, given the unchanged powers of chief constables and the absence of anything approaching countervailing powers in either of these schemes, remains highly unlikely. For those sections of the community not represented or involved, so far little appears to have changed. Since these are the groups for whom they were ostensibly initiated, our conclusion as to their likely contribution to producing more effective policing has to be sceptical.

(3) *Partnership Monitoring*

The 1980s have seen a growth in the awareness of the need to involve the public in crime prevention. This strand of police–community contact is characterized by a mushrooming of neighbourhood watch schemes, and has seen the development of a more formal partnership emerging between the police and the community, building on the established tradition of 'good neighbour' schemes already in existence in many police forces.

Cheshire, it seems, claims to have established the first neighbourhood watch scheme in 1982. Morgan and Maggs (1985) report 29 forces with 3,909 schemes between them by 1 April 1985. In the Metropolitan Police, neighbourhood watch schemes were positively endorsed and encouraged in Commissioner Newman's plans for policing London, and by the end of 1985 there were 3,770 such schemes (*Policing London*, no. 22 July–August 1986). Indeed, Donnison, Skola and Thomas (1986) argue that Newman, then MPD Commissioner, saw the emergence of neighbourhood watch schemes as one means whereby the police become accountable to the public;

> I can think of no better forum to canvass and discuss local problems of policing priorities than in the context of local neighbourhood watch meetings all over London. (Quoted in Donnison, Skola and Thomas, 1986, p. 11)

Given the rapid growth of such schemes and the apparent importance placed on them in some areas, it is useful to examine these schemes in a little more detail.

Donnison, Skola and Thomas (1986) identify three elements to neighbourhood watch schemes in the London area, elements which appear to be relevant to other parts of the country. First they are intended to be the means by which local residents act as the 'eyes and ears' of the police; looking out for suspicious people or vehicles and passing on such information to the police. Secondly, participants in such schemes are offered the facility of property marking schemes, window stickers and street signs as a means of deterring would-be criminal activity. Finally, advice on home security in general is available. The impetus for establishing a neighbourhood watch scheme can come either from a group of residents or from a process of police targeting areas, in the light of crime rates and/or victimization rates, where they feel neighbourhood watch might be of benefit. It is usual to appoint a scheme co-ordinator who is given advice on what kind of information might be relevant to police activity.

A number of studies are emerging which have attempted to evaluate the effectiveness of such schemes. One of the early schemes, at Kingsdown in Bristol, claims to have reduced the crime rate by 25 per cent. Such claims need to be examined carefully, given the known difficulties associated with counting crime. Bennion *et al.* (1985), in comparing and contrasting the effectiveness of two schemes, one in a middle-class area, the other in an inner-city council estate, conclude:

> There is as yet little evidence from police sources to prove that Neighbourhood Watch succeeded in preventing crime or increas-

ing detection, but the police objective of reducing the fear of crime
does seem to have been met for those people perceiving benefits in
Neighbourhood Watch. (Bennion *et al*., 1985, p. 46).

This finding has been confirmed by a more recent study by Bennett
(1987) conducted in Acton and Wimbledon. What both Bennion *et al*.
(1985) and the Donnison, Skola and Thomas (1986) studies point to is
the extent to which in both surveys neighbourhood watch has become
identified most effectively in middle-class owner occupied areas.
Bennion *et al* also note 'that police crime prevention activities would
be concentrated in such areas, thus creating further divisions between
middle class and working class areas' (1985, p. 45).

Thus, as a partnership monitoring of crime, it may well be, as
Weatheritt (1986) suggests, that neighbourhood watch may be
successful in some circumstances, if not in others. It may also be that
neighbourhood watch is successful in affecting some aspects of
participants' behaviour. Bennett(1987, p. 45) found that residents in
Wimbledon had made improvements in home security, for example.
Whether, however, they constitute another strand of an increased
democratically accountable police force providing more effective
policing for *all* sections of the community is another matter. Kinsey,
Lea and Young (1986) trace the origins of neighbourhood watch to
Detroit and state that

> The NWS was set up in the context of a radical administration with
> considerable democratic powers over policing. Thus the alienation
> of the public from the police was assuaged not only by the crime
> prevention programme and its consequent publicity, but by the
> palpable movement towards police accountability. (pp. 95–6)

There has been no such increase in democratic powers in this
country, and whilst neighbourhood watch schemes might provide
certain benefits to parts of the community, the possibility remains that
through such schemes policing may build on and exacerbate existing
social divisions. In this connection, the concern by some that neighbourhood watch simply widens the net of surveillance and increases
the amount of intelligence-gathering, with all the threats to civil
liberties such activities pose, is not an idle one. Moreover, as with the
lay visiting schemes, there is the question of their limited scope. They
are basically concerned only with a narrow range of crimes that are
easily observable and liable to be reported. This leaves a whole range
of police activities of known concern to the public, including public

order policing and the use of police powers, completely outside their remit. Any notion of acceptable or effective policing, however, cannot possibly be so exclusive.

(4) *Monitoring by Crime Surveys*

Official crime statistics, as we know, are subject to numerous distortions (Box, 1981, chs 3 and 6). These can result from inadequate knowledge (the unknown tax evaders for example), different perceptions (one person's 'family tiff' is another's criminal assault) and decisions about whether to report and to record (is it serious enough to be worth the bother? will anybody do anything about it?). Such distortions occur at each *stage* of the process of transforming certain behaviours into criminal statistics, and can be produced by any of the *parties* involved, which means, principally, victims or other 'reporters', and the police. Criminal victimization surveys, or crime surveys as they are popularly called, are basically attempts to produce a picture of the extent of crime without the distortions produced by police perceptions and decisions. In asking a random sample of the population directly about their experiences as victims of certain crimes, the basic method of crime surveys, and then grossing these up to produce an estimate of the extent of these crimes, one source of distortion (the police input) is eliminated. Though the resulting crime picture is fuller, it is by no means a 'true' picture. Serious distortions, to which we return later, none the less remain. In addition, crime surveys have increasingly included a range of crime related questions: for example, on the impact of crime and the fear of crime; on public attitudes to policing, punishment, neighbourhood watch and victim support schemes; and on public evaluations of crime seriousness, police responses, etc.

Although national crime surveys have been carried out in the USA since 1972, the first National British Crime Survey (BCS) was not conducted until 1982. It has been repeated subsequently in 1984 and 1986 (see, for the main findings in England and Wales, Hough and Mayhew, 1983 and 1985; and, for Scotland, Chambers and Tombs, eds, 1984). Local surveys have followed, in Nottinghamshire and adjacent counties (Farrington and Dowds, 1985), on Merseyside (Kinsey, 1984; 1985a; 1985b), and in Islington (Jones, MacLean and Young, 1986). The last two of these locally based studies – those on Merseyside and Islington – have increased further the scope of the topics covered. The authors of these studies have also become more ambitious about what locally based surveys can be used for. In particular, they regard such surveys as the key 'monitoring' weapon in the struggle for more responsive policing and crime control (cf. Kinsey, Lea and Young, 1986). This more directly political use of the crime survey – part of a broader intellectual/political project which has been dubbed 'the new realism' – has been accompanied by a certain blindness to the inherent limitations of survey methodology and a tendency, in consequence, to 'over-read' data. In describing and evaluating survey findings and their likely contribution to more acceptable policing, we shall focus on this shift, from the 'academic' Home Office-funded National Crime Surveys to the politicized 'new realist' (largely) council-funded local surveys.

Summarizing the findings of the British Crime Surveys is a risky business, mainly because of their sheer number taken individually. However, concentrating selectively on the key findings, in line with perhaps their dominant broad interpretation to date, the general 'message' of the first two surveys 'sweeps' reads something like this. There were far more offences committed than ever found their way into the official crime statistics. The reporting rate varied enormously by offence but overall was about 1 in 3. The majority of unreported crimes were not serious, an important factor in the decision not to report them, and generally, risks of serious injury or substantial loss from crime were small. For example, vehicle crime was the most common form of crime, accounting for about 1 in 3 of all reported offences, and was the most costly to victims. Although the rise in crime between 1981 and 1983 was roughly in line with the police recorded rise (BCS, 10 per cent, Police, 12 per cent), the police recorded rise in domestic burglaries between 1972 and 1983 (namely, 100 per cent) was far in excess of the 20 per cent figure produced by combining data of the BCS and the General Household Survey. This vividly demonstrated the role increased reporting and increased recording can play in crime trends. Despite the predominance of non-violent, low-value property crimes, anxiety about crime was wide-spread, especially about serious and violent crimes, such as robbery, rape and burglary. This was particularly the case among women, the elderly and those in inner cities. Such anxiety affected behaviour, particularly among women, as many as half of whom avoided going out unaccompanied after dark. Much of the fear was excessive, based on an overestimation of the actual risks of being a crime victim. Indeed, taking particular groups, the fear of crime was inversely related to victimization, so that the most fearful group – elderly females – were least likely to be victims. The figures produced for some offence categories – for example, domestic violence and sexual offences – were clearly underestimates, because of the reluctance of victims to talk about such offences with strangers. Other offences too, because they had no individual victims, such as shoplifting and fraud, could not be compared with police figures.

The implications drawn from all this were modest. On measurement, it was suggested that crime surveys could prove a useful supplement to police figures, showing, for example, where police figures provide a perfectly adequate guide (for example, vehicle theft), or providing the basis for producing a classification of crimes based on 'seriousness of harm' rather than merely legal criteria. The arguments for encouraging more reporting of crime had to be balanced against the difficulty of doing much about many of them. What could be done about crime prevention was improved security measures and more encouragement to 'target hardening' measures (more locks and bolts). And better information about the real risks of crime victimization should help to reduce anxiety about crime.

When we move forward to the second 'new realist' wave of crime surveys (Kinsey's Merseyside Crime Survey (MCS) and the Jones, MacLean and Young, Islington Crime Survey (ICS)), there has been a dramatic change. Though the methodology remains the same, and the questionnaires are heavily based on those of the two British Crime Surveys and that of the PSI (1983) study on policing in London, there is a new sense of mission behind the work. The introduction to the ICS makes it clear. The development of mass victimization studies in the USA as a guide to public policy had social-democratic origins – a guiding vision of social justice. The rise of the right was to change all this. Victimization studies became absorbed by the new administrative criminology, being used as a guide to the allocation of resources in a never-to-be won war against crime (Jones, MacLean and Young, 1986, p. 2) and not used to address questions about the structural inequalities causing crime and how such injustices might be eliminated. Feminism's concern with domestic violence, rape and sexual harassment revealed the hidden connection between the study of victims and a radical criminology concerned with social injustice. The result was to force radical criminologists to confront the fact that much crime was intra-class and intra-racial, and to take seriously the question of working-class and black victims. The result: a radical *realist* criminology which added the reality of the victim's experiences to its other concerns, namely, the offender, informal social control and the state. Despite the fact that, theoretically, the victim became one of *four* things to be studied, in practice it was placed centre-stage, and the offender, informal social control and the state were left waiting in the wings. Moreover, the extension in the range of questions, to include the police and attitudes to penality, etc., in order to begin 'to provide the sort of empirical basis necessary for a realist criminology'

(Jones, MacLean and Young, 1986, p. 4) began to suggest, implicitly anyway, *everything* else was to be studied *only* through its refraction in victims' experiences, perceptions and attitudes. Whether that is the intention is not entirely clear. But what is clear is that the sole reliance on victims produces a range of distortions which are not adequately addressed by the methodological precautions taken, as we shall see.

Once again, there is the problem of summarizing a whole variety of findings adequately. Given that, we shall focus on the ICS and on the main differences from the BCS, both in terms of findings and implications. On the question of crime itself, ICS claimed that because of its more focused attention, geographically and within group, it has uncovered what the BCS masked – a high level of victimization among particular groups, who tended to be victims over and over again. In particular, its methodological innovations managed to uncover far more instances of domestic violence and sexual assaults on women than the BCS, with the result that 'women appear to be at greater risk of crime than men generally' (ICS, p. 84). Ethnic minorities suffer more victimization than whites and all this within the context of 'a high number of criminal occurrences' (ICS, p. 83).

These experiences of crime were 'matched' by perceptions: 7 out of 10 residents see crime as a 'problem', many think it is getting worse, around half worry about being burgled or robbed in the street and, when totals are broken down in sub-populations 'perception of risk is often related to . . . relative vulnerability' (ICS, p.35). Fears and anxieties are not 'unrealistic'.

In line with these experiences and perceptions, there was a broad cross-community consensus that police priorities should be street robberies and sexual assaults on women, followed by hard drug use and domestic burglaries. Yet substantial minorities thought police spent too much time on prostitution and cannabis, two offences that came near the bottom of the list, and a majority regard the police as 'unsuccessful' in their handling of street robberies, burglaries, vandalism, sexual assaults on women and women being molested or pestered. There is, in short, 'a tendency for the public to see the police as unsuccessful at dealing with those crimes which they prioritize and see as becoming more common, and vice versa' (ICS, p. 114). Most contact with police is crime-related. And there is widespread belief, especially among the young, even more so among blacks, that police act unfairly, and that the police should be more democratically accountable.

The net result of this set of findings is an inversion of the suggestions made by the BCS. The fear of crime is not to be educated away but taken seriously because the fears do relate to levels of victimization.

Similarly, experiences match perceptions when it comes to beliefs about police fairness and malpractice. Thus the public should be taken seriously. What the public want is speedier reaction to calls, criminal investigation and officers on the beat as deterrence, that is, crime-related rather than order-maintenance or service activities, which is not in accord with current police policy in London. A shift in priorities in accord with community priorities should occur which would involve more time investigating burglaries, taking violence against women and racist violence more seriously, and foot stops being severely curtailed. Developing performance indicators using surveys would help, as would rationalizing police tasks towards crime control and away from service tasks and minor disputes which might be better dealt with by community controlled 'pre-legal mitigation'. Neighbourhood watch, too, as part of a consultative, multi-agency, multi-problem directed strategy, rather than police and crime-centred as at present, could also have a role. So, too, could council directed crime prevention: 'target hardening' and security measures, as well as a variety of measures to lessen the impact of crime such as council insurance for all tenants, shelters for battered women, etc. And, finally, a unified multi-agency approach, not police-centred, but participatory and democratic, is needed to produce 'a unified crime control plan' (ICS, p. 216).

The thrust of this evaluation will suggest that the shift from 'administrative' to 'new realist' victimization studies, towards the overtly political use of the crime survey as a key tool monitoring 'what sort of crime control the public wants' and 'how well it is being provided with it', has produced a compounding of the original limitations.

Let us start with the original limitations. As the BCS is quick to admit there are all kinds of possible errors, due to technical limitations in survey methodology, which prevent surveys counting accurately what it is they wish to count. Distortions can arise from sampling error, interviewer error, respondent error and questionnaire error. The problem of representativeness, and the biases ensuing from systematic omissions in the sampling frame from which the sample is drawn, is endemic. Then there are the 'voluntary' omissions resulting from those who refuse to take part. This is particularly problematic for infrequent crime events like robbery. The 'errors' produced by interviewers arise when they make any of a number of mistakes, from misreading questions, misleading respondents, inaccurately completing questionnaires and so on. Respondent errors can result from forgetfulness, inaccurate recall (remembering an incident happening *before* the reference period and including it in an answer, and vice versa), unwillingness to divulge (e.g. women and sexual assaults), misunderstandings and lying. And there are the errors resulting from the basic tool – the questionnaire. Sticking only with the apparently most factual part of that, questions concerning people's experiences of crime, there is always a gap between the *meaning* of the question to the interviewer and its *meaning* to the interviewee. At its simplest, the victim's perception of whether s/he has been victimized – say assaulted – in the reference period, will not necessarily coincide with a legal definition of 'assault', nor with the perceptions of other victims. Again, one person's 'tiff' is another's assault. So, whether the interviewer's questions 'count' the same things as the victim's answer is inherently problematic.

But interviewees can only answer questions posed. So, 'error' can arise through the decison about which questions to ask, and which to omit. The principal omission in crime surveys are crimes which do not have clearly identifiable victims.

> Most surveys, including the BCS, have restricted themselves to crimes against individuals and their private property. It is considerably more difficult to survey corporate victims – public services, schools, shops and businesses, though attempts have been made to do this. And of course, crime surveys are poorly suited to the measurement of offences involving drug and alcohol abuse and consensual sexual offences. (Hough and Mayhew, 1985, p. 3)

And, as the BCS authors go on to admit, 'this partial coverage of crime categories has the insidious effect of distracting attention from important but less easily countable offences, especially "white collar crimes" ' (ibid., p. 6).

Of course there are methodological conventions designed to arrest the impact of these limitations, and for some types of questions tolerably accurate counts are achievable. This is not intended as a counsel of despair; but it is intended as a warning against over pressing the claims of crime survey.

Now, whilst the later 'new realist' surveys make some claims to have overcome some of these limitations, especially the claim to have broken the barrier with women victims and divulging sexual attacks, there is no claim to have overcome these limitations, which are in any case general and inherent, as a whole. But nor is there any strong acknowledgement that these exist and should inform readings. Indeed the extension of the scope of the original questionnaires has worsened these endemic problems; and an overreading of the subsequent data has compounded them yet further.

The worsening of the problem has resulted from including more questions based not on experiences (reasonably factual events) but on perceptions and attitudes. (The BSC had some of these. ICS and MCS have included more.) Asking respondents about their perceptions of, for example, 'offences on which they believe the police spend more time than necessary' is to introduce a much more subjective dimension than one about crime victimization. Because perceptions are not necessarily based on extensive, concrete knowledge, they can stem either from a limited direct experience, knowledge gleaned from friends, or from the media. Such limited, selective or 'biased' exposure can lead to *mis*perceptions: people's perceptions can be simply wrong, like the white racist who thinks immigrants are taking the white men's jobs because *he* is unemployed and his black neighbour is not. Worst of all are attitudes. Attitudes are very complex: attitudes to crime may be situationally based (thefts from shops being regarded differently from 'perks' from work), have a 'private' face (condonation) different from a 'public' face (condemnation), be susceptible to a desire to hold the 'right' attitudes, or vary from time to time, or be unknown to the respondent because s/he has never had to 'have' the attitude being sought (and so may provide the interviewer with a clichéd 'hand me down' answer). It probably goes without saying that these difficulties – with perceptions and attitudes – make asking about them, getting the questions right, that much harder. It should also make the reading of the answers that much more tentative and qualified, since their meaning is not going to be transparent. Unfortunately, both the ICS and MCS adopt a reading of their data which suggests the reverse: that the meanings are clear and unambiguous. But this is only managed at the expense of ignoring awkward anomalies.

Let us end with some examples. Take Kinsey's use of both ICS and MCS data in his *Marxism Today* article (Kinsey, 1986). At the risk of oversimplifying, he outlines basically what the surveys found on people's view of crime, points out how police priorities differ, and suggests that if the two were brought into line things would be much better. In terms of perceptions, the argument's subtext is that we should base policing on people's (accurate) perceptions of the crime problem and not, as at present, on police (mis)perceptions of the problem. But are people's immediate perceptions that sound a basis for action? Kinsey's reading suggests they are. But his data are less certain. For example, he tells us that 'in Liverpool 8 some 37% of males under 30 reported that they had been stopped *and searched* by the police at least once during the past year. However, not only are such stops highly unproductive and wasteful of police time – in Merseyside only 43 arrests made per thousand stops – they are highly selective and discriminatory' (Kinsey, 1986, p. 8, italics in original). We can agree – but his survey respondents do not.

> *It also appears that a substantial majority of Merseysiders believe that, stop and searches happen only occasionally or hardly ever and that this is what they 'think is about right'. This is true even in those areas where the survey results suggest a high level of both stops and searches, half or more of those interviewed believing that stops and searches 'hardly ever' or only 'occasionally' take place and this was as it should be.* (Kinsey, 1984, p. 43, italics in original)

So, on the basis of their own (limited) experience, most Merseysiders *mis*perceive what is happening to their young people. That *mis*perception forms the basis of their complacency. Kinsey's more extensive knowledge produces his more accurate perception of the discriminatory stopping of young people in Liverpool 8, and he rightly condemns it. But it is an overreading of his survey data.

Similar overreadings occur in the ICS. For example, the gloss on one of their tables, 'Theft from person (by age, race and gender)' which shows that young people, 16–24, and black people have the highest victimization rates per 1000 households suggests that it 'illustrates that it is the less powerful who are most often preyed upon by this type of crime' (ICS, p. 57). However, two pages further on, a table illustrating 'Theft from person (by socio-economic categories)' shows that the employed have a higher rate of victimization per 1000 households than the unemployed (162:117) and, apart from squatters, the most vulnerable group are the richest, i.e. those with an income over £12,000 p.a. There is no mention in the gloss of how this piece of information relates to that contained in the table we have just referred to. More than that, though it mentions that 'people in the highest income brackets are the most vulnerable to crime', it still chooses to emphasize the plight of the poor.

> Due to the relative rarity of high income households in Islington, it would appear once more as if the bulk of the theft is aimed at working class persons in the low to middle income categories. (ibid., p. 59)

The irony that that particular statement is true by definition and did not need an elaborate and expensive survey to 'prove', seems to escape the authors. But it is, once more, a case of overreading. The poor, it appears, are worse off when their victimization rates are highest *and* when they are not. With political championing of that order, who needs surveys.

There are other examples that illustrate the sheer complexity of the data, the occasionally *contradictory* character and the consequent *difficulty* (and danger) of taking a *singular* (highly political) message from it all. The truth is that whilst it would be nice (and convenient) to think that complex public policies could be based directly on people's experiences, perceptions and attitudes, it is anything but realistic. The reality is that people's limited experiences, unreconstructed perceptions and shifting attitudes do not translate immediately and un-problematically into socially just policies – even if a survey could get at them accurately. As Gramsci (1971) said long ago, the task for those interested in social justice is not to build a position on the basis of the people's *common sense* – but to look for the elements of *good sense* and build on these. Such a view entails the possibility that victims are not always the best judge of an appropriate and just crime control policy. Victimization studies clearly have an important role to play in *assisting* us to get a clearer picture of crime and criminal justice in our society. Nothing is gained – though much credibility may be lost – by over-selling their potentiality.

This critical view of crime surveys is one shared by Sim, Scraton and Gordon (1987). In a trenchant critique, they upbraid the 'new realist' project for its failure to recognize, not only the methodological problems with crime surveys, but the complexities of all the other relevant aspects: crime itself; the relationship between police, accountability and the state; the role of 'information' in improving the detection rate; and the relationship between effective crime control and civil liberties. This is as damning as the implicit critique supplied by other surveys. Jones (1983), for example, in her survey of police–public relations in Devon and Cornwall and Greater Manchester, concluded with two points of relevance to the 'new realism':

(a) 'the public' is not a homogeneous entity with a single set of policing needs;
(b) the 'public' judged police effectiveness, *not* by their success in crime control (as police were prone to think) *but* in terms of the quality of service, in human terms, offered.

We cannot arbitrate here between the findings of the new realists and those contrary ones. We introduce them here to demonstrate once more the need for caution. If crime surveys do have a role to play in producing more effective police work, it is certainly a limited one; it might also prove a misleading one unless its 'new realist' advocates begin to face up more rigorously to the many difficulties involved.

(5) *Independent Monitoring Groups*

Independent monitoring groups are the last of the recent policy initiatives to be considered here. Such groups see themselves as an important part of the campaign for a democratically accountable police force, whose function is to inform their police committee/ authority and their community on policing matters, especially those which are controversial, unacceptable or generally demonstrate the current lack of accountability. In addition they are intended to keep contact with and reflect the 'grassroots' on policing matters, by establishing contact with those sections of the community not represented by the existing formal structures of elected bodies and community meetings. Starting in London, the absence of an elected police authority produced the Greater London Council (GLC) Labour Party response of an unofficial, campaigning police committee with the funds to support independent monitoring groups. Some London boroughs followed suit, and subsequently certain big cities, Manchester in particular. Such groups, with their grass roots connections, are becoming increasingly recognized as important, particularly in a radical restructuring of accountability. The reason seems to be twofold:

(a) Policing, as we have argued throughout, has always been directed primarily against the variously dispossessed and power-less (see especially Chapters 4, 5 and 6). Unsurprisingly, these are the least well-represented groups. Such groups are often as critical of councillors as police. Hence, the importance of a 'grass-roots' connection, even to a radically reformed police committee.

(b) The campaign for democratic accountability has centred its attention on structural questions: the form the framework of policing should take. The content of policing, by contrast, has been relatively neglected.

This second reason, the neglect of the question 'what kind of policing?', has allowed some to argue that 'political' control of policing would lead to policing simply reflecting an area's political complexion: 'Tory policing' in Tory areas and 'Labour policing' in Labour areas. This could lead to the oppression of minorities. Worse, the fear is that nothing might change.

One of our constant nightmares is that, if there was a completely democratic control of the police in areas such as Hackney, the resulting police force would look exactly the same as the present Hackney police force. (Lea and Young, 1984, p. 270)

Others, it should be added, are more optimistic, even arguing, as Scraton does, that monitoring offers 'the *only effective* means by which police operational policies and practices can be opened to public scrutiny' (Scraton, 1985, p. 176, italics in original). What is certain, however, is that the 'grass-roots' connection supplied by monitoring groups, speaking on behalf of, if not directly representing, the most policed groups, offers at least the promise of a radically revised content.

If monitoring is becoming recognized as an essential component of a radical system of accountability, and if the above reasons explain why, then two linked issues are placed on the agenda. The first concerns how to ensure that the various sections of the community, and especially the most disadvantaged and least vocal, get their voices heard by the authorities responsible for policing. The second, following on from that, concerns how to establish criteria for arbitrating between *competing* community demands on policing, so that the answer to the question 'what kind of policing' proves satisfactory to *all*.

The lack of representation of the most disadvantaged, and their mistrust of elected representatives, is a reminder that elected representation is but one feature of a democracy. Equally important are questions of participation and information. Low levels of participation and information may mean elected representatives end up simply representing themselves and their like, using a discourse whose terms they define and over which they exercise a near monopoly. The alienated might well see this as descriptive of the present system, including the other forms of monitoring already discussed. So, the question is how to ensure all sections of the community, including the powerless, actively participate within the police debate on an informed basis.

Improving the availability of information has been a feature of monitoring work. For example, the GLC Police Committee published prolifically, including a monthly *Policing London*, free to all Londoners. And the Manchester unit deliver their *Policewatch* to all Manchester households. Obviously, the quality of the information is only as good as the available sources (which in secretive Britain means official obstruction and the constant threat of the Official Secrets Act) and as available resources allow; serious, quality, research-based monitoring costs money.

But, assuming adequate levels of representation, participation and information (no easy assumption, it should be said, and issues that are problems for *all* the external initatives mentioned; see Jefferson, McLaughlin and Robertson, 1988), there is still the question of criteria for choosing between rival claims on scarce police resources. The idea of community policing or community consultation can rest on a simplistic notion of a homogeneous community agreed about their policing needs. The reality, of course, especially in the areas where the issue is most urgent – the inner cities – is that communities are heterogeneous and often divided on their conceptions of policing priorities. The most developed response to this problem is the suggestion that conceptions of *justice* ought to enter the debate. Justice in a democracy concerns ensuring the protection of the rights and common interests of all or equal treatment of all under the law. In talking of the rights of *all*, not simply the rights of individuals, it is a notion of *public justice*, not individual justice, we have in mind. 'However, there are different versions of justice according to the conception of rights held. The first *assumes* substantive equality between individuals and therefore justice consists of treating all alike. Stemming from the philosophy of individualism, it gives rise to a notion of individualist justice. The second *recognises* substantive inequalities between individuals and therefore justice consists of, where necessary, unequal treatment in order to compensate for these inequalities' (Jefferson, 1986, pp. 279–80, italics in original). This second is socialist justice. Given the existing social inequalities in our society, a guiding definition of socialist justice would provide the monitoring group (or whoever) with an effective criterion for choosing between rival priorities in such a way that the interests of equality (or effective policing) would be met, *and* such a definition would also provide a criterion for judging *existing* police effectiveness, again in the interests of equality (cf. Jefferson and Grimshaw, 1984, pp. 154–68).

Downes and Ward draw explicitly on the idea of socialist justice in suggesting that 'Labour controlled Police Authorities should, given the power, apply socialist principles of justice to police strategies, even if this runs counter to the view of the majority of population who are relatively unaffected by existing police practices. To act democratically does not mean blindly following public opinion; it also involves respecting the rights of minorities' (Downes and Ward, 1986, p. 62). Other commentators, in various relatively underdeveloped ways, recognize the problem to be confronted. Lustgarten in discussing the local–central balance, argues that while a local-based administration will be attuned to local needs, a central dimension is required for 'standard-setting, equalisation and protection of minorities' (Lustgarten, 1986, p 178). Reiner, in defining 'democratic' policing, suggests somewhat abstractly that it means 'that they respect due process rights, do not discriminate unjustifiably in enforcement practices, and follow priorities which are in line with popular sentiment where this is clear, or which discreetly balance contending priorities in a divided community)' (Reiner, 1985a, pp. 180–1). Jones, MacLean and Young talk of equalizing experiences of, and attitudes to, the police:

> We must press for a situation where our surveys can detect little difference between the experiences of contact with the police between different sub-groups of the population – between young and old, black and white, male and female, working class and middle class, and where *all* groups have a belief in police fairness. (Jones, MacLean and Young, 1986, p. 205)

Finally, a Council for Racial Equality proposal to monitor the conduct of officers, put to Lord Scarman in phase 2 of his inquiry, seems to be employing just such a notion of justice. The proposal suggested that the following be added to the general orders of the Metropolitan Police.

An officer not below the rank of Chief Superintendent and not based at the material station shall:

(a) monitor the stop and arrest statistics of every station, and
(b) where the statistics so require, investigate and
(c) where the result of the investigation warrants it, lay a disciplinary charge of discrimination wherever the statistics or other information show:

    (i) that one or more officers have stopped or arrested a substantially higher proportion of persons belonging to ethnic or national minorities than the proportion of such minorities in the local population, or

    (ii) that the proportion of members of ethnic or national minorities stopped or arrested for a particular class of offence substantially exceeds the proportion of such persons in the local population. (Scarman, 1982, para. 5.39)

While appreciative of the intention, Scarman found the proposal too rigid. Perhaps. But it does not seem just fortuitous to us that representatives of a highly disadvantaged group should have produced a proposal in line with our criterion of social justice.

Summary and Conclusions

The initiatives outlined above constitute a range of mechanisms through which it is thought a better, more informed relationship between the police and the community might develop. The first three are seen very much as ways to improve communication (internal monitoring) and increase the flow of information between the police and the community (public monitoring, partnership monitoring) to enable the police and the police authority to provide a better service – a service more open and in tune with the community, and consequently more efficient, but a service in which it has been assumed that the process of enforcement is relatively impartial. An examination of these initiatives has revealed the divided nature of the community embraced by them, and therefore questions concerning their likely effectiveness need to be asked. In addition, because questions concerning legal powers have not been raised, these initatives have left the legal structure of accountability (Chapter 7) unchanged and hence afford scope for an unreconstructed cop culture (Chapter 3) to operate regardless of these initiatives.

The fourth kind of initative, monitoring by crime survey, is also about increasing the quality of information about crime so as to produce more realistic policework. Yet, whilst a more informed picture of crime victimization does emerge from such monitoring, serious distortions still remain. These distortions, and the subjective, common-sense nature of victims' perceptions of and attitudes to crime and policework, make survey results alone a very problematic basis upon which to construct an adequate set of policework policies. While it is true that 'radical realism' does also raise the question of accountability in arguing for the need for a democratically account-able police force, this tends to be introduced rhetorically rather than as an integral part of the argument.

The last kind of monitoring, the independent monitoring group, sees its role not as an adjunct to the present system, but as providing information which constitutes a critique of the present system. In this way independent monitoring recognizes the partial nature of law enforcement and stands as a means by which such policing policy and practice may be closely scrutinized and criticized in the interests of those on the receiving end of such partial practice. Its conception of the community is one which recognizes that certain sections of the com-munity's interests are not being met by the present system and is an attempt, albeit in a hazy fashion at present, to rectify this.

The first three approaches constitute a traditional understanding of the question of accountability, the last a radical one, with monitoring

by crime survey sitting uneasily between the two. The first three are
traditional in their approach primarily because they see the existing
structure of accountability as basically sound: all that is necessary is
that the police organization should pay more attention to its public
and offer more open reassurance with respect to police activities. The
last is radical in so far as it recognizes that the current system represents
only part of the community's interests and therefore needs to be made
more democratic by ensuring that the voice of those groups not
represented by the current structure is heard.

Penetrating the problem of accountability as discussed in this text
requires an approach which penetrates the permissiveness of the law
enshrined in the doctrine of constabulary independence which gives
the chief constable and the officer on the beat the discretionary power
they have. The independent monitoring group, in campaigning for
greater accountability, at least embraces this problem (though has by
no means 'solved' questions of representation, participation, etc.; see
Jefferson, McLaughlin and Robertson, 1988). The failure on the
whole of the initiatives discussed here to tackle the issues involved at
this level means that, while they may have some limited success in
improving the flow of information between the police, sections of the
public, and elected representatives, the partial process of law enforcement and the endemic problems associated with it will remain.

Finally, the problem for all approaches involves the question of
content. In so far as the accountability debate has been preoccupied
with the question of *who* should decide policework policies, the 'what'
of policework and criteria for deciding this have been all but neglected.
To begin to address this question, a notion of *public justice* has to enter
and affect the debate.

Suggestions for Further Reading

On Consultative Committees
Morgan, R., and Maggs, C. (1985), *Setting the PACE*, Bath Social Policy
    Papers no. 4 (University of Bath).

On Neighbourhood Watch
Bennett, T. (1987), *An Evaluation of Two Neighbourhood Watch Schemes in
    London, Executive Summary*, Final Report to the Home Office Research and
    Planning Unit (Cambridge: Institute of Criminology).

On Crime Surveys
Hough, M., and Mayhew, P. (1983), *The British Crime Survey: First Report*,
    Home Office Research Study no. 76 (London: HMSO).

Jones, T., MacLean, B., and Young, J. (1986), *The Islington Crime Survey* (Aldershot, Gower).

General
Downes, D., and Ward, T. (1986), *Democratic Policing* (London: Labour Campaign for Criminal Justice).

9 *Conclusion*

We have now finished our journey from psychology to the post-Scarman initiatives, via micro-sociology, history, macro-sociology and accountability. And we hope we have stayed true to our intention: a fair overview of the available literature focused through an argument stemming from our reading of the evidence. If we have managed that, the chapters can be usefully read whether or not our argument convinces. Naturally, we hope to persuade, but not at the expense of a full overview of the material. The test of that, however, will be whether those who do not share our bias concede, never-theless, that our case has not been constructed through the simple distortion and omission of arguments we do not agree with, and the selection only of evidence that supports our case.

Let us, finally, return to the stories we mentioned in Chapter 1 and the questions we briefly posed. Reference to the chapters in which problems were discussed is given in brackets. First, the Holloway Road incident and the question of whether improved selection, training and supervision will prove sufficient to prevent van loads of officers roaming the streets looking for trouble. In thinking about your answer, it might be worth bearing in mind certain salient facts about the case: the victims were male youths, two of them black, walking home from a fairground; the officers had been cooped up together in the van, many of them for a double shift, and had been the object of taunting by youths earlier in the evening; the police had a sergeant present in the van with them who witnessed the attack (who was gaoled for failing to protect the schoolboys and for covering up the affair); and they were members of a District Support Unit – a mobile support unit comprised of locally based officers. The District Support Units (DSUs) replaced the Special Patrol Group (SPG), the mobile support unit whose paramilitary reputation took a terminal nose-dive after the death of an anti-fascist demonstrator, Blair Peach, in 1979, was widely attributed to a SPG officer. The Holloway Road incident led to the disbandment of the DSUs and a return to the SPG concept of 'hand picked' and specially trained officers – only this time under a new name, namely, Territorial Support Groups. So, a group of local DSU officers who might be thought to be closer to local

communities than the SPG they replaced, under the constant supervision of a sergeant, still managed an unprovoked attack on five
schoolboys.

Does the historical relationship between the police and working-
class culture (Chapters 4 and 5) and the present relationship between
police and male youths (Chapter 6) help sort out your thoughts on this
incident? And do these relationships help explain why a van load of
officers were patrolling the streets in that vicinity (near a fairground)
and at that time (late into the evening), presumably on the lookout for
youthful 'trouble'. What about supervision? Did the Metropolitan
Police just promote the wrong man, a man who, according to the
judge, 'failed miserably', or does the idea of 'cop culture' help here?
Can tighter formal rules or better supervision simply override the
informal cop culture (Chapter 7)? And how does the Met. deal with
the paradoxical consequences of 'professionalism' (Chapter 5): the
idea, as Paul Keel put it, 'that the very *esprit de corps* which it [the Met.]
is anxious to instil could foster the reluctance to inform on colleagues
which obstructed the Holloway Road inquiry' (*Guardian*, 17 July
1987, p. 2)? What sustains the *esprit de corps* and its fierce loyalty? Is it
the type of recruits and the values they bring to the job (Chapter 2)? Is it
the immediate demands and conditions of the job itself (Chapter 3)?
Or has it more to do with the broader social functions of policework
(Chapters 4 and 5)?

Second, there was the story about the new Met. Commissioner and
his problems with 'partnership policing' in the inner city, a result, he
thought, of 'political opposition' (by some Labour-controlled
borough councils) and 'misunderstanding' as to the purpose and
intentions of the schemes. Is this a new problem (Chapter 4)? If not,
should we be surprised at the difference between suburban and inner
city attitudes? What is it about the inner city that makes the idea of
partnership policing perennially difficult? Do inner city residents
simply 'misunderstand' the police? In the light of these 'difficulties',
what are we to make of the notion of policing by consent (Chapter 4)?
Who does and who does not 'consent' to policing? Is there a pattern
here? And, if so, what sense can we make of it (Chapter 6)? Does the
distinction between 'efficient' and 'effective' policing help here
(Chapter 8)?

Thirdly, there were the stories about police oppression and
brutality involving youth, peacewomen, 'terrorists' and black
people. How best can these be explained? Are they a result of poor
selection, training and supervision (Chapter 2), a consequence of the
interactional dynamics of conflictual situations (Chapter 3), an
enduring legacy of the police's historically acquired social role

(Chapters 4 and 5), or a combination of these factors? And linking up with stories about accountability, how is such behaviour to be prevented in the future (Chapter 7)? Do we need to change the personnel, the rules, or the culture? Where is it most important to start, and why? How effective are the new post-Scarman initiatives likely to be in addressing this issue – and why (Chapter 8)?

The other theme in the stories on accountability centred on the appropriate relationship between the police, the Home Secretary and local police authorities. Who should decide what kind of policing we get? Is the decision to use plastic bullets best left to the police as experienced professionals, or are such decisions political and therefore the proper province of the community and its representatives? (Presently the courts have decided in favour of the police. See *Guardian*, Law Report, 20 November 1987, p. 5.) Is the line to be drawn between police (i.e. legal) decisions and political (i.e. democratic) decisions in the right place at the moment? If not, where should it be drawn? How is such a line to be 'policed' (Chapter 7)? Where do the new initiatives fit in all this (Chapter 8)?

More questions than answers, of course. But, we hope in thinking about these stories and the questions we have raised, you will be able to work out what our answers might look like. More importantly, we hope the material presented will assist you to work out your *own* answers. And not only in relation to the above stories; but also in relation to any other 'police' stories that will continue to appear in the media daily, posing dilemmas, demanding 'solutions'. We can only hope your 'answers' will prove more thoughtful and informed as a result of reading this book.

References

Adler, Z. (1987), *Rape on Trial* (London: Routledge & Kegan Paul).

Adorno, T. W., Freukel–Brunswick, E., Levinson, D. J., and Sanford, R. N. (1950), *The Authoritarian Personality* (New York: Harper).

Advisory Committee on Police in Schools (1986), *Policing Schools* (London: Advisory Committee on Police in Schools).

Ainsworth, P., and Pease, K. (1987), *Police Work* (London: Methuen).

Albini, J. L. (1975), 'Mafia as method: a comparison between Great Britain and the USA regarding the existence and structure of types of organised crime', *International Journal of Criminology and Penology*, vol. 3, pp. 295–305.

Ascoli, D. (1979), *The Queen's Peace* (London: Hamish Hamilton).

Bahn, C. (1973), 'The problem of counter training', *Personnel Journal*, vol. 52, no. 12, pp. 1068–72.

Bahn, C. (1984), 'Police socialization in the eighties', *Journal of Police Science and Administration*, vol. 12, no. 4, pp. 390–4.

Bailey, V. (ed.) (1981), *Policing and Punishment in the Nineteenth Century* (London: Croom Helm).

Balch, R. W. (1972), 'The police personality: Fact or fiction?', *Journal of Criminal Law, Criminology and Police Science*, vol. 63, no. 1, pp. 106–19.

Baldwin, R., and Kinsey, R. (1982), *Police Powers and Politics* (London: Quartet Books).

Ball, J., Chester, L., and Perrott, R. (1979), *Cops and Robbers* (Harmondsworth: Penguin).

Banton, M. (1964), *The Policeman in the Community* (London: Tavistock).

Banton, M. (1973), *Police Community Relations* (London: Collins).

Banton, M. (1985), 'Back to the drawing board', *Police*, vol. 17, no. 6, pp. 44–5.

Batta, I. D., Mawby, R. I., and McCulloch, J. W. (1978), 'Crime, social problems and Asian immigration: the Bradford experience', *International Journal of Contemporary Sociology*, vol. 18, pp. 135–68.

Baxter, J., and Koffman, L. (eds) (1985), *Police: The Constitution and the Community* (Abingdon: Professional Books).

Bayley, D., and Mendelsohn, H. (1969), *Minorities and the Police* (New York: Free Press).

Becker, H. (1963), *Outsiders: Studies in the Sociology of Deviance* (New York: Free Press).

Belson, W. A. (1975), *The Public and the Police* (London: Harper & Row).

Benn, M. (1985), 'Policing women', in Baxter and Koffman (eds), pp. 124–39.

Bennett, T. (1979), 'The social distribution of criminal labels', *British Journal of Criminology*, vol. 19, no. 2, pp. 134–45.

Bennett, T. (1987), *An Evaluation of Two Neighbourhood Watch Schemes in London, Executive Summary*, Final Report to the Home Office Research and Planning Unit (Cambridge: Institute of Criminology).

Bennion, C., Davie, A., Hesse, B. H., Joshua, L., McGloin, P., Munn, G., and Tester, S. (1985), *Neighbourhood Watch: The Eyes and Ears of Urban Policing?*, Occasional Papers in Sociology and Social Policy, no. 6 (University of Surrey).

Benyon, J. (1986), *A Tale of Failure: Race and Policing*, Policy Papers in Ethnic Relations, no. 3 (University of Warwick).

Bethnal Green and Stepney Trades Council (1978), *Blood on the Streets* (London: Bethnal Green and Stepney Trades Council).

Binney, V., Harkell, G., and Nixon, J. (1981), *Leaving Violent Men: A Study of Refuges and Housing for Battered Women* (England: Women's Aid Federation).

Bittner, E. (1967), 'The police on Skid Row: a study in peacekeeping', *American Sociological Review*, vol. 32, no. 5, pp. 699–715.

Bittner, E. (1970), *The Functions of the Police in Modern Society* (Rockville, MD: National Institute of Mental Health, Centre for Studies of Crime and Delinquency).

Black, D. (1971), 'The social organization of arrest', *Stanford Law Review*, vol. 23, June, pp. 1087–1111.

Black, D., and Reiss, A. J. (1967), *Studies of Crime and Law Enforcement in Major Metropolitan Areas* Vol. 2 (Washington DC: Government Printing Office).

Blom-Cooper, L., and Drabble, R. (1982), 'Police perception of crime', *British Journal of Criminology*, vol. 22, no. 1, pp. 184–7.

Boehringer, G. (1971), 'Towards a theoretical orientation in the sociology of policing: The Northern Ireland case', unpublished MS (McQuarrie University, Australia).

Bordua, D. J. (ed.) (1967), *The Police: Six Sociological Essays* (New York: Wiley).

Bottomley, K., and Pease, K. (1986), *Crime and Punishment: Interpreting the Data* (Milton Keynes: Open University Press).

Box, S. (1981), *Deviance, Reality and Society*, 2nd edn (Sussex: Holt, Rinehart & Winston).

Box, S. (1983), *Power, Crime and Mystification* (London: Tavistock).

Box, S., and Russell, K. (1975), 'The politics of discreditability', *Sociological Review*, vol. 23, no. 2, pp. 315–46.

Boydstun, J. E. (1975), *San Diego Field Interrogation: Final Report* (Washington DC: Police Foundation).

Boyle, J. (1977), *A Sense of Freedom* (Edinburgh: Canongate).

Bradley, D., Walker, N., and Wilkie, R. (1986), *Managing the Police* (Brighton: Harvester).

Brady, J. (1982), 'The revolution comes of age: Justice and social change in contemporary Cuba', in C. Sumner (ed.), *Crime, Justice and Underdevelopment* (London: Heinemann), pp. 248–300.

Brewer, J., and Styles, J. (1980), *An Ungovernable People* (London: Hutchinson).

Bridges, L. (1983a), 'Policing the urban wasteland', *Race and Class*, vol. 25, no. 2, Autumn, pp. 31–47.

Bridges, L. (1983b), 'Extended views: the British Left and law and order', *Sage Race Relations Abstracts*, February, pp. 19–26.

Brodeur, J. P. (1983), 'High policing and low policing: Remarks about the policing of political activities', *Social Problems*, vol. 3, no. 5, pp. 507–20.

Brogden, M. (1982), *The Police: Autonomy and Consent* (London: Academic Press).

Brogden, M. (1983), 'Rules, regulations and Christmas Boxes', paper given at the conference on Law, Labour and Crime, University of Warwick, September.

Brogden, M. (1987), 'The emergence of the police: the colonial dimension', *British Journal of Criminology*, vol. 27, no. 1, pp. 4–15.

Brogden, M., and Brogden, A. (1984), 'From Henry III to Liverpool 8: the unity of police street powers', *International Journal of the Sociology of Law*, vol. 12, no. 1, pp. 37–58.

Brown, C. (1984), *Black and White Britain: the Third PSI Report* (London: Heinemann).

Bryant, L., Dunkerley, D., and Kelland, G. (1985), 'One of the boys?' *Policing*, vol. 1, no. 4, pp. 236–44.

Bull, R. (1984), 'Police awareness training', *Policing*, vol. 1, no. 3, pp. 109–23.

Bull, R., and Horncastle, P. (1986a), *Metropolitan Police Recruit Training: an Independent Evaluation* (London: Police Foundation).

Bull, R., and Horncastle, P. (1986b), 'The gunmen who are a figment of the nervous policeman's imagination', *Guardian*, 15 January, p. 13.

Bull, R., Bustin, B., Evans, P., and Gahagan, D. (1983), *Psychology for Police Officers* (Chichester: Wiley).

Bunyan, T. (1977), *The Political Police in Britain* (London: Quartet Books).

Bunyard, R. S. (1978), *Police Organisation and Command* (Plymouth: MacDonald & Evans).

Burbeck, E., and Furnham, A. (1984), 'Personality and police selection: Trait differences in successful and non-successful applicants to the Metropolitan Police', *Journal of Personality and Individual Differences*, vol. 5, pp. 257–63.

Burbeck, E., and Furnham, A. (1985), 'Police officer selection: a critical review of the literature', *Journal of Police Science and Administration*, vol. 13, no. 1, pp. 58–69.

Burney, E. (1985), 'Inside the Nick', *New Society*, 8 November, pp. 239–40.

Butler, A. J. (1984), *Police Management* (London: Gower).

Cain, M. (1973), *Society and the Policeman's Role* (London: Routledge & Kegan Paul).

Cain, M. (1979), 'Trends in the sociology of police work', *International Journal of the Sociology of Law*, vol. 7, no. 2, pp. 143–67.

Cain, M., and Sadigh, S. (1982), 'Racism, the police and community policing: a comment on the Scarman Report', *Journal of Law and Society*, vol. 9, no. 1, pp. 87–102.

Carlen, P. (ed.) (1985), *Criminal Women* (Cambridge: Polity Press).

Carson, W. G., and Wiles, P. (eds) (1971), *Crime and Delinquency in Britain: Sociological Readings* (London: Martin Robertson).

Chambers, G., and Millar, A. (1983), *Investigating Sexual Assault* (Edinburgh: Scottish Office).

Chambers, G., and Tombs, J. (eds) (1984), *The British Crime Survey: Scotland* (Edinburgh: HMSO).

Chambliss, W. (1971), 'A sociological analysis of the law of vagrancy', in W. G. Carson and P. Wiles (eds), pp. 206–19.

Chatterton, M. (1979), 'The supervision of patrol work under the Fixed Points System', in S. Holdaway (ed.), pp. 83–101.

Christina, D., and Carlen, P. (1985), 'Christina: in her own time', in Carlen (ed.), pp. 59–103.

Cicourel, A. V. (1968), *The Social Organization of Juvenile Justice* (New York: Wiley).

Cochrane, R., and Butler, A. J. (1980), 'The values of police officers, recruits and civilians in England', *Journal of Police Science and Administration*, vol. 8, no. 8, pp. 205–11.

Cohen, P. (1979), 'Policing the working-class city', in B. Fine, R. Kinsey, J. Lea, S. Picciotto and J. Young (eds) *Capitalism and the Rule of Law* (London: Hutchinson), pp. 118–36.

Cohen, S. (1971), 'Mods, rockers and the rest: community reactions to juvenile delinquency', in Carson and Wiles (eds), pp. 226–36.

Cohen, S. (1973), *Folk Devils and Moral Panics* (London: Paladin).

Cohen, S. (1979), 'The punitive city: notes on the dispersal of social control', *Contemporary Crises*, vol. 3, no. 4, pp. 339–63.

Cohen, S. (ed.) (1971), *Images of Deviance* (Harmondsworth: Penguin).

Coleman, A. M., and Gorman, P. L. (1982), 'Conservatism, dogmatism and authoritarianism in British police officers', *Sociology*, vol. 16, no. 1, pp. 1–11.

Cook, D. (1987), 'Rich law, poor law: the differential treatment of tax and supplementary benefit law', paper given at the British Criminology Conference, University of Sheffield, July.

Cook, P. M. (1977), 'Empirical survey of police attitudes', *Police Review*, vol. 85, pp. 1042, 1078, 1114, 1140.

Corrigan, P. (1979), *Schooling the Smash Street Kids* (London: Macmillan).

Coulter, J., Miller, S., and Walker, M. (1984), *State of Siege* (London: Canary Press).

Cox, B., Shirley, J., and Short, M. (1977), *The Fall of Scotland Yard* (Harmondsworth: Penguin).

Critchley, T. A. (1970), *The Conquest of Violence* (London: Batsford).

Critchley, T. A. (1978), *A History of Police in England and Wales*, 2nd edn (London: Constable).

Daniel, S., and McGuire, P. (eds) (1972), *The Paint House* (Harmondsworth: Penguin).

Ditchfield, J. A. (1976), *Police Cautioning in England and Wales*, Home Office Research Study no. 37 (London: HMSO).

Ditton, J. (1980), *Controlology: Beyond the New Criminology* (London: Macmillan).

Dobash, R. E., and Dobash, R. (1980), *Violence Against Wives* (London: Open Books).

Donnison, H., Scola, J., and Thomas, P. (1986), *Neighbourhood Watch: Policing the People* (London: The Libertarian Research and Education Trust).

Downes, D. (1966), *The Delinquent Solution* (London: Routledge & Kegan Paul).

Downes, D., and Ward, T. (1986), *Democratic Policing: Towards a Labour Party Policy on Police Accountability* (London: Labour Campaign for Criminal Justice).

Draper, H. (1978), *Private Police* (Sussex: Harvester).

Edgar, J. M., and Lubans, V. (1979), *Policing by Objectives: A Handbook for Improving Police Management* (Connecticut: Social Development Corporation).

Edwards, S. (1986), *The Police Response to Domestic Violence in London* (London: Polytechnic of Central London).

Edwards, S. (1987), 'Provoking her own demise from common assault to homicide', in Hanmer and Maynard (eds), pp. 152–68.

Ehrlich-Martin, S. (1980), *Breaking and Entering: Policewomen on Patrol* (University of California Press).

Emsley, C. (1983), *Policing and its Context, 1750–1870* (London: Macmillan).

Ericson, R. V. (1982), *Reproducing Order: A Study of Police Patrol Work* (University of Toronto Press).

Eve, M., and Musson, D. (eds) (1982), *The Socialist Register 1982* (London: Merlin).

Faragher, T. (1981), 'The police response to violence against women in the home', in J. Pahl (ed.), *Private Violence and Public Policy: the Needs of Women and the Response of the Public Services* (London: Routledge & Kegan Paul), pp. 110–24.

Farrington, D. P., and Bennett, T. (1981), 'Police cautioning of juveniles in London', *British Journal of Criminology*, vol. 21, no. 2, pp. 123–35.

Farrington, D., and Dowds, E. (1985), 'Disentangling criminal behaviour and police reaction', in D. Farrington and J. Gunn (eds) *Reactions to Crime: the Public, the Police, Courts and Prisons* (Chichester: Wiley).

Farrington, D. P., Gallagher, B., Morley, L., St Ledger, R. J., and West, D. J. (1986), 'Unemployment, school leaving and crime', *British Journal of Criminology*, vol. 26, no. 4, pp. 335–56.

Field, J. (1981), 'Police, power and community in a provincial English town: Portsmouth 1815–75', in Bailey (ed.), pp. 42–64.

Field, S., and Southgate, P. (1982), *Public Disorder*, Home Office Research Study no. 72 (London: HMSO).

Fielding, N. (1984), 'Police socialization and police competence', *British Journal of Sociology*, vol. 35, no. 4, pp. 568–90.

Fine, B., and Millar, R. (eds) (1985), *Policing the Miners' Strike* (London: Lawrence & Wishart).

Fogelson, R. (1977), *Big-City Police* (Cambridge, Mass.: Harvard University Press).

Foucault, M. (1979), *Discipline and Punish: the Birth of the Prison* (Harmondsworth: Penguin).

Fryer, P. (1984), *Staying Power: The History of Black People in Britain* (London: Pluto).

Geary, R. (1985), *Policing Industrial Disputes: 1893–1985* (Cambridge University Press).

Gibson, J. (1987), 'Is Homewatch worth it?', *Police Review*, vol. 95, no. 4922, 24 July.

Gill, O. (1977), *Luke Street: Housing Policy, Conflict and the Creation of the Delinquent Area* (London: Macmillan).

Gillis, J. R. (1975), 'The evolution of juvenile delinquency in England 1890–1914', *Past and Present*, no. 67, pp. 96–126.

Gilroy, P. (1982), 'The myth of black criminality', in Eve and Musson (eds), pp. 47–56.

Gilroy, P., and Sim, J. (1985), 'Law, order and the state of the Left', *Capital and Class*, no. 25, Spring, pp. 15–55.

Gladstone-Smith, P. (1970), *The Crime Explosion* (London: Macdonald).

Goffman, E. (1959), *The Presentation of Self in Everyday Life* (Harmondsworth: Penguin).

Goffman, E. (1968), *Asylums* (Harmondsworth: Penguin).

Gordon, P. (1981), *Passport Raids and Checks* (London: Runnymede Trust).

Gordon, P. (1983), *White Law: Racism in the Police, Courts and Prisons* (London: Pluto).

Gramsci, A. (1971), *Selections from the Prison Notebooks* (London: Lawrence & Wishart).

Greater London Council (1983), *A New Police Authority for London*, Discussion Paper no. 1 (London: GLC).

Greater London Council (1984), *Racial Harassment in London* (London: GLC).

Grimshaw, R., and Jefferson, T. (1987), *Interpreting Policework: Policy and Practice in Forms of Beat Policing* (London: Allen & Unwin).

Gutzmore, C. (1983), 'Capital, "Black Youth" and crime', *Race and Class*, vol. 25, no. 2, pp. 13–30.

Hall, S. (1985), 'Cold Comfort Farm', *New Socialist*, no. 32, November, pp. 10–12.

Hall, S., and Jefferson, T. (eds) (1976), *Resistance Through Rituals: Youth Subcultures in Post-War Britain* (London: Hutchinson).

Hall, S., Critcher, C., Jefferson, T., Clarke, J., and Roberts, B. (1978), *Policing the Crisis* (London: Macmillan).

Hanmer, J., and Maynard, M. (eds) (1987), *Women, Violence and Social Control* (London: Macmillan).

Harring, S. (1983), *Policing a Class Society* (New Brunswick: Rutgers University Press).

Harring, S. L., and McMullin, L. M. (1975), 'The Buffalo Police 1872–1900: labour unrest, political power and the creation of the police institution', *Crime and Social Justice*, no. 4, Fall–Winter, pp. 5–14.

Hay, D. H. (1983), 'Manufacturers and the Criminal Law', in *Police and Policing*, Past and Present Colloquium, July (Oxford: Past and Present Society), pp. 1–70.

Hebdige, D. (1974), *The Kray Twins: A Study of a System of Closure*, stencilled

Occasional Paper no. 21 (Centre for Contemporary Cultural Studies, University of Birmingham).

Heidensohn, F. (1985), *Women and Crime* (London: Macmillan).

Her Majesty's Chief Inspector of Constabulary (HMCIC) (1985), *Annual Report for 1984* (London: HMSO).

Holdaway, S. (1977), 'Changes in urban policing', *British Journal of Sociology*, vol. 28, no. 2, pp. 119–37.

Holdaway, S. (1983), *Inside the British Police* (Oxford: Blackwell).

Holdaway, S. (ed.) (1979), *The British Police* (London: Edward Arnold).

Home Office (1967), *Police Manpower, Equipment and Efficiency* (London: HMSO).

Home Office (1981), *Racial Attacks* (London: HMSO).

Home Office (1983), *Lay Visitors to Police Stations: Guidelines; Provincial Forces* (London: Home Office).

Home Office (1984), *Cautioning by the Police: a Consultative Document* (London: Home Office).

Honeycombe, G. (1975), *Adam's Tale* (London: Arrow).

Hopper, M. (1977), 'Becoming a policeman: socialization of cadets in a police academy', *Urban Life*, vol. 6, no. 2, pp. 149–70.

Hough, M., and Mayhew, P. (1983), *The British Crime Survey: First Report*, Home Office Research Study no. 76 (London: HMSO).

Hough, M., and Mayhew, P. (1985), *Taking Account of Crime: Key Findings from the Second British Crime Survey*, Home Office Research Study no. 85 (London: HMSO).

Hunte, J. (1966), *Nigger Hunting in England* (London: West Indian Standing Conference).

Ignatieff, M. (1978), *A Just Measure of Pain* (London: Macmillan).

Institute of Race Relations (1979), *Police Against Black People* (London: IRR).

Institute of Race Relations (1987), *Policing Against Black People* (London IRR).

Irving, B. (1983), 'Psychology and policing: past and present', paper given at British Psychological Society, December.

Irving, B. (1985), 'The Police and Criminal Evidence Act 1984: in the police station', paper given at the conference on Police and Criminal Evidence Act 1984, University of Leicester, January.

James, D. (1979), 'Police–black relations: the professional solution', in Holdaway (ed.), pp. 66–82.

Jefferson, T. (1986), 'Policing the miners: law, politics and accountability', in M. Brenton and C. Ungerson (eds) (1986), *The Yearbook of Social Policy 1985–6* (London: Routledge & Kegan Paul), pp. 265–86.

Jefferson, T. (1987), 'The Police', Block 3, Part 1a, Delivering Justice, '*Crime, Justice and Society*' (D310) (Milton Keynes: Open University Press), pp. 9–38.

Jefferson, T., and Grimshaw, R. (1982), 'Law, democracy and justice: the question of police accountability', in D. Cowell, T. Jones and J. Young (eds), *Policing the Riots* (London: Junction Books), pp. 82–117.

Jefferson, T., and Grimshaw, R. (1984), *Controlling the Constable: Police Accountability in England and Wales* (London: Muller/Cobden Trust).

Jefferson, T., McLaughlin, E., and Robertson, L. (1988), 'Monitoring the monitors: accountability, democracy and policewatching in Britain', *Contemporary Crises*, vol. 12, no. 2.

Jefferson, T., and Smith, J. (1985), 'Watching the police', *Critical Social Policy*, vol. 13, Summer, pp. 124–33.

Jeffreys, S., and Radford, J. (1984), 'Contributory negligence or being a woman? The car rapist case', in P. Scraton and P. Gordon (eds), *Causes for Concern* (Harmondsworth: Penguin), pp. 154–83.

Johnson, D. R. (1979), *Policing the Urban Underworld* (Philadelphia: Temple University Press).

Johnson, N. (1985), 'Police, social work and medical responses to battered women', in N. Johnson (ed.), *Marital Violence*, Sociological Review Monograph, 31, pp. 109–23.

Johnson, T. (1972), *Professions and Power* (London: Macmillan).

Jones, D. (1982), *Crime, Protest, Community and Police in Nineteenth Century Britain* (London: Routledge & Kegan Paul).

Jones, J. M. (1980), *Organizational Aspects of Police Behaviour* (Farnborough: Gower).

Jones, S. (1983), 'Police–public relations: a study of public and police perceptions of each other. Summary of main findings', unpublished report (Department of Social Administration, University College, Cardiff).

Jones, S. (1987), *Policewomen and Equality* (London: Macmillan).

Jones, S., and Levi, M. (1983), 'The police and the majority: the neglect of the obvious?', *Police Journal*, vol. 56, no. 4, pp. 351–64.

Jones, S., and Joss, R. (1985), 'Do police officers survive their training?', *Policing*, vol. 1, no. 4, pp. 206–25.

Jones, S., and Silverman, E. (1984), 'What price efficiency? Circular arguments. Financial constraints on the police in Britain', *Policing*, vol. 1, no. 1, pp. 31–48.

Jones, T., MacLean, B., and Young, J. (1986), *The Islington Crime Survey: Crime Victimization and Policing in Inner-City London* (Aldershot: Gower).

Kettle, M. (1985), 'The national reporting centre and the 1984 miners' strike', in Fine and Millar (eds), pp. 23–33.

King, P. (1984), 'Decision-makers and decision-making in the English Criminal Law, 1750–1800', *Historical Journal*, vol. 27, no. 1, pp. 25–58.

Kinsey, R. (1981), 'Police cut question time', *New Statesman*, 12 June, p. 3.

Kinsey, R. (1984), *Merseyside Crime Survey First Report* (Liverpool: Merseyside County Council).

Kinsey, R. (1985a), *Survey of Merseyside Police Officers First Report* (Liverpool: Merseyside County Council).

Kinsey, R. (1985b), *Merseyside Crime and Police Surveys: Final Report* (Liverpool: Merseyside County Council).

Kinsey, R. (1986), 'Crime in the city', *Marxism Today*, May, pp. 6–10.

Kinsey, R., Lea, J., and Young J. (1986), *Losing the Fight Against Crime* (Oxford: Blackwell).

Klug, F. (1982), *Racist Attacks* (London: Runnymede Trust).

Lambert, J. (1970), *Crime, Police and Race Relations* (Oxford University Press).

Lambeth Council Working Party (1981), *Final Report of the Working Party into Community/Police Relations in Lambeth* (London: Borough of Lambeth).

Landau, S. (1981), 'Juveniles and the police', *British Journal of Criminology*, vol. 21, no. 1, pp. 27–46.

Landau, S., and Nathan, G. (1983), 'Selecting delinquents for cautioning in the London Metropolitan Area', *British Journal of Criminology*, vol. 28, no. 2, pp. 128–49.

Lane, R. (1967), *Policing the City: Boston 1822–1885* (Cambridge, Mass.: Harvard University Press).

Lane, R. (1980), 'Urban police and crime in nineteenth-century America', in N. Morris and M. Tonry (eds), *Crime and Justice: An Annual Review of Research, Vol. 2* (Chicago University Press), pp. 1–43.

Laycock, G., and Tarling, R. (1985), 'Police force cautioning: policy and practice', *Research Bulletin*, no. 19 (London: Home Office Research and Planning Unit), pp. 23–6.

Lea, J., and Young, J. (1984), *What is to be done about Law and Order?* (Harmondsworth: Penguin).

Lee, J. A. (1981), 'Some structural aspects of police deviance in relations with minority groups', in C. Shearing (ed.), *Organizational Police Deviance* (Toronto: Butterworths), pp. 49–82.

London Strategic Policy Unit (1986), *Police Response to Domestic Violence* (London: LSPU).

Loveday, B. (1985), *The Role and Effectiveness of the Merseyside Police Committee* (Merseyside County Council).

Lucas, N. (1969), *Britain's Gangland* (London: Pan).

Lundman, R. J. (1980), *Police and Policing: An Introduction* (New York: Rinehart & Winston).

Lundman, R. J., Sykes, R. E., and Clark, J. P. (1978), 'Police control of juveniles: a replication', *Journal of Research in Crime and Delinquency*, vol. 15, no. 1, pp. 74–91.

Lustgarten, L. (1986), *The Governance of Police* (London: Sweet & Maxwell).

Lyman, J. L. (1964), 'The Metropolitan Police Act of 1829', *Journal of Criminal Law, Criminology and Police Science*, vol. 55, pp. 141–54.

Mack, J. (1975), *The Crime Industry* (Farnborough: Saxon House/Lexington).

Maier, P. (1970), 'Popular uprisings and civil authority in eighteenth-century America', *William and Mary Quarterly*, vol. 27, pp. 3–35.

Manning, P. K. (1977), *Police Work: The Social Organization of Policing* (Cambridge, Mass.: MIT).

Manning, P. K. (1979), 'The social control of police work', in Holdaway (ed.), pp. 41–65.

Manning, P. K. (1980), 'Violence and the police role', in L. W. Sherman (ed.), *Annals of the American Academy*, 452, November (Philadelphia: Annals, AAPSS), pp. 135–44.

Manning, P., and Van Maanen, J. (eds) (1978), *Policing: A View from the Street* (Santa Monica, Calif.: Goodyear).

Marshall, G. (1965), *Police and Government* (London: Methuen).

Marshall, G. (1984), *Constitutional Conventions* (Oxford University Press).

Matthews, R. (1986), *Policing Prostitution: A Multi-Agency Approach*, Centre for Criminology, Paper 1 (London: Middlesex Polytechnic).

Matza, D., and Sykes, G. (1957), 'Techniques of neutralization: a theory of delinquency', *American Sociological Review*, vol. 22, pp. 664–70.

Mawby, R. (1979), *Policing the City* (London: Gower).

Mayo, P. E. (1969), *The Making of a Criminal* (London: Weidenfeld & Nicolson).

Mays, J. B. (1954), *Growing up in the City* (Liverpool University Press).

Mays, J. B. (1975), *Crime and its Treatment*, 2nd edn (London: Longman).

McBarnet, D. (1978), 'The police and the state: arrest, legality and the law', in G. Littlejohn, B. Smart, J. Wakeford and N. Yuval-Davis (eds) (1978), *Power and the State* (London: Croom Helm), pp. 196–216.

McCabe, S., and Sutcliffe, F. (1978), *Defining Crime* (Oxford: Blackwell).

McConnell, B. (1969), *The Evil Firm: The Rise and Fall of the Brothers Kray* (London: Mayflower).

McConville, M., and Baldwin, J. (1981), *Courts, Prosecutions and Conviction* (Oxford University Press).

McIntosh, M. (1975), *The Organization of Crime* (London: Macmillan).

McKenzie, I. K., and Irving, B. (1987), 'Police interrogation; the effects of PACE', *Policing*, vol. 3, no. 1, Spring, pp. 4–22.

McLeod, E. (1981), 'Man-made laws for men? The street prostitutes' campaign against control', in B. Hutter and G. Williams (eds), *Controlling Women* (London: Croom Helm), pp. 61–78.

McMullan, J. I. (1982), 'Criminal organization in sixteenth and seventeenth-century London', *Social Problems*, vol. 29, no. 3, pp. 311–23.

McNamara, J. H. (1967), 'Uncertainties in police work: the relevance of police recruits' background and training', in Bordua (ed.), pp. 163–252.

Mead, G. H. (1934), *Mind, Self and Society* (University of Chicago Press).

Meehan, P. (1978), *Innocent Villain* (London: Pan).

Merricks, W. (1983), 'Police interviews – getting it taped', *New Law Journal*, 21 January, pp. 51–2.

MIL Research Ltd (1979), *Attitudes to the Police: Report on a Survey Amongst West Indians* (London: MIL).

Monkkonen, E. H. (1981), *Police in Urban America 1860–1920* (Cambridge University Press).

Morgan, R. (1987), 'Police accountability: the implications of local consultative committees', paper given at the Socio-Legal Group Conference, University of Sheffield, March.

Morgan, R., and Maggs, C. (1985), *Setting the PACE*, Bath Social Policy Papers no. 4 (University of Bath).

Morris, A., Giller, H., Szwed, E., and Geach, H. (1980), *Justice for Children* (London: Macmillan).

Morse, M. (1965), *The Unattached* (Harmondsworth: Penguin).

Mouzelis, N. P. (1967), *Organization and Bureaucracy* (London: Routledge & Kegan Paul).

Moylan, J. (1934), *Scotland Yard* (London: Putnam).

Muncie, J. (1984), *The Trouble with Kids Today* (London: Hutchinson).

Muncie, J. (1986), 'Youth and the reforming zeal', Block 2, Part 4, Law and Disorder: Histories of Crime and Justice, *'Crime, Justice, and Society'* (D310) (Milton Keynes: Open University Press), pp. 3–28.

National Council for Civil Liberties (1986), *Armagh Strip Searches* (London: NCCL).

Newsam, Sir Frank (1954), *The Home Office* (London: Allen & Unwin).

Pahl, J. (1978), *A Refuge for Battered Women: A Study of the Role of a Women's Centre* (London: HMSO).

Park, R. E., and Burgess, E. W. (1925), *The City* (University of Chicago Press).

Parker, H. (1974), *The View from the Boys* (Newton Abbot: David & Charles).

Payne, L. (1973), *The Brotherhood* (London: Michael Joseph).

Pearson, G. (1983), *Hooligan: A History of Respectable Fears* (London: Macmillan).

Pearson, J. (1973), *The Profession of Violence* (London: Panther).

Phillips, D. (1977), *Crime and Authority in Victorian England* (London: Croom Helm).

Phillips, D. (1980), ' "A New Engine of Power and Authority": the institutionalization of law enforcement in England 1780–1830', in V. A. C. Gatrell, B. Lenman and G. Parker (eds), *Crime and the Law* (London: Europa), pp. 155–89.

Piliavin, I., and Briar, S. (1964), 'Police encounters with juveniles', *American Journal of Sociology*, vol. 70, pp. 206–14.

Player, E. (1984), 'Women and the criminal justice system', paper given at the Howard League for Penal Reform.

Plumridge, M. D. (1985), 'Dilemmas of police management and organisations', in J. R. Thackrah (ed.), *Contemporary Policing* (London: Sphere), pp. 173–90.

Policy Studies Institute (1983), *Police and People in London*, Vol. 1, Smith, D. J., *A Survey of Londoners;* Vol. 2, Small, S., *A Group of Young Black People*; Vol. 3, Smith, D. J., *A Survey of Police Officers*; Vol. 4, Smith, D. J., and Gray, J., *The Police in Action* (London: PSI).

Potter, L. J. (1977), 'Police officer personality', M.Ed. thesis, University of Bradford.

Powis, D. (1977), *The Signs of Crime* (London: McGraw Hill).

Pratt, J. (1986), 'Diversion from the Juvenile Court', *British Journal of Criminology*, vol. 26, no. 3, pp. 212–33.

Price, Sir Norman (1987), *Report of Working Party on the Enforcement of Law Relating to Social Security* (London: NACRO).

Pryce, K. (1986), *Endless Pressure*, 2nd edn (Bristol Classical Press).

Punch, M. (1979), *Policing the Inner City: A Study of Amsterdam's Warmoesstraat* (London: Macmillan).

Punch, M. (1985), *Conduct Unbecoming* (London: Tavistock).

Punch, M. (ed.) (1983), *Control in the Police Organization* (Cambridge, Mass.: MIT).

Radford, J. (1987), 'Policing male violence – policing women', in Hanmer and Maynard (eds), pp. 30–45.

Radzinowicz, L. (1955), *A History of English Criminal Law, Vol. 3* (London: Stevens).

Reiner, R. (1978), *The Blue Coated Worker* (Cambridge University Press).

Reiner, R. (1984), 'Is Britain turning into a police state?' *New Society*, August, pp. 51–6.

Reiner, R. (1985a), *The Politics of the Police* (Brighton: Wheatsheaf).

Reiner, R. (1985b), 'Police and race relations', in Baxter and Koffman (eds), pp. 149–87.

Reiss, A. J. (1971), *The Police and the Public* (New Haven: Yale University Press).

Reith, C. (1952), *The Blind Eye of History: A Study of the Origins of the Present Police Era* (London: Faber).

Reuss-Ianni, E. (1983), *The Two Cultures of Policing* (New Brunswick, NJ: Transaction).

Richardson, T. J. (1970), *The New York Police: Colonial Times to 1901* (New York: Oxford University Press).

Riley, D. (1984), 'Contacts between police and teenagers', *Research Bulletin*, no. 18 (London: Home Office Research and Planning Unit), pp. 19–21.

Riley, D. (1986), 'Sex differences in teenage crime: the role of lifestyle', *Research Bulletin*, no. 20 (London: Home Office Research and Planning Unit), pp. 34–8.

Robertson, G. (1976), *Reluctant Judas* (London: Temple-Smith).

Robinson, C. (1978), 'The deradicalisation of the policeman', *Crime and Delinquency*, vol. 24, no. 2, pp. 129–51.

Rock, P. (1985), 'Law, order and power in late seventeenth- and early eighteenth-century England', in S. Cohen and A. Scull (eds), *Social Control and the State* (Oxford: Blackwell), pp. 191–221.

Rowse, A. L. (1950), *The England of Elizabeth: The Structure of Society* (London: Macmillan).

Rutherford, A. (1986), *Growing out of Crime* (Harmondsworth: Penguin).

Samuel, R., Bloomfield, B., and Boanas, G. (eds) (1986), *The Enemy Within* (London: Routledge & Kegal Paul).

Scarman, Lord (1982), *The Scarman Report: the Brixton Disorders 10–12 April 1981* (Hardmonsworth: Penguin). Originally published in 1981 as Cmnd. 8427 by HMSO.

Schneider, J. C. (1980), *Detroit and the Problem of Order, 1830–1880* (Nebraska: Lincoln).

Scraton, P. (1985), *The State of the Police* (London: Pluto).

Scraton, P. (1986), 'Policing society, policing crime' in Block 2, part 5, Law and Disorder: Histories of Crime and Justice, *Crime, Justice and Society* (D310) (Milton Keynes: Open University), pp. 29–79.

Scull, A. (1979), *Museums of Madness* (London: Allen Lane).

Sharpe, J. A. (1983), 'Policing the parish in early modern England', in *Police and Policing*, Past and Present Colloquium, July (Oxford: Past and Present Society), pp. 1–24.

Sherman, L. J. (1975), 'An evaluation of policewomen on patrol', *Journal of Police Science and Administration*, vol. 3, no. 4, pp. 434–8.

Sherman, L. W. (1980), 'Causes of police behaviour: the current state of quantitative research', *Journal of Research in Crime and Delinquency*, vol. 17, no. 1, pp. 69–100.

Silver, A. (1967), 'The demand for order in civil society', in Bordua (ed.), pp, 1–24.

Sim, J. (1982), 'Scarman: the police counter-attack', in Eve and Musson (eds), pp. 57–77.

Sim, J., Scraton, P., and Gordon, P. (1987), 'Introduction: Crime, the state and critical analysis', in P. Scraton (ed.), *Law, Order and the Authoritarian State* (Milton Keynes: Open University Press), pp. 1–70.

Simey, M. (1985), *Government by Consent: The Principle and Practice of Accountability in Local Government* (London: Bedford Square Press).

Sivanandan, A. (1985), 'Britain's gulags', *New Socialist*, no. 32, November, pp. 13–15.

Skolnick, J. (1966), *Justice without Trial* (New York: Wiley),

Smith, A. C. H., Blackwell, T., and Immirzi, E. (1975), *Paper Voices: The Popular Press and Social Change 1935–1965* (London: Chatto).

Smith, D. (1986), 'West Indian hostility to the police in relation to personal experience', unpublished MS (London: Policy Studies Institute).

Smith, D., and Visher, C. (1981), 'Street level justice: situational determinants of police arrest decisions', *Social Problems*, vol. 29, no. 2, pp. 167–77.

Softly, P. (1985), 'Police interrogation: an observational study in four police stations', in K. Heal, R. Tarling and J. Burrows (eds), *Policing Today*, Home Office Research and Planning Unit Publication (London: HMSO), pp. 115–30.

Southgate, P. (1982), *Police Probationer Training in Race Relations*, Research and Planning Unit Paper 8 (London: Home Office).

Southgate, P. (1984), *Racism Awareness Training for the Police*, Research and Planning Unit Paper 29 (London: Home Office).

Southgate, P., and Ekblom, P. (1984), *Contacts between Police and Public: Findings from the British Crime Survey*, Home Office Research Study no. 77 (London: HMSO).

Southgate, P., and Ekblom, P. (1986), *Police–Public Encounters*, Home Office Research Study no. 90 (London: HMSO).

Sparks, R. F., Genn, H. G., and Dodd, D. J. (1977), *Surveying Victims* (Chichester: Wiley).

Spencer, S. (1985a), 'The eclipse of the policy authority', in Fine and Millar (eds), pp. 34–53.

Spencer, S. (1985b), *Called to Account: The Case for Police Accountability in England and Wales* (London: National Council for Civil Liberties).

Spitzer, S., and Scull, A. (1977), 'Social control in historical perspective: from private to public responses to crime', in D. F. Greenberg (ed.), *Corrections and Punishment* (Beverley Hills: Sage), pp. 265–86.

Stanko, E. (1985), *Intimate Intrusions: Women's Experience of Male Violence* (London: Routledge & Kegan Paul).

Stead, P. (ed.) (1977), *Pioneers in Policing* (New Jersey: Patterson Smith).

Stedman Jones, G. S. (1977), 'Class expression versus social control? A critique of recent trends in the social history of leisure', *History Workshop*. vol. 4, pp. 162–70.

Steer, D. (1970), *Police Cautions: A Study in the Exercise of Police Discretion* (Oxford: Blackwell).

Stevens, P., and Willis, C. (1979), *Race, Crime and Arrests*, Home Office Research Study no. 58 (London: HMSO).

Stevens, P., and Willis, C. (1981), *Ethnic Minorities and Complaints Against the Police*, Research and Planning Unit Paper 5 (London: Home Office).

Stinchcombe, J. B. (1979), 'Beyond bureaucracy: a reconsideration of the professional police', *Criminology and Criminal Law*, vol. 17, pp. 49–61.

Storch, R. (1975), 'The plague of the blue locusts: police reform and popular resistance in northern England 1840–57', *International Review of Social History*, vol. 20, pp. 61–90.

Stretch, C. (1981), 'Women in the police', *The Leveller*, no. 56, May, pp. 12–14.

Styles, J. (1980), 'Our traitorous moneymakers', in Brewer and Styles (eds), pp. 172–249.

Sykes, R. E., Fox, J. C., and Clark, J. P. (1976), 'A socio-legal theory of police discretion', in A. Niederhoffer and A. S. Blumberg (eds), *The Ambivalent Force*, 2nd edn (Hinsdale, Ill.: Dryden Press), pp. 171–83.

Taylor, L., Lacey, R., and Bracken, D. (1980), *In Whose Best Interests?* (London: Cobden Trust/Mind).

Toner, B. (1982), *The Facts of Rape* (London: Arrow).

Trevelyan, G. W. (1941), *England Under the Stuarts* (London: Longman).

Tuck, M., and Southgate, P. (1981), *Ethnic Minorities, Crime and Policing*, Home Office Research Study no. 70 (London: HMSO).

Van Maanen, J. (1973), 'Observations on the making of policemen', *Human Organizations*, vol. 32, no. 4, pp. 407–18.

Visher, C. (1983), 'Gender, police arrest decisions and notions of chivalry', *Criminology*, vol. 21, no. 1, pp. 5–28.

Walker, M. A. (1987), 'Interpreting race and crime statistics', *Journal of the Royal Statistical Society* Series A (General), vol. 150, Part 1, pp. 39–56.

Walker, S. (1977), *A Critical History of Police Reform* (Lexington, Mass.: Heath).

Walker, S. (1983), *Police in America* (New York: McGraw Hill).

Walklate, S. (1986a), *The Merseyside Lay Visiting Scheme First Report: The Lay Visitors* (Liverpool: Merseyside Police Authority).

Walklate, S. (1986b), *The Merseyside Lay Visiting Scheme Second Report: The Custody Officer* (Liverpool: Merseyside Police Authority).

Warren, K., and Tredinnick, D. (1982), *Protecting the Police* (London: Conservative Political Centre).

Weatheritt, M. (1986), *Innovations in Policing* (London: Police Foundation/ Croom Helm).

Weinberger, B. (1981), 'The police and public in mid nineteenth-century Warwickshire', in Bailey (ed.), pp. 65–93.

Westley, W. (1970), *Violence and the Police: a Sociological Study of Law, Custom and Morality* (Cambridge, Mass.: MIT).

Whitaker, B. (1979), *The People in Society* (London: Eyre/Methuen).

Wilkins, L. T. (1964), *Social Deviance* (London: Tavistock).

Willis, C. (1983), *The Use, Effectiveness and Impact of Police Stop and Search Powers*, Research and Planning Unit Paper 15 (London: Home Office).

Willmott, P. (1966), *Adolescent Boys of East London* (London: Routledge & Kegan Paul).

Wilson, D., Holdaway, S., and Spencer, C. (1984), 'Black police in the United Kingdom', *Policing*, vol. 1, pp. 20–30.

Wilson, J. Q. (1968), *Varieties of Police Behaviour* (Cambridge, Mass.: Harvard University Press).

Young, J. (1971), 'The role of the police as amplifiers of deviancy', in Cohen (ed.), pp. 27–61.

Index of Subjects

Index of Names